Drugs, Oil, and War

ALSO BY PETER DALE SCOTT

PROSE

The Politics of Escalation (1967, in collaboration)
The War Conspiracy: The Secret Road to the Second Indochina War (1972)
The Assassinations: Dallas and Beyond (1976, in collaboration)
Crime and Cover-Up: The CIA, the Mafia, and the Dallas-Watergate Connection
  (1977)
The Iran-Contra Connection (1987, in collaboration)
Cocaine Politics: Drugs, Armies, and the CIA in Central America (1991, 1998,
  in collaboration)
Deep Politics and the Death of JFK (1993, 1996)
Deep Politics Two: Oswald, Mexico and Cuba (1995)
Drugs, Contras, and the CIA: Government Policies and the Cocaine Economy
  (2000)

SECULUM: A POETIC TRILOGY

Coming to Jakarta (1988)
Listening to the Candle (1992)
Minding the Darkness (2000)

OTHER POETRY

Crossing Borders: Selected Shorter Poems (1995)

War and Peace Library
Series Editor: Mark Selden

Biological Warfare and Disarmament:
New Problems/New Perspectives
Edited by Susan Wright

Drugs, Oil, and War

The United States in Afghanistan, Colombia, and Indochina

Peter Dale Scott

ROWMAN & LITTLEFIELD PUBLISHERS, INC.
Lanham • Boulder • New York • Oxford

GIB
SCO

ROWMAN & LITTLEFIELD PUBLISHERS, INC.

Published in the United States of America
by Rowman & Littlefield Publishers, Inc.
A Member of the Rowman & Littlefield Publishing Group
4501 Forbes Boulevard, Suite 200, Lanham, Maryland 20706
www.rowmanlittlefield.com

P.O. Box 317, Oxford OX2 9RU, United Kingdom

British Library Cataloguing in Publication Information Available

Library of Congress Cataloging-in-Publication Data

Scott, Peter Dale.
    Drugs, oil, and war : the United States in Afghanistan, Colombia, and Indochina /
Peter Dale Scott.
        p. cm. — (War and peace library)
    Includes bibliographical references and index.
    ISBN 0-7425-2521-X (cloth : alk. paper)—ISBN 0-7425-2522-8 (pbk. : alk. paper)
    1. Intelligence service—United States—History—20th century. 2. United States.
Central Intelligence Agency. 3. United States—Foreign relations—20th century. 4.
Narcotics, Control of—Political aspects. 5. Drug traffic—History—20th century. 6.
Petroleum industry and trade—Political aspects. 7. United States—Foreign relations—
Indochina. 8. Indochina—Foreign relations—United States. 9. United States—Foreign
relations—Colombia. 10. Colombia—Foreign relations—United States. 11. United
States—Foreign relations—Afghanistan. 12. Afghanistan—Foreign relations—United
States. I. Title. II. Series.
    JK468 .I6S35 2003
    327.1273'009'045—dc21   2002155383

Printed in the United States of America

9/15/04   *Amb*

Contents

viii   *Contents*

Abbreviations and Acronyms

AAA	Alianza Anticomunista Americana (American Anticommunist Alliance)
AID	Agency for International Development
AIPAC	American Israel Public Affairs Committee
AIUSA	Amnesty International USA
APACL	Asian People's Anti-Communist League
ASC	American Security Council
AUC	Autodefensas Unidas de Colombia (United Self-Defense Forces of Colombia)
AVG	American Volunteer Group
BCCI	Bank of Credit and Commerce International
BP	British Petroleum
CAMCO	Central Aircraft Manufacturing Company
CAT	Civil Air Transport [later Air America]
CATCL	Civil Air Transport Co., Ltd.
CDI	Center for Defense Information
CDNI	Committee for the Defense of National Interests
CIA	Central Intelligence Agency
CINCPAC	Commander in Chief Pacific
COSVN	Central Office for South Vietnam
DEA	Drug Enforcement Administration
DIA	Defense Intelligence Agency
EAST	Eagle Aviation Services and Technology Inc.
ECAFE	United Nations Economic Commission for Asia and the Far East
ELINT	electronics intelligence
ELN	National Liberation Army
FARC	Revolutionary Armed Forces of Colombia

FBIS	Foreign Broadcast Intelligence Service
FBN	Federal Bureau of Narcotics
FCRA	Free China Relief Agency
FPRI	Foreign Policy Research Institute
FRUS	*Foreign Relations of the United States* (publication)
ICA	International Cooperation Administration
IMF	International Monetary Fund
IMU	Islamic Movement of Uzbekistan
ISI	Inter-Services Intelligence
JCS	Joint Chiefs of Staff
KKK	Khmer Kampuchea Krom
KMT	Kuomintang
MAS	Muerte a Sequestradores (Death to Kidnappers)
MPRI	Military Professional Resources Inc.
NAVOCEANO	U.S. Naval Oceanographic Office
NLF	National Liberation Front [of Vietnam]
NSC	National Security Council
NSDD	National Security Decision Directive
NSIA	National Security Industrial Association
ODCCP	United Nations Office for Drug Control and Crime Prevention
ONI	Office of Naval Intelligence
OPC	Office of Policy Coordination
OPEC	Organization of Petroleum Exporting Countries
OSS	Office of Strategic Services
PRC	People's Republic of China
PRG	Provisional Revolutionary Government [of Vietnamese NLF]
RAND	Research and Development Corporation
SALT II	Strategic Arms Limitations Talks II
SAT	Southern Air Transport
SEATO	Southeast Asia Treaty Organization
SOG	Studies and Operations Group
TRW	Thompson-Ramo-Wooldridge
UNCND	United Nations Commission on Narcotic Drugs
Unocal	Union Oil of California
UNRRA	United Nations Relief and Rehabilitation Administration
USAF	United States Air Force
WACL	World Anti-Communist League

Preface

This book, *Drugs, Oil, and War: The United States in Afghanistan, Colombia, and Indochina*, explores the underlying factors that have engendered a U.S. strategy of indirect intervention in Third World countries through alliances with drug-trafficking proxies. This strategy was originally developed in the late 1940s to contain communist China; it has since been used to secure control over foreign petroleum resources. The result has been a staggering increase in the global drug traffic and the mafias assorted with it, a problem that will worsen until there is a change in policy.

The book also traces some of the processes by which covert interventions have escalated into war. Parts I and II include lengthy new chapters on Afghanistan and Colombia. Part III consists of five updated chapters from my 1972 book *The War Conspiracy: The Secret Road to the Second Indochina War*.

This book explores ongoing causal patterns that have helped shape U.S. foreign policy, sometimes at a deeper level than was recognized even by bureaucrats in high places. Under pressure from interested outsiders, decisions were made by the United States, after World War II in Burma and again in Laos in 1959–1965, to back armies and governments that were supporting themselves through the drug traffic. This has led to a linked succession of wars, from Vietnam to Afghanistan, which have suited the purposes of international oil corporations and U.S. drug proxy allies, far more than those of either the U.S. government or its people. Those decisions were also major causes for the dramatic increase in drug trafficking over the last half century.

Today drug networks are important factors in the politics of every continent. The United States returns repeatedly to the posture of fighting wars in areas of petroleum reserves with the aid of drug-trafficking allies (or what I call drug proxies) with which it has a penchant to become involved. Surprisingly, this is true even in Colombia, where we are nominally fighting a war on drugs; yet the chief drug-trafficking faction, the paramilitaries, are allies of our allies, the

Colombian army. Worse, they are the descendants of yet another clever CIA notion—to train terrorists to fight the left—which has once again come back to haunt us.

This is the situation that has recently engaged the United States in Afghanistan, a country through which until 1998 a U.S. oil company, Unocal, hoped to build oil and gas pipelines. The drug-trafficking network of al-Qaeda and Osama bin Laden, a former CIA ally operating out of caves designed and paid for by the CIA, has just been defeated with the help of another drug proxy, the Afghan Northern Alliance. In the pursuit of bin Laden, the United States defeated his allies, the Taliban (which in 2000 had enforced a total ban on opium cultivation in its area), with the aid of the Northern Alliance (which in the same period had overseen a trebling of opium cultivation in its area).

As this book goes to press, the new interim Afghan government has initiated a nominal ban on opium cultivation. But the United States has not given the Hamid Karzai regime enough financial support to make the ban work. Clearly the drug traffic itself is now a well-financed transnational power player in the region, and there are no serious current plans to reduce it. (There are only minimal plans to repair the devastation wrought by U.S. bombing on an Afghan economy that was already in ruins after decades of international and civil war.)

Even if there were an effective ban on opium production and trafficking in Afghanistan, one could still predict with some confidence that it would increase in a neighboring area, such as Tajikistan or Kyrgyzstan. As the drug traffic grows in the new area, it will help destabilize the host states in the region, none of which is too secure to begin with. Without a change in policy, the United States, which has already sent troops into the region, will sooner or later be confronted with another crisis that calls for intervention.

These problems facing America are by no means entirely of its own making. But one recurring cause, commonly recognized, is U.S. dependence on foreign oil and its need to control international oil markets. Past U.S. support for drug proxies is another more covert and less recognized contributing factor, one that must be acknowledged if the root causes for these crises are to be addressed.

Conversely, the great resistance that still exists to acknowledging past U.S. involvement in and responsibility for covert intrigues contributes to our present inability to bring true peace and security to the rest of the world. The agencies responsible for past errors are too concerned to preserve not only their reputations but their alliances and, above all, the corrupt social systems in which such alliances have thrived. Consequently an international drug traffic, which the United States helped enlarge, continues to thrive.

I shall argue in this book that covert operations, when they generate or reinforce autonomous political power, almost always outlast the specific purpose for which they were designed. Instead they enlarge and become part of the hostile forces the United States has to contend with. To put it in terms I find more precise, _parapolitics_, the exercise of power by covert means, tends to metastasize into *deep politics*, an interplay of unacknowledged forces over which the original parapolitical agent no longer has control. This is the heart of the analysis.

In my book *Deep Politics and the Death of JFK* (pp. 7–8), I give a seminal example of this process: U.S. *parapolitical* use of Mafia figures like Vito Genovese in postwar Italy. This was a conscious operation that soon led to the *deep political* dominance of Italian party politics by a Mafia out of control. That example will serve in miniature for the history of all U.S. interventions since then in Asia. In 1951 a decision was made to ship arms and supplies to the armies of the Kuomintang (KMT) drug network in Burma. This led to a fivefold increase in Burmese opium production in less than a decade, from eighty to four hundred tons. By 1999, the peak year before the ban imposed by the Taliban took effect, world opium production had reached 7,000 tons. Of this, 4,700 tons, or 70 percent, was being grown in Afghanistan and trafficked by heirs of the mujahedin who in the 1980s had been financed, armed, and supported by the CIA.

Again, the United States was not solely responsible for this growth. Some of it would have occurred anyway, possibly (as the U.S. government used to contend) under the guidance of a hostile power such as China or the Soviet Union. The point is that the drug problem cannot be understood, let alone properly addressed, until the parapolitical consequences of CIA involvement have been acknowledged and corrected.

OIL

The presence of drug trafficking in the background of these interventions is paralleled by considerations about oil. Here too decisions made freely after World War II have helped to enmesh the United States in a problematical situation—the risks from terrorism are continuously increasing and extrication will not now be easy.

Right after World War II, building on the so-called Quincy Agreements with Saudi Arabia in 1945, the United States moved to dominate a global system for the production and distribution of oil. Starting with the Truman Doctrine in 1946, U.S. geostrategic thinking was oil based. What began as a strategy for containment of the Soviet Union has become more and more nakedly a determination to control the oil resources of the world. This pursuit has progressively deformed the domestic U.S. economy, rendering it more and more unbalanced and dependent on heavy military expenditures in remote and ungovernable areas—most recently Afghanistan. It has also made the United States an increasingly belligerent power, fighting wars, especially in Asia, where it turns time after time to allies and assets prominent in the global drug traffic.

From the outset U.S. strategy in Southeast Asia envisaged protecting what President Eisenhower once referred to as "the rich empire of Indonesia," whose primary export was oil.[1] In the 1970s, as opium production in Asia shifted west from the Golden Triangle to the Golden Crescent, so also U.S. interventions, first covert and then overt, shifted from Indochina to Afghanistan.

I do not mean to suggest that domination of oil resources was the sole consideration on the minds of U.S. policy planners. On the contrary, they believed in their own rhetoric of defending the so-called free world from communist domination, whether Soviet or Chinese. But inasmuch as what they feared above all was communist control of oil resources, the result of their planning was continuously to strengthen U.S. domination of an increasingly unified global oil system.

From Iran in 1953 to Indonesia in 1965 and Ghana in 1966 the CIA was involved in the covert overthrow of governments around the world that (as Michael Tanzer noted years ago) had threatened to nationalize their oil industries.[2] As U.S. interventions overseas increased in the 1960s, so did U.S. dependence on overseas oil to meet its growing demands. When this exposure led to the oil shocks of the 1970s, the United States was forced into a double policy of controlling the international flow of oil and petrodollars. As we shall see, it solved the latter problem by means of secret agreements that maintained the strength of the U.S. dollar at the expense of the Third World.

The resulting impoverishment of the Third World has been accompanied by a disastrous increase in global terrorism, which has now become a major focus of U.S. foreign policy. Yet, as Frank Viviano observed in the *San Francisco Chronicle* (September 26, 2001),

> The hidden stakes in the war against terrorism can be summed up in a single word: oil. The map of terrorist sanctuaries and targets in the Middle East and Central Asia is also, to an extraordinary degree, a map of the world's principal energy sources in the 21st century. The defense of these energy resources—rather than a simple confrontation between Islam and the West—will be the primary flash point of global conflict for decades to come, say observers in the region.[3]

Although it was not part of his subject, Viviano's observations can be applied also to other regions of oil and terrorism, such as Indonesia, Colombia, Somalia, and (because of oil pipelines) Chechnya and even Kosovo.

In short the etiology or origin of global terrorism is rooted partly in the historical context of previous U.S. policy decisions with respect to both drugs and oil. I say this not to cast blame but to suggest the proper direction to search for solutions. Decision makers of a half century ago cannot be faulted for lacking the foreknowledge that comes more easily in retrospect. It is, however, not too late to address the legacy they have left us—a suspect affluence grounded in part on the impoverishment of the rest of the world. As long as that legacy is not corrected, we can be sure that the problem of terrorism will remain with us.

WHAT TO DO

The problem will not be solved by putting more and more U.S. troops abroad, from Colombia to Kyrgyzstan. (Both countries, as it happens, are in oil regions and are experiencing a rapid increase in drug trafficking). The quintessential example of such a buildup of U.S. arms and personnel was Iran in the 1970s—a major cause, as is now obvious, for the Iranian revolution against the U.S. client shah. Hundreds of millions of U.S. dollars for the Somali dictator Siad Barre encouraged him to pursue increasingly oppressive policies, which led in 1991 to his overthrow.

With respect to drugs, I will only say that the United States must end those repressive policies whose result (and often intention) is to maintain the high drug prices that strengthen and enrich the international drug traffic. With respect to oil, we must intensify the search for technological ways to reduce consumption at home and move toward a more multilateral and equitable oil system abroad. Above all, the United States must return to the multilateral system of global regulation that it helped establish after World War II and renounce the fatal temptation to become a hegemon. We must not repeat the follies of Napoleon and Hitler in the heartlands of Eurasia.

This shift will require a different strategy to deal with the dollar and with petrodollars, particularly those from Saudi Arabia and its neighbors in the Persian Gulf. At present the United States balances its payments by secret agreements with Saudi Arabia to recycle petrodollars to the United States and to ensure that OPEC sales all over the world are denominated in U.S. dollars. These arrangements to ease pressure on the U.S. currency have helped, as an inevitable consequence, to create debt crises all over the Third World.

The same secret agreements, discussed in chapter 2 of this volume, are perhaps the prime example of how secret U.S. policies, barely documented, can give rise to global conditions of misery and unrest. People's strategies of public opposition to official policies, such as the rallies that activists like Noam Chomsky indefatigably address, are in my opinion unlikely to succeed until they expose the unjust secret arrangements and deals on which these official policies are based. The U.S. political establishment, seemingly unassailable on its surface, becomes more vulnerable when the private, covert, and sometimes conspiratorial origins of what passes for public policy are exposed. This book is dedicated to examining war policies at this deeper level.

Meanwhile, official strategies that enrich the United States by impoverishing the rest of the world diminish the possibilities of peace and progress for this country. And our security is put still more at risk by giving military aid to unpopular dictators. The United States tried this strategy in Vietnam in the 1960s, Iran in the 1970s, and Somalia in the 1980s, to name a few. We are still suffering from the anti-American reactions these policies produced. Yet today, as if we had learned nothing, we are establishing bases and giving military aid to the dictator of Uzbekistan—an ex-Soviet *apparatchik* with no program for dealing with his extensive Muslim opposition except to imprison them.

We cannot expect a reversal of these strategies from America's present leaders of either party, constrained as they are by an increasingly oppressive global system that is in large part of those parties' own making. Recent revelations have shown the extent to which contributions from energy companies have constrained both parties in America as they have politicians abroad. What we hear instead from Washington, although not without opposition, are increasingly strident calls for unilateralist policies in an allegedly unipolar world. Triumphal unilateralism in the United States and terroristic Islamism abroad have become more and more similar to (and dependent on) each other, with each invoking its opposite to justify its excesses.

The future of American democracy rests on our ability to recognize and separate our nation from the causal factors that lie at the heart of U.S. global policies—policies that have produced such harmful results, not only for those who have been victimized on a world scale but also for Americans.

To these ends I offer, hopefully, the findings of this book. Part III of what follows is from my 1972 book *The War Conspiracy,* chapters long on detail but short on deep political analysis. At the front of the book are six chapters on the deep politics of U.S. engagements in Afghanistan, Colombia, and Indochina. The patterns in each case are, I believe, more easily discerned by a comparative analysis of the others. Above all, we see the recurring lobbying activities of groups like the American Security Council, in which oil companies are represented, as well as the lobbying activities of airlines with government contracts for arms shipments, and with alleged involvement also in drug trafficking and/or organized crime.

The point of these chapters, and of the book, is not to compete with what I describe as the archival histories of these events, which chronicle them from the documented perspective of the policy makers. It is to focus on deeper causal patterns arising from less documented sectors of society, which have tended to be overlooked in serious academic analysis. It is at this level, I submit, that we can isolate and expose factors more easily amenable to correction.

It would be folly to suggest that this book can bring peace to the world. But I do believe that it suggests new ways in which to search for peace. Above all I hope that it may help Americans understand how they may love their country and still come to accept its share of responsibility for an international order that cries out for amendment.

Just as some in the U.S. government demonize others as terrorists forming an "axis of evil," so others turn such epithets back on the U.S. government itself. I myself see little value in depicting either the United States or its enemies as an intractable other, to be opposed by means that may well prove counterproductive. Just as Islamism needs to be understood in its complexity, so does U.S. power, which is at least as complex. Above all we have to recognize that U.S. influence is grounded not just in military and economic superiority but also in so-called soft power (an "ability . . . that shapes the preferences of others," that "tends to be associated with intangible power resources such as an attractive culture, ideology, and institutions").[4]

We need a "soft politics" of persuasion and nonviolence to address and modify this country's soft power. Such a proposal is not utopian: the soft politics of the antiwar movement helped, despite many key errors of strategy, to hasten U.S. disengagement from Vietnam. As it becomes increasingly clear that that war "dealt a major blow to the United States' ability to remain the world's dominant economic power,"[5] even the exponents of America's hard power may come in time to express their gratitude to critics of the Vietnam War.

As this book goes to press, this country is facing the prospect of yet another needless and disastrous intervention in Iraq. For our sake as well as for the sake of the rest of the world, we must continue to develop alternative soft processes of change.

Note: For the most part I have made only necessary corrections and amplifications to part III, "Indochina," first published in 1972 in *The War Conspiracy.* Though I have updated a few of the terms (e.g., "Hmong" in place of "Meos"), I have generally avoided *pinyin* substitutions ("Guomindang" in place of "Kuomintang") except where the context is recent.

ACKNOWLEDGMENTS

Chapter 9 was originally published as "Laos: The Story Nixon Won't Tell," *New York Review of Books,* April 9, 1970, 35–45. © 1970 NYREV, Inc.

I am grateful to Susan McEachern, my editor at Rowman & Littlefield, for her advice, wisdom, encouragement, and patience, and also to her long-suffering assistant Jessica Gribble. I am indebted to those involved in the production of the book: April Leo, Chrisona Schmidt, and Lynn Gemmell. I particularly want to acknowledge Michael Leon and Rex Bradford for their long hours spent on the text. My thanks to my agent Virginia Shoemaker, to Mike Ruppert for having encouraged this project in the first place, and also to Bill Firth and Frank Dorrel for their early support. I am grateful to scholars who took the time to read and sometimes comment on the text, above all Mark Selden, Bruce Cumings, David Kaiser, Fredrik Logevall, Edwin Moïse, and Carl Trocki. I owe an immeasurable debt to the work and wisdom of other researchers, notably Alfred McCoy, Alan A. Block, and Lawrence Lifschultz. I also want to thank Barnett Rubin for advice on a crucial issue and George Hunsinger for keeping me apprised of relevant breaking news as the book went to press. Above all I am grateful to my best friend, Daniel Ellsberg, for his astute comments and guidance on and beyond the text of this book.

My biggest debt by far is to my wife and inspiration, Ronna Kabatznick, not only for her help with the book but for her love and companionship, which have strengthened me in a difficult engagement with both poetry and this world.

AUTHOR'S NOTE

In 2001, having completed a book consisting of parts II and III in this volume, I wrote a preface about America's recurring alliances with drug traffickers to gain control over oil resources. The preface was completed and dated August 31, 2001, eleven days before the events of 9/11. My first reaction to the 9/11 crisis was to consider my remarks passé; but on reflection I have decided my analysis was more relevant than ever, especially as the U.S. dependence on the drug-trafficking Northern Alliance became more and more evident. Portions of that original preface are preserved in the following author's note.

Writing this expanded version of my 1972 book has sharpened my sense of the deep politics of our country, especially of deep causes for our involvement in irrational conflicts: conflicts that do not serve the interests of either the invaded country or the American people. Plan Colombia in particular is another phase, hopefully but not necessarily the last, of Cold War practices inimical to democracy that have outlived any possible justification yet will prove hard to eradicate.

Central to these practices is the habit of intervening militarily in the Third World on the side (and with the assistance) of repressive forces organized around the drug traffic. Such covert arrangements with drug traffickers require systematic lying to the American people, a practice of lying that entraps not only U.S. government officials but their allies in the so-called responsible U.S. press.

I had a chance to observe the viciousness of this corrupt system in 1987, when I spent six months in Washington at a think tank, supplying documentation to the Kerry congressional subcommittee investigating the drug trafficking of Contras and their supporters. Less alarming to me than the facts were their consequences for those who knew of or reported them. One conscientious witness, a Republican businessman and Reagan supporter, suffered credible death threats that appear to have been partly acted on. Another for his pains was similarly menaced and directly targeted by Oliver North in the White House as a "terrorist threat."

Even members of our think tank were interrogated by the FBI, which was perhaps the least bothersome inconvenience suffered by those promoting the truth. Others were placed under twenty-four-hour surveillance by forces the Washington police could not identify, or deprived of their professional jobs. In an arrangement that was probably illegal, a CIA-type propaganda campaign was funded through the State Department against the American people, targeting for defeat those who had opposed the Contras in Congress.

Although there was no longer any Cold War pretext for this crude approach, the coercive forces had become stronger than ever. It is clear that, at a minimum, the lies are continuing today. The nation is being slowly dragged into a conflict with alleged Colombia "narco-guerrillas," whose share of coca production was officially estimated in 2001 to be 2.5 percent of the total. Our arms and assistance are going to the Colombian military, who work in coordination with drug-trafficking paramilitary death squads. In 2001 these death squads' share of the drug trade was estimated, officially by the Colombian government, at 40 percent.

This fundamental Orwellian absurdity of our misnamed "war on drugs" is (as far as I can determine) totally ignored by the U.S. press today. This is part of a predictable pattern, just as in the past the U.S. press ignored the drug trafficking of our allies in Vietnam, Afghanistan, Central America, and most recently Kosovo. Also completely ignored by the U.S. press is the extent to which U.S. oil companies have lobbied for Plan Colombia, just as in the 1960s the press ignored the vigorous campaign of Socony Mobil for an escalated involvement in Vietnam.

I do not say these things out of despair, nor from a dislike of the United States. On the contrary, I have written this with the conviction that if the American people understand the truth about Plan Colombia, they will finally mobilize to end it, just as in the 1960s and 1970s they mobilized against Vietnam. But reaching this understanding will not be easy. The channels of information and communication in this country, though the most developed in the world, are also deeply flawed.

Only to this extent am I a pessimist: I believe that if U.S. Colombian policy is left in the hands of those now running and informing this country, it will lead to more and more killings of Colombians and Americans alike. Whether or not we have a new Vietnam War will depend on concerned people like the readers of this book.

NOTES

1. Dwight D. Eisenhower, speech, August 4, 1953; *The Pentagon Papers: The Defense Department History of United States Decisionmaking on Vietnam*, Senator Gravel ed. (Boston: Beacon, 1971–1972), 1:592.

2. Michael Tanzer, *The Political Economy of International Oil and the Underdeveloped Countries* (Boston: Beacon, 1969).

3. Frank Viviano, *San Francisco Chronicle*, September 26, 2001, www.sfgate.com/cgi-bin/article.cgi?file = /chronicle/archive/2001/09/26/MN7098 3.DTL.

4. Joseph S. Nye Jr., *The Paradox of American Power: Why the World's Only Superpower Can't Go It Alone* (Oxford: Oxford University Press, 2002), 9.

5. Immanuel Wallerstein, "The Eagle Has Crash Landed," *Foreign Policy,* July–August 2002, www.foreignpolicy.com/issue_julyaug_2002/wallerstein.html.

PARAPOLITICS AND DEEP POLITICS:
DEFINITIONS AND USAGE

I. (From *The War Conspiracy*, p. 171, chapter epigraph)

"**par·a·pol·i·tics** (păr′ ə pŏl′ ə tĭks), *n*. **1.** a system or practice of politics in which accountability is consciously diminished. **2.** generally, covert politics, the conduct of public affairs not by rational debate and responsible decision-making but by indirection, collusion, and deceit. Cf. *conspiracy*.[1] **3.** the political exploitation of irresponsible agencies or parastructures, such as intelligence agencies.

Ex. **1.** 'The Nixon doctrine, viewed in retrospect, represented the application of parapolitics on a hitherto unprecedented scale.' **2.** 'Democracy and parapolitics, even in foreign affairs, are ultimately incompatible.'

1. Notes for an unwritten future dictionary."

II. (From *Deep Politics and the Death of JFK*, pp. 6–7)

"the investigation of *parapolitics*, which I defined (with the CIA in mind) as a 'system or practice of politics in which accountability is consciously diminished.' . . . I still see value in this definition and mode of analysis. But parapolitics as thus defined is itself too narrowly conscious and intentional . . . it describes at best only an intervening layer of the irrationality under our political culture's rational surface. Thus I now refer to parapolitics as only one manifestation of *deep politics*, all those political practices and arrangements, deliberate or not, which are usually repressed rather than acknowledged."

III. (From "America's Worst Enemy: The CIA's Secret Powers")

"Covert power is like nuclear power: it produces noisome and life-threatening by-products which cumulatively are more and more threatening to the environment supposedly served. The by-products of covert power include trained terrorists who in the end are likely to target their former employers, the incriminating relations to government which hinder these terrorists' prosecution, and the ensuing corruption of society at large. The result is deep politics: the immersion of public political life in an immobilizing substratum of unspeakable scandal and bad faith. The result in practice is 9/11."

Introduction

The Deep Politics of U.S. Interventions

In 1969–1970, the year of Cambodia and Kent State, I wrote a book, *The War Conspiracy*. In it I described what I considered hidden, undiscussed forces that helped lead the United States into the Vietnam War. My book looked behind official U.S. policy statements to other more powerful factors not generally recognized, and some of my friends considered this approach pessimistic. It was not. It was optimistic, inspired by the old-fashioned hope that a better understanding of these factors might help contribute to bringing them under control.

As I explored instances of hidden manipulations, whether at the highest or at subordinate levels, I coined a term, "parapolitics," to cover "the conduct of public affairs . . . by indirection, collusion, and deceit." But "parapolitics" does not cover the full range of events in this book. "Parapolitics" describes intentional controlling behavior, mostly executive and bureaucratic. My later chapters looked more at societal factors outside government that did not fit the definition—notably the lobbying and other activities of oil companies and the aircraft industry, often in conjunction with the military. The last two chapters dealt with matters of relevance to U.S. interventions today: the impact on U.S. foreign policy of oil strategies and the drug traffic.

Today I would speak of "deep politics" or deep political processes rather than conspiratorial events, meaning a series of practices, at odds with the laws and mores of society, "which are usually repressed rather than acknowledged."[1] Deep political processes include parapolitical ones but are more open-ended. Parapolitics is a means of control. Deep politics can refer to any form of sinister, unacknowledged influence.

The distinction, easy enough to make in theory, is much harder to make in practice. Some of the bureaucratic manipulations described in this book, such as those involving Air America in Laos, strike me as parapolitical intrigue. But underlying Southeast Asian history in these years was the politically significant narcotics traffic. The CIA was intimately connected to this traffic, chiefly through

1

its proprietary Air America. But it was not securely in control of this traffic and probably did not even seek to be. What it desired was "deniability," achieved by the legal nicety that Air America, which the CIA wholly owned, was a corporation that hired pilots and owned an aircraft maintenance facility on Taiwan. Most of its planes, which often carried drugs, were 60 percent owned and frequently operated by Kuomintang (KMT) Chinese.

The CIA was comfortable in this deniable relationship with people it knew were reorganizing the postwar drug traffic in Southeast Asia. The U.S. government was determined to ensure that drug-trafficking networks and triads in the region remained under KMT control, even if this meant logistic and air support to armies in postwar Burma whose chief activity was expanding the local supply of opium. The complex legal structure of the airline CAT—known earlier as Civil Air Transport and later as Air America—was the ideal vehicle for this support. (Some CAT pilots were involved in smuggling during World War II, before the CIA connection.)[2]

The acquisition of CAT was part of a larger strategy whose principal advocate was its original owner, Major General Claire L. Chennault. Chennault predicted in the late 1940s that the victory of Mao Tse-tung in mainland China would be followed by a massive expansion of communist influence: first to Indochina and then Thailand, Malaya, Burma, and possibly even India. Knowing that the commitment of U.S. troops in response to this threat was not politically possible, Chennault proposed an alternative: using his airline as logistical support for a KMT Chinese army, strengthened by American military advisers.[3] Chennault's project, unpopular at first inside the government, was eventually forced on a reluctant Truman administration with the support of Henry Luce's *Life* magazine and China lobby representatives in Congress.[4]

The Chennault plan deserves to be recognized as the prototype of the U.S. use of drug proxies, which has survived down to the 2001 U.S. intervention in Afghanistan.[5] This working alliance with a drug network, implemented in the 1950s in Burma, would have been dangerous enough if politically neutral. An even more dangerous milieu for conspiratorial intrigue emerged in the early 1960s, as President Kennedy gradually disengaged from the goals of the KMT and the powerful China lobby, still scheming for the recovery of the Chinese mainland.[6]

Urged on by the growing evidence of a Chinese–Soviet split, Chiang Kai-shek in 1962 talked openly of an imminent invasion of mainland China. As discussed below, his proposal to Washington for an expanded Bay of Pigs–type operation on the mainland was endorsed by Ray Cline, the former Taiwan CIA station chief (later CIA deputy director of intelligence). It was backed also by Admiral Harry D. Felt, commander in chief of the Pacific (CINCPAC). Many top U.S. military leaders and the CIA were also sympathetic.[7] One supporter who went even further was Air America board chairman and former CINCPAC Admiral Felix B.

Stump, who called publicly for the defeat of communism in the Far East, using tactical nuclear weapons if necessary. As is often pointed out, Chiang's efforts in mainline China resulted only in the killing or capture of his agents. But KMT allies played a successful conspiratorial role with Air America (formerly Chennault's airline, CAT) in destabilizing Laos in 1960–1964. And even more conspicuously they succeeded, with the help of CAT, in building up the postwar drug traffic. Both of these roles were probably more significant in the Laotian crises than the role attributed by U.S. intelligence at the time to the Chinese People's Republic.[8] KMT political objectives, assets, and allies in Laos cannot be dissociated from their stake, by then considerable, in the international drug traffic.

The CIA fiascoes in Laos should concern us again today, as the U.S. plays the drug card in Colombia and Afghanistan. The CIA's convenience or milieu of deniability, as opposed to secure control, gave rise to many episodes in the 1960s that are still imperfectly understood but had lasting and disastrous consequences. Those mistakes, which contributed enormously to the spread of the international drug traffic, are apparently being repeated today.

THE CHENNAULT/CAT LEGACY: DRUG PROXY ASSETS, INFRASTRUCTURES, AND LOBBIES

The following chapters study, in reverse chronology, the evolution of the energies of the CIA–Air America–KMT complex into the current deep politics of oil and drugs in Afghanistan and Colombia. The overall picture is complex, but certain general propositions tend to prevail. One is that initially small, covert operations, lacking proper supervision, become budget opportunities to be exploited by a number of different lobbies, from oil to herbicides.

A second proposition is that off-the-book proprietaries, like Air America, survive through the war scares they help generate. In Air America's wake, there are now a number of outsourced, nominally private corporations, such as DynCorp, which serve as trainers and infrastructure for proxy U.S. assets abroad. All of these, lacking a regular standing budget, require continuity of U.S. intervention if they are to remain in business as adjuncts to the U.S. defense establishment. They not only need the business but can help ensure that it happens.

A third proposition is that where wisdom calls for moderation and excessive U.S. response will generate a larger budget, excess will tend to prevail. As I quote from former U.S. Ambassador Robert White in chapter 6 of this book, "If you put over 90 cents of your foreign policy dollar into the Pentagon and the CIA, then your policy is going to emphasize a military approach, a secretive, under the [table] approach, to the problems."[9] This 9–1 ratio becomes even greater when we compare lobbying by profit-motivated interests to that by public interest groups.

An underreported factor in the political corruption of U.S. Asian policy has been the input of money, including drug money, from foreign governments through their lobbyists and PR firms. This book will talk about cash injected into the U.S. political system by the China lobby, allegedly drug financed, to back pro-KMT politicians like the young Richard Nixon.[10] As the China lobby waned in the 1960s, its place was taken by the Korea lobby, with Anna Chennault, the general's young Chinese wife, playing an important role in both.[11] To this day money from Sun Myung Moon's Unification Church, an offspring of the KCIA and of the related Asian People's Anti-Communist League (APACL, later the World Anti-Communist League or WACL), continues to subsidize the right-wing *Washington Times*.[12]

Two deeper factors reinforce the continuity sketched in the preceding paragraph. One is the continuing close involvement of regular or "rogue" CIA officers, such as Ray Cline or Edwin Wilson, at every stage.[13] Another, not unrelated, is the recurring allegations that the China lobby, the Unification Church, and the APACL have all derived their considerable budgets from the drug traffic.[14] At the origins of this insidious influence one finds the undoubted drug involvement of the CIA's airline CAT (later Air America).[15]

These foreign sources lobbying for successive U.S. wars were supported by domestic Washington lobbies, such as the American Security Council (with major oil corporations as members).[16] We also see the role of oil companies and their own ad hoc lobbying groups in lobbying directly for heightened commitments in Vietnam, Afghanistan, and Colombia—Socony Mobil in Vietnam, the Foreign Oil Companies Group in Afghanistan, the U.S.-Colombia Business Partnership in Colombia.[17] These ongoing lobbies undergirded the emergence of front lobbying groups whose names were less revealing of economic interest— the American Friends of Vietnam in the 1950s and 1960s, the Committee for a Free Afghanistan in the 1980s.[18]

Such lobbying activities have ranged over a wide spectrum, from overt media activity to covert corruption. Oil companies do not hesitate to associate themselves publicly with the ASC and other overt lobbying groups. At the latter, deep level are detected indirect links to the funds and principals of institutions connected to the drug traffic. But in practice the two are intertwined, as we shall see when we look more closely at the example of Afghanistan in the 1980s.

A CASE STUDY IN POLICY DEFORMATION: THE STINGERS FOR AFGHANISTAN

An exemplary case of deep political boondoggle enlarging official policy is the story of how the United States, in 1986, provided Stinger antiaircraft missiles to the mujahedin in Afghanistan. According to conventional accounts, beginning in October 1986, certain resistance groups began to receive US-made Stinger missiles through the CIA arms pipeline. . . . The Stinger was the most important of the many new weapons used in the war; by the end of 1986 it provided the mujahideen with a credible air defense for the first time. Reports of incredible accuracy induced the Soviets to change their hitherto successful air war strategy.[19]

Another book claims that "The CIA's most notable and important success was introducing the Stinger antiaircraft missile, which would begin to turn the tide of the war in 1985 [i.e., 1986], forcing Soviet attack aircraft and helicopter gunships to keep to ineffective high altitudes."[20]

The first point is that it is by no means clear that the Stingers, as so often reported, "turned the tide." On the contrary, a subsequent analysis of the Soviet Politburo records by political scientist Alan J. Kuperman convinced him that

although counterintuitive and contrary to popular wisdom, it appears the U.S. counterescalation of 1985–1986 was largely irrelevant to the Soviet withdrawal decision of November 1986. . . . This is clearly the case for the Stinger, which was not utilized in Afghanistan until September 1986, a mere two months before the Politburo's decision to adopt a withdrawal deadline. At the key November 1986 Politburo meeting, no mention was made of the Stinger nor any other U.S. escalation.[21]

Furthermore, the program to supply Stingers, so often touted as a successful policy, became an acute problem of "blowback." As critics had warned, the Stingers soon fell into the wrong hands:

In the fall of 1986, for example, Soviet commandoes ambushed a group of rebels and captured two Stingers. In June 1987, Iranian revolutionary guards either seized or bought at least 16 Stinger missiles from the Afghan rebel forces of Yunis Khalis. One of the Stingers and a launcher turned up in the fall of 1987 on an Iranian speedboat that was captured after it fired on American Navy helicopter gunships in the Persian Gulf.[22]

The CIA in 1989–1990 had to allocate millions in a desperate attempt, only minimally successful, to buy the unused Stingers back.[23] Fear that the Taliban might possess as many as three hundred of them was the reason that the United States, in 2001, initially conducted its air war in Afghanistan from such high altitudes.[24]

The leading impetus to supply the Stingers did not come from the CIA, as many accounts assert, but from members of Congress and their staffs, with lobbies behind them. The army was bitterly opposed, fearing that this state-of-the-art weapon might fall into Soviet hands and be copied.[25] The CIA "warned that supplying the mujahideen with Stingers might provoke Soviet retaliation against Pakistan, the base for the CIA's rebel-support effort."[26]

Although other senators and congressmen were involved, the key instigator

was a Democrat, Representative Charles Wilson, associated with the American
Security Council:

> In the fall of 1983, Representative Charles Wilson, Democrat of Texas, started a
> campaign to supply the guerrillas with a more effective antiaircraft weapon. "Oppo-
> sition to the Stinger was so great that we had to settle for something less than a
> missile," he said, recalling that even William J. Casey, the Director of Central Intel-
> ligence, would not push for Stingers. At the end of 1983, Mr. Wilson persuaded his
> colleagues to provide $40 million for weapons, and much of it went for a powerful
> 20-millimeter antiaircraft gun made by a Swiss company, Oerlikon. The guerrillas
> began to get the automatic cannon in late 1984, Mr. Wilson said in an interview. . . .[27]
> For several months, conservative groups had harshly criticized John N. McMahon,
> who was Deputy Director of Central Intelligence, on the ground that he was blocking
> efforts to send Stingers to the guerrillas. In early March 1986, Mr. Reagan approved
> delivery of such missiles. At about the same time, Mr. McMahon, who had served
> 35 years with the agency, resigned for what he described as "personal reasons."
> He said his resignation was not "an expression of discontent with the President's
> policies."[28]

From an archival historian's perspective (discussed below), the decision to provide Stingers in 1986 flowed from National Security Decision Directive 166 of
March 1985, signed as President Reagan looked beyond support to victory in
Afghanistan. Clearly, however, the momentum shifted in 1983–1984, when U.S.
covert military aid to the Afghan rebels (until then stable in the level of $30–$35
million annually) more than doubled.[29] The final 1986 Stinger decision was an
outgrowth of congressional lobbying in the pre-1985 period—lobbying by the
same kind of interests who would lobby later for Colombia and had lobbied earlier for Vietnam.

One such interest was the American Security Council, which took an active
interest in lobbying for an increased effort in Vietnam in the 1960s, and in
Afghanistan in the 1980s. Charles Wilson himself was a member of the American
Security Council Task Force on Central America.[30] An ASC staff member, Odilie
English, toured Afghanistan several times in the 1980s, before becoming the PR
director for the Committee for a Free Afghanistan, and more recently lobbyist for
the Northern Alliance.[31] The chair of the Committee for a Free Afghanistan,
Major General Milnor Roberts (ret.), was vice president of the ASC.[32]

THE DARKER SIDE OF COVERT ASSETS

A more dubious, "deeper" influence was Farhad Azima, a contributor to both
political parties.[33] As we shall see, Azima's airline, Global International Airways,
became involved in the 1980s U.S. arms pipeline to Afghanistan. It was also part
of a complex of CIA-linked contract cargo airlines that included Air America

(in Vietnam), Southern Air Transport (doing business with the Contras and in Colombia), and Azima's RACE Aviation (flying U.S. arms to Iran).[34] Azima founded Global International in 1978. "With money borrowed from an Arabian international bank, Global International quickly became one of the nation's largest charter airlines."[35] An FBI agent told author Pete Brewton that some Global flights "had munitions and arms going out and narcotics coming in."[36] Azima also had a contract for Global to fly junkets for high rollers to the Dunes Hotel and Casino in Las Vegas. Furthermore Azima allegedly sponsored a loan to the Dunes from the mob-controlled Indian Springs State Bank in Kansas City (where Azima himself had loans).[37]

This apparent digression into trails leading from covert operations to political influence, and ultimately to drug airlines and mob-controlled banks, is the story that I first explored in *The War Conspiracy* and again (with respect to the Contras) in *Cocaine Politics*.[38] (CIA involvement with drug airlines shocked even an aide to Oliver North.)[39] This story is not one that I fully understand. But essentially the same lobbies and their milieus, with oil prominent at the overt level, and mob and drug links at the deeper covert level, play recurring roles. For example, there is a striking continuity between the activities of Paul Helliwell, the OSS veteran and eventual CIA officer who was counsel to Meyer Lansky's bank,[40] who arranged for Civil Air Transport (later Air America) to become a CIA proprietary, and the succession of later banks with CIA, drug, and mob connections: Castle Bank of the Bahamas (a Helliwell creation), the World Finance Corporation, the Nugan Hand Bank, and most notoriously the Bank of Credit and Commerce International (BCCI).[41]

Unscrupulous individuals and groups can make fortunes through supplying covert operations. Richard Secord of Iran-Contra fame (a Nugan Hand client) first made millions, with Farhad Azima and Global International, delivering arms to Egypt through Secord's company, EATSCO.[42] Secord made more money by negotiating Iran-Contra arms deals to Iran, in company with David Kimche of Israel's Mossad (one shipment of twenty-three tons was flown in July 1986 by Azima's Madrid airline, RACE Aviation).[43] Finally in 1992 Secord and Kimche were reportedly in Azerbaijan, trying to negotiate the sale of arms from Israel. One year later Gulbuddin Hekmatyar, the chief drug trafficker among the leaders of the Afghan mujahedin, was "observed recruiting Afghan mercenaries [i.e., foreign mercenaries trained in Afghanistan] to fight in Azerbaijan against Armenia and its Russian allies."[44]

COVERT OPERATORS, LOBBIES, AND OIL

The experience of Iran-Contra demonstrated that, at least with an oilman like Casey running the CIA, such intrigues could escalate to the level of a U.S. constitutional crisis. They would not normally lead to war. Similarly the biggest defense expenditure items, for strategic weapons and their delivery systems, have not led us into wars. Wars have emerged instead in smaller countries of interest to oil companies and their lobbies, but whose names at the time were barely known to most Americans—names like Vietnam, Afghanistan, Kuwait.

Nations of Central Asia could play a role in our future, such as (to take a random example) Azerbaijan. Since 1994 Azerbaijan's state oil company has had an $8 billion, thirty-year contract with BP, Unocal, Exxon, and other foreign oil companies to develop oilfields that may be among the largest in the Caspian basin. Such forward investments create pressures for U.S. government commitments to secure them, and in this case to secure agreements for the pipelines necessary for financial return. There are recurring allegations that U.S. oil companies, either directly or through cutouts, engage in covert operations; in Colombia (as we shall see) a U.S. security firm working for Occidental Petroleum took part in a Colombian army military operation "that mistakenly killed 18 civilians."[45] We shall see in chapter 1 that in the Caspian basin the major drug routes are where the oil companies are, as for example in Azerbaijan.[46]

The entire Caspian basin is such an area, with additional major insecure U.S. oil investments in Kazakhstan and Turkmenistan. Especially since 9/11, we have watched Central Asia receive forward deployments of U.S. troops from Georgia to Kyrgyzstan. Nearly all of these states are unstable and their governments have faced armed opposition. The short-term effect of oil investment is usually to increase instability by encouraging corruption, ostentatious living for a few, and increasingly oppressive dictatorship. Awareness of this instability in turn feeds the demand for irrational but definitive shows of U.S. force (as of this writing in 2002 for a U.S. invasion of Iraq).

The reasons why the United States has engaged in wars against the Third World have been articulated in terms of high-minded strategy. But before the high-minded papers appear, the energies for involvement have been generated by the interests, and with them the campaign contributions, of private sectors frequently financed by oil, by drugs, or both.

This is especially true of U.S. official policies in Asia, where America's two most powerful lobbies—the oil cartels and the pro-Israel lobby—have become so hypertrophied in their continuous opposition to each other that they are now both almost beyond mention in polite public discourse.[47] It is customary to refer to AIPAC—the American Israel Public Affairs Committee—as "the most influential and one of the best-organised lobbies in Washington."[48] But AIPAC, though famous for being underreported in the media, is relatively high profile compared to the opposing oil lobbies discussed in this book, such as the Foreign Oil Companies Group.[49]

AIPAC works at least partly through Congress; the oil lobbies usually work chiefly in the silent halls of the State Department, National Security Council, and CIA. It has been said that "the oil lobby is . . . in itself a subgovernment, with roots planted deep in the soil of the real government."[50] AIPAC and the oil lobby have developed largely in conflict with each other, but occasionally their interests converge. In 2002 they have at least two active interests in common: both favor the current forward projection of U.S. power into Central Asia and a U.S. invasion of Iraq.

The conflict of unmentionable special interests, going back to World War I, has deformed the evolution of U.S. attitudes toward Asia and especially Islam. Worse, it has deformed the evolution of Asia itself, starting with the artificial national boundaries drawn by the Western powers at Versailles.

PSYCHOLOGICAL RESISTANCE TO RECOGNITION OF DEEP POLITICAL INTRIGUE

I have mentioned elsewhere the psychological resistance that inhibits frank recognition of the dysfunctional and sometimes even criminal underpinnings of our political establishment. This resistance is particularly acute in the case of U.S. policies in Asia, dominated by the machinations of special interests. I hope to show in part I a particularly sensitive thread—the role of the international drug traffic in influencing U.S. interventions from Vietnam to Afghanistan.

I would not apply the term "conspiracy" to this process, although I did earlier, inspired by my early researches into the KMT, the related airline Air America, the China lobby, and the China lobby's undoubtedly conspiratorial dealings with Richard Nixon in 1968. The word conspiracy inevitably connotes a specific group or cabal, and the arc of my research soon embraced a larger milieu. On the other hand, I encountered among other pro–Vietnam War forces a similar ongoing, even predictable conspiratorial mentality, one that could be counted on to seek to thwart conditions of peace imposed by either presidents or Congress.

Events since the publication of my book have amply proved that this mentality is still with us. Violations of law to pursue warlike ends were officially documented in the case of Iran-Contra, which led ultimately, if indirectly, to indictments and guilty pleas.[51] A decade later, it was discovered that the Pentagon had continued lethal training of so-called elite elements of the Indonesian army that were known to have committed war crimes, despite explicit congressional prohibitions.[52] Such violations of law do not surprise long-term observers of the CIA and the Pentagon. It is part of the culture of these organizations to be impatient at restraints from outside, and part of public American political culture to be shocked and surprised anew at each disclosure.

In truth "conspiracy" has associations too strong for all of what I am describing, just as alternative words like "mentality" would be assuredly too weak. But, at least in the 1960s, it was necessary to understand that war decisions and actions were not always reached or implemented in conditions of openness and candor, but through deceptions and intrigues outside the sites of policy discussion. We can treat the developing U.S. presence in Colombia as a test to determine whether such conditions still exist.

Perhaps, instead of the word "conspiracy," I should have used the older English word "conspiration." By analogy with the word "aspiration," this would suggest a collusive mentality per se, rather than any particular group engaged in it.[53] Indeed it might be more fitting to talk of presidents in a "peace conspiration," since major presidential initiatives for peace regularly had to be prepared in conditions of secrecy. Eisenhower's remarks about the "military-industrial complex"—a theme of this book—surprised even his close advisers. Kennedy's June 1963 speech at American University, calling for a greater effort for peace with the Soviet Union, "was written in the White House without Pentagon or State Department clearance."[54] When Nixon dispatched Kissinger to meet in Beijing with Chou En-lai, total secrecy was maintained collusively, with the cover story that Kissinger had retreated to the mountains because of stomach problems.[55]

The difference is that such peace conspiration was within the lawful power of its perpetrators. The war conspiracy, in contrast, repeatedly exhibited efforts, going at times beyond the law, to resist or frustrate that lawful power. This is an instructive paradox: presidents have found it necessary to conspire, almost in isolation, for peace, while many cabals have engaged in dysfunctional efforts for war.

DEEP SOURCES OF DYSFUNCTION IN WAR

The word "dysfunction" suggests irrationality, which I intend. A number of historians have stressed the irrationality of the overall Vietnam campaign, since (in the words of David Kaiser) a war fought to preserve U.S. "credibility and the integrity of its commitments" ultimately "undermined its credibility and threatened its ability to fulfill other commitments."[56]

Another historian, Fredrik Logevall, has located this dysfunction in the White House itself, claiming that, at least in 1964, "the driving force in American Vietnam policy" was not national credibility but party or even personal credibility.[57] This argument is keyed to his thesis that at no point in 1964 "were American leaders hemmed in on Vietnam. They always had considerable freedom about which way to go in the war."[58]

Logevall's noble case for freedom in history is in rebuttal to those who (like Leslie Gelb or David Dallek) claim that the American entry into the Vietnam War was so overdetermined that no real choice was available to stop it. But his analysis of our engagement would be trivialized if we attributed it to personality defects of either Lyndon Johnson or his top advisers like Robert McNamara. These men were actors in a larger social system that severely restricted their policy options. The choice to act differently cannot be imagined without a significant reorientation of the power structure that empowered them in the first place.

Specifically, Johnson feared to escalate the war as he wished until after the 1964 election, just as Kennedy feared to withdraw significant numbers of U.S. troops before that date.[59] Though the two men were very different, both knew that their ability to lead was severely conditioned by forces resistant to their control—in Congress, the media, their political backing, and the nation.

This point is very relevant to the alternative analysis in this book. Without derogating from the importance of analyses at the top of policy, one can point to other, less visible factors from below, which cumulatively over the years were also important in influencing outcomes. More to the point, one cannot imagine counterbalancing these hidden factors until they have been exposed.

In my book I began with a quasi-autonomous infrastructure—Civil Air Transport (later called Air America). I showed how it and its CIA handlers were able to influence policy in Laos in a way that, although deleterious to stated U.S. policy goals, made total sense in terms of the needs of the airline itself (as well as of the Kuomintang and of Pan Am, the government and civilian airline with which it interfaced.)[60]

This subrationality, or rationality of the part, is a common denominator for much of the systemic dysfunction discussed in this book. Elements in the U.S. Navy and U.S. Air Force strove to induce or sustain strategies and tactics of bombing that were contrary to U.S. diplomatic objectives. Those who controlled the most secret intelligence sources (electronic and communications intelligence) allowed them to be manipulated to influence policy outcomes as well as to deceive Congress. Those who feared that the war would be lost through negotiations (rather than on the battlefield) repeatedly applied pressure to prevent the threat of diplomatic peace. Oil interests aware of untapped reserves in the South China Sea lobbied vociferously and successfully for an increased U.S. commitment in Indochina, well in advance of the nation's nominal decision makers. Powerful lobbies like the American Security Council veiled, in patriotic rhetoric, cases for intervention and escalation that in fact masked the budget priorities of their corporate subscribers. My book focuses on these deeper factors.

In short the bureaucratic decision-making process can be compared to the human one. The sense of free choice people enjoy is partly illusory when viewed against deeper influences that are normally hidden. Bureaucracies and societies, just like the psyche, have their own inertias that impel them in sordid, unjustifiable directions. On the macro- as on the microlevel, moreover, there is denial and resistance to this kind of unflattering recognition. I will deal shortly with instances of such resistance and denial among our best Vietnam historians.

I intend this deep political analysis of the Vietnam War to refine, rather than counter, Weberian notions of institutional rationality. I have incorporated five chapters from *The War Conspiracy* in my new book, because I find them both relevant and useful, as this country is poised on the brink of new distant wars in Iraq and Colombia.

In some ways the Pentagon has learned to fight wars differently since Vietnam, above all by relying on air power to reduce U.S. casualties. But in some ways the underlying infrastructures, both in-house and outsourced, remain the same. Air America no longer exists. But in Colombia there is a sister airline, a successor to the CIA's other major airline proprietary Southern Air Transport. Here too there is a need to generate business to sustain military airlift capacity from the nation's civilian air transport services.[61]

Above all we see in Colombia, as previously in Indochina, the mysterious overlap of the CIA with both oil and the international drug traffic, the latter with its own quintessentially deep political agendas.

We will see both continuities and differences in the evolution of U.S. interventions since Indochina. Perhaps the biggest difference has been the increase of corporate power at the expense of bureaucratic power, especially inside the Pentagon. Nevertheless, I submit that a closer examination of hidden continuities is necessary if the public is ever to achieve control over the process that leads this country repeatedly into war.

VIETNAM AND DENIAL: A DEEP POLITICAL CRITIQUE OF ARCHIVAL VIETNAM HISTORIES

As the United States wavers on the verge of new Vietnam-style involvements, my deep political analysis from 1970 remains relevant. It is true that a vast archivally based literature now exists that explores government decision making over Vietnam in a way not possible in 1970. In particular the State Department has released seven volumes of Vietnam records for 1961–1965 in its archival series, *Foreign Relations of the United States.*

However, mounting documentation has not produced consensus: the debate continues between those who (like Michael Lind) see Vietnam as *The Necessary War* and those who (like David Kaiser and, for that matter, myself) see it as *An American Tragedy.*[62] From the best of these books (in my view, those of Kaiser and Fredrik Logevall) we see two important points that I tried to articulate in *The War Conspiracy.*

The first is that Presidents Eisenhower, Kennedy, and Johnson faced policy establishments that were continuously pressing from below for escalation. The second is that escalations were undertaken, time and again, from the fear that the war might be lost—not on the battlefield but in a quite different sense, by the alienation of Congress, by the defections of the Joint Chiefs, who preferred a more unlimited campaign, by the defection of Saigon allies to the temptations of neutralization, or by the willingness of enemies to negotiate.

But nearly all of this literature shares what might be called the archival bias that I in my book question—that the truth about policy should be studied chiefly from recorded bureaucratic discussions, statements, and rationalizations. With the increasing sophistication of such books (and many of them are truly excellent) we risk losing sight of the possibility that a significant part of the process lies elsewhere, in deeper forces that articulate themselves obliquely in other arenas or not at all.[63] And with the increasing wealth of policy records, relevant alternative sources, such as the Foreign Broadcast Intelligence Service (FBIS), or Defense Department Contract Awards, are now looked at more sparsely or ignored altogether.

The archival bias is particularly dangerous with respect to Indochina. As the United States became a major player there, its intelligence became not only more voluminous but more unreliable. The better historians are aware of this problem and have responded to it commendably, but in different ways. Kaiser, who perhaps best understands the degree to which crises in Laos engendered war in Vietnam, is careful to balance his accounts of the first Laotian crisis in 1959 with Bernard Fall's outsider account, as well as the records from the FRUS (Foreign Relations of the United States) series. Fall's classic *Anatomy of a Crisis* goes only up to 1961.

Kaiser's accounts of the subsequent Laotian tangles, disappointingly, do not include facts long available from other standard works such as Arthur Dommen or Hugh Toye.[64] For example, Kaiser, citing FRUS, repeats U.S. claims that in April 1963 Pathet Lao troops "had moved against Kong Le's forces."[65] He ignores the explanation that "the resumed fighting . . . in April 1963 was chiefly, if not entirely, between the two neutralist factions, rather than with the Pathet Lao."

THE NEED FOR ARCHIVAL SKEPTICISM

Kaiser's work includes a great deal of the U.S. paranoia (not entirely baseless but certainly exaggerated) about communist aggression in Laos after 1962, but very little about the reverse paranoias of the other side, which were at least equally grounded.[66] As a Canadian I find this a major shortcoming of these passages. Many wars, like the Laotian one, arise out of facing paranoias that feed on each other and with better communications might have been resolved peacefully. But it is surely time for U.S. histories to look more closely at the North Vietnamese grievances and acknowledge that in Laos, North Vietnam had far better reasons to fear and respond to what the United States was doing than vice versa.

Perhaps I should explain my perspective by clarifying how Laos led to my writings and actions about Vietnam. Until 2002 I had never visited Asia; during my last two years in the Canadian Foreign Service (1959–1961) I was in Poland. As it happened, both Canada and Poland were represented, along with India, on the International Control Commission, which was created to help implement the 1954 Geneva Accords on Indochina.

Depressing stacks of cables arrived in every diplomatic pouch to be read by the most junior officer—me. There was far more detail there than I could retain as I moved in 1961 from Warsaw to a new career at Berkeley. But I came away with a sense that nearly all the nations most friendly to the United States differed with Washington when it came to Indochina. Canada was not alone in wanting to uphold the 1954 Geneva Accords; the United States was virtually alone in seeking to subvert them, at what terrible cost we now know. In 1959–1961, when I was in Warsaw, the focus of this dissatisfaction was the behavior of U.S. officials in Laos.[67] More than I realized at the time, what I read encouraged my future skepticism about U.S. governmental behavior abroad, which has survived my growing respect and admiration for the American people.

I do not find enough of this skepticism in the archivally based histories, even the best ones. For example, Kaiser's book purports to look at "The Origins of the Vietnam War," yet (like Logevall's) it does not mention the pressures exerted on Kennedy and Johnson by the American Security Council and other important lobbies. As mentioned above, the book deserves praise for its awareness of how U.S. Vietnam policy was steered by Laos, yet it includes only two passing references to Air America, a major U.S. presence in Laos.[68] Both books seemingly assume (erroneously in my view) that Air America was a passive instrument of U.S. policy, not a player with a KMT component capable of independently influencing outcomes.[69]

The problem of deficiencies in the bureaucratic policy-making record is small compared with our ignorance of hidden pressures from bureaucratic and corporate interest groups. In chapter 10 I mention what I take to be a revealing anecdote—Nixon shared his secret decision to send U.S. troops into Cambodia with "private citizens" linked to the American Security Council two days before he revealed it to congressional leaders. It seems clear that this extraordinary violation of security would not have occurred if there had not been lobbying for the action from this sector.

Much of my chapter on Cambodia documents, from obscure UN Economic Commission sources, how U.S. Navy planes were conducting aeromagnetic surveys of Cambodian offshore waters at a time when a concession for oil drilling there had been obtained by Union Oil of California, a backer of the ASC and Nixon. To my knowledge no other book (and certainly not William Shawcross's supposedly definitive *Sideshow*) has shown how U.S. defoliation of French rubber plantations contributed, almost inevitably, to the military overthrow of the neutralist Sihanouk government in a coup that was necessary in order for oil companies to exploit Cambodia's petroleum resources.

HOW UNACKNOWLEDGED PROGRAMS
CAN METASTASIZE

The unacknowledged defoliation program, which eventually complemented the unacknowledged Cambodian bombing program conducted by Nixon, is a good example of how sub rosa programs, separated from public evaluations of policy, can grow beyond any rational justification. I wish I had written more about the defoliation program practiced in Indochina (and now being repeated in Colombia). What began as a way of clearing back hedgerows escalated into a practice of rendering whole regions uninhabitable (see table I.1).

What is most revealing about these escalating figures is that by October 1967 the RAND Corporation had concluded that the defoliation program had harmed residents in the vicinity of crop destruction targets, had alienated the rural South Vietnamese population from the government, had aroused much hostility toward the United States and its South Vietnamese allies, was not considered necessary or useful by the rural population, and might well be counterproductive.[70]

One month later this negative assessment was endorsed by Assistant Secretary of Defense Alain Enthoven. Nevertheless, over half of the total gallons of herbicides sprayed over Vietnam occurred afterward, between 1968 and 1971. Even the apparent drop-off in 1969 is deceptive, since in that year the U.S. Air Force shifted to comparably massive defoliation of French rubber plantations in Cambodia.[71]

This is only one example of how programs with lucrative contracts can metas-

Table I.1.   Statistical Summary of Herbicidal Warfare in Vietnam
Operation Trail Dust: August 10, 1961–October 31, 1971 (3,735 days)

| Year | Summary by Year | | |
	Total Gallons Used	*Total Acres Affected*	*Total Square Miles Affected*
1962	17,171	5,724	27
1963	74,760	24,920	117
1964	281,607	93,869	440
1965	664,657	221,552	1,039
1966	2,535,788	845,263	3,962
1967	5,123,353	1,707,784	8,005
1968	5,089,010	1,696,337	7,952
1969	4,558,817	1,519,606	7,123
1970	758,966	252,989	1,186
1971	10,039	3,346	16
Unknown	281,201	93,734	439
TOTAL	19,395,369	6,465,123	30,305

Source: Figures from William A. Buckingham Jr., *Operation RANCH HAND: The Air Force and Herbicides in Southeast Asia, 1961–1971* (Washington, D.C.: Office of the Air Force Historian, 1981).

tasize and expand, even following rational assessments that they do not work. I have not done the research that might show, with respect to herbicides, how perceived communities of interest developed between the suppliers of a commodity or service and those using it in the armed forces.[72] In *The War Conspiracy* I showed a comparable example (an important one in my view) with respect to Air America and strategic military airlift. I described how Air America, whose managers overlapped with those of the CIA in one direction and of Pan Am in another, was thrust into an escalating role in Laos that was contrary to U.S. interests but supplied Pan Am with the needed military airlift business to survive in the Far East.[73] I invite researchers to test my hypothesis that Plan Colombia today is helping create badly needed airlift business for the successor lines to Southern Air (formerly Air America's sister CIA airline).

Vietnam, in other words, was not an isolated event. It was the product of ongoing war-creating energies located chiefly in this country, which to this day have not yet been properly identified and countered. Of these forces, none is deeper and more mysterious than the involvement yet again of the CIA, and airlines working for it, with major drug traffickers—not in Indochina this time, but in Colombia and Afghanistan.[74] Such forces will continue to haunt us until they are better understood.

In the past, the U.S. government has been the chief force preventing this understanding. Throughout the 1950s reverse propaganda concealed the KMT's active role in smuggling drugs to the United States. The principal source was Harry Anslinger, the head of the U.S. Federal Bureau of Narcotics, who charged repeatedly, and falsely, that the United States was being inundated by communist China with a flood of Yunnan opium.[75] But he was backed by a powerful China lobby inside and outside government, powerful enough to suppress the only book in that period which referred to the KMT role in drug trafficking.[76]

The U.S. government has persisted in this practice of projective or reverse drug propaganda, blaming communists for drug trafficking that is in fact conducted by covert allies. In the 1980s Reagan blamed Sandinistas for the cocaine flood that in fact was being principally attributed by DEA to traffickers who were Contra supporters.[77] In the 1990s Clinton's drug czar, General Barry McCaffrey, attributed to "narco-guerrillas" the flood of cocaine that in fact was principally attributed by the Colombian government to the right-wing paramilitaries.

Clearly the prodigious task of stopping new Vietnam Wars in Colombia or Afghanistan will require a better understanding of the global drug traffic as well as its links to oil companies and other economic interests, and to this goal I dedicate this book. Assuredly it is not definitive. But it is focused on deep political issues that other books, more sophisticated in their own way, tend to ignore.

NOTES

1. *Deep Politics and the Death of JFK* (Berkeley: University of California Press, 1996), 7.

2. Martha Byrd, *Chennault: Giving Wings to the Tiger* (Tuscaloosa: University of Alabama Press, 1987), 277–78. See also Peter Dale Scott, "Opium and Empire: McCoy on Heroin in Southeast Asia," *Bulletin of Concerned Asian Scholars*, September 1973, 49–56 (a review of Alfred W. McCoy et al., *The Politics of Heroin in Southeast Asia*). For more on the complex CIA relationship to the airline, see William M. Leary, *Perilous Missions: Civil Air Transport and CIA Covert Operations in Asia, 1946–1955* (University, Ala.: University of Alabama Press, 1984); Christopher Robbins, *Air America* (New York: Avon, 1985).

3. Leary, *Perilous Missions*, 67–68. See also Byrd, *Chennault*, 325–28.

4. Byrd, *Chennault*, 312, 327–28, 334.

5. Chennault was one of the first to propose fighting communism with the aid of the Muslims of western China, some of whom eventually served in the Afghan mujahedin (Byrd, *Chennault*, 322–23).

6. Gordon H. Chang, *Friends and Enemies: The United States, China, and the Soviet Union, 1948–1972* (Stanford: Stanford University Press, 1990), 224–25.

7. Chang, *Friends and Enemies*, 225–26.

8. Not until I wrote chapter 11 in 1971–1972 did I realize how CIA-backed efforts in 1960–1964 to install and maintain a military government in Laos resulted in delivering the country into the hands of drug traffickers.

9. Center for Defense Information, *Show Transcript: Colombia in Crisis*, www.cdi.org/adm/1315/transcript.html. Quoted at greater length in chapter 6, note 98. Over 50 percent of the *overall* Fiscal 2002 federal discretionary budget is devoted to military spending. Center for Defense Information, www.cdi.org/issues/budget/fy'02/index.html.

10. See chapter 8.

11. Anna Chennault became a force in the George Town Club organized by Tongsun Park, a trained Korean CIA officer who used money derived from his connections to the South Korean government and KCIA "to bribe influential members of Congress and to pay the enormous costs of subsidizing The George Town Club." Susan B. Trento, *Power House: Robert Keith Gray and the Selling of Access and Influence in Washington* (New York: St. Martin's, 1992), 97–103. See also Scott, *Deep Politics*, 234–38.

12. Scott Anderson and Jon Lee Anderson, *Inside the League* (New York: Dodd Mead, 1986), 122–29.

13. Anderson and Anderson, *Inside the League*, 55–56 (Cline); Trento, *Power House*, 101–3 (Wilson). Cline after his retirement continued to attend meetings of WACL, which he had helped create. Wilson was a key figure at the George Town Club.

14. Anderson and Anderson, *Inside the League*, 129 (Unification Church); Peter Dale Scott and Jonathan Marshall, *Cocaine Politics* (Berkeley: University of California Press, 1998), 86–87 (APACL/WACL).

15. See chapters 8 and 11. Some of this foreign right-wing propaganda was also paid for by U.S. client governments supported ultimately by the U.S. taxpayer. In the 1970s the puppet Lon Nol government of Cambodia lavishly distributed from its Washington embassy the right-wing propaganda of the Sun Myung Moon Unification Church.

16. The line between domestic and foreign should not be too sharply drawn. Tongsun Park "came from a family with long ties to Korean intelligence, and American oil companies that did business in Korea" (Trento, *Power House*, 97).

17. For the overlapping activities of the oil industry, the State Department, and the U.S. Navy, see Daniel Yergin, *The Prize: The Epic Quest for Oil, Money, and Power* (New York: Simon & Schuster, 1991); Ovid Demaris, *Dirty Business* (New York: Avon, 1975), 191–289.

18. For analyses of defense and foreign policy lobbying, see Jerry W. Sanders, *Peddlers of Crisis: The Committee on the Present Danger and the Politics of Containment* (Boston: South End, 1983); Russell Warren Howe, *The Power Peddlers: How Lobbyists Mold America's Foreign Policy* (Garden City, N.Y.: Doubleday, 1977).

19. Larry P. Goodson, *Afghanistan's Endless War: State Failure, Regional Politics, and the Rise of the Taliban* (Seattle: University of Washington Press, 2001), 68.

20. John K. Cooley, *Unholy Wars; Afghanistan, America, and International Terrorism* (London: Pluto, 1999), 75.

21. Alan Kuperman, *Political Science Quarterly,* Summer 1999. See also Alan J. Kuperman, "The Stinger Missile and U.S. Intervention in Afghanistan," in Demetrios James Caraley, ed., *The New American Interventionism: Lessons from Successes and Failures* (New York: Columbia University Press, 1999). Goodson's own footnotes concede that "analysis of data on air losses from issues of Afghanistan Report indicates no appreciable immediate increase after the introduction of Stinger missiles" (p. 209). For a contrary assessment, see, e.g., Robert Gates, *From the Shadows* (New York: Simon & Schuster, 1996), 350.

22. *New York Times,* March 12, 1989. In April 1990 the FBI foiled an attempt by Colombians from the Medellin Cartel to buy 120 Stingers in Florida (*Washington Post,* May 8, 1990).

23. This has led to additional criticism of the CIA "for concentrating on recovering the hardware that had done so much damage to the Soviet military forces and neglecting the larger problems of the political vacuum left in Afghanistan when the Soviet forces pulled out in 1989. The CIA campaign to retrieve the Stingers reflected this misplaced sense of U.S. priorities, according to one intelligence source, who said the focus on the weaponry seemed to blind Washington—including even the intelligence community—to the danger caused by political disintegration in Afghanistan after the Russian withdrawal and the collapse of any effective central government" (*International Herald Tribune,* September 26, 2001).

24. *Chicago Tribune,* October 21, 2001.

25. Howard Means, *Colin Powell: Soldier/Statesman—Statesman/Soldier* (New York: D.I. Fine, 1992), 208–10.

26. *Ottawa Citizen,* October 6, 2001. Ahmed Rashid's claim that the initiative came from CIA director Casey (*Taliban* [New Haven: Yale University Press, 2001], 129) is disputed by the true initiator, Charles Wilson, who claims that even Casey "would not push for Stingers" (*New York Times,* April 18, 1988, see next note). Robert Gates, who was later CIA director (DCI), agrees that the original "catalyst" was not Casey but Charles Wilson (*From the Shadows,* 320). Another strong proponent was Senator Orrin Hatch (R-Utah), who flew to first China and then Pakistan, allegedly persuading General Zia (but compare next note) "to accept the Stingers. Six months later, after a lengthy internal Reagan administration fight that pitted a reluctant CIA and U.S. Army against bullish Pentagon and State intelligence officials [including Morton Abramowitz], the Stinger supply program began. In retrospect, many senior U.S. officials involved see the decision as a

turning point in the war and acknowledge that Hatch's clandestine lobbying played a significant role" (*Washington Post*, July 20, 1992). Hatch traveled with his aide, Michael Pillsbury, who later continued to champion the provision of Stingers as assistant secretary of defense. Pillsbury's unexplained connections to BCCI figure Mohammed Hammoud were later explored in Senate Committee Foreign Relations Committee, *The BCCI Affair*, a Report to the Senate Foreign Relations Committee by Senators John Kerry and Hank Brown, 102d Cong., 2d sess., Senate Print 102–140 (Washington, D.C.: GPO), 470–72. Others have attributed the Stinger idea to Zia, or even bin Laden (this book, 132).

27. Wilson claimed that the proposal to supply the Oerlikon gun "was Pakistani President Zia's idea." See Bob Woodward, *Veil: The Secret Wars of the CIA, 1981–1987* (New York: Simon & Schuster, 1987), 316. In January 1987 Andrew Eiva, director of the Federation for American-Afghanistan Action, complained that only eleven of the promised forty Oerlikon weapons had reached the mujahedin, prompting speculation that the funds were being diverted for other purposes (*Washington Post*, January 13, 1987).

28. *New York Times*, April 18, 1988. See also Woodward, *Veil*, 316–18, 372.

29. Goodson, *Afghanistan's Endless War*, 146. Cf. Woodward, *Veil*, 372.

30. Russ Bellant, *Old Nazis, the New Right, and the Republican Party* (Boston: South End, 1988). Wilson may also have had a personal financial stake in the $40 million program he advocated. As David Isenberg noted in 1997, "The Voice of America reported earlier this week that the Swiss Supreme Court ruled the Swiss government can help the United States in its investigation of a weapons-bribery case involving a member of Congress and his partner. The U.S. case, which involves allegations that the Congressman received kickbacks from companies delivering arms to Afghan rebels, dates back to 1983 when the Congress approved $40 million in aid to purchase weapons for the rebels. Most of that went to purchase antiaircraft guns provided by a company recommended by the Congressman. The U.S. government accuses the two men of having received some four million dollars in bribes for providing weapons to the mujahedin. Although the identities of the two suspects are being kept secret, the Swiss tribunal says that the U.S. representative's family name begins with stet'W.' That is a dead giveaway to those with long memories who remember those rollback days of the Reagan Doctrine. The unidentified legislator conceivably could be former Rep. Charles Wilson, a Republican from Texas" (David Isenberg, "The Stinger That Keeps on Stinging," Center for Defense Information, *Weekly*, www.cdi.org/weekly/1997/Issue11.

31. *Pittsburgh Post-Gazette*, October 10, 2001, www.post-gazette.com/columnists/20011010sally1010p1.asp.

32. One could go on and on. For example, Jim Guirard, national affairs director of the ASC Foundation, was a board member of the Committee to Free Afghanistan and a leading member of the Coalition for Peace Through Strength's 1980s Task Force on Nicaragua.

33. *New York Times*, February 9, 2000 (Democrats); *Washington Weekly*, July 14, 1997 (Fred Thompson, R); Associated Press, September 30, 1997.

34. See Pete Brewton, *The Mafia, CIA, and George Bush* (New York: S.P.I. Books, 1992), 197–204; Stephen Pizzo, Mary Fricker, and Paul Muolo, *Inside Job* (New York: McGraw-Hill, 1989), 89–91, 341–42; Anthony Kimery, "Failed Banks and Farhad Azima," www.microsp.com/sources/azima.html.

35. Pizzo et al., *Inside Job*, 89. It is suspected, but not established, that the bank was the drug-linked Bank of Credit and Commerce International, or BCCI. Pete Brewton, in

his investigation of the Indian Springs bank collapse, was told that FBI had not followed up on Indian Springs because the CIA informed them that Azima was "off-limits" (Brewton, *Mafia*, 211; *Houston Post*, February 8, 1990). Similarly, the assistant U.S. attorney handling the Indian Springs investigation was told to "back off from a key figure in the collapse because he had ties to the CIA" (Gary W. Potter, "Organized Crime, the CIA, and the Savings and Loan Scandal," www.policestudies.eku.edu/POTTER/International/ S&L.htm.)

36. Brewton, *Mafia*, 211.

37. Pizzo et al., *Inside Job*, 90–91. Compare the junket airline Jet Avia in Las Vegas, said to have flown for the CIA in Colombia; this book, page 91.

38. *War Conspiracy*, 209–13; reprinted in this volume as chapter 11; *Cocaine Politics* (Berkeley: University of California Press, 1998), 92–94.

39. Robert Owen reported to Oliver North that a DC-4 supplying the Contras "was used at one time to run drugs and part of the crew had criminal records. Nice group the Boys [CIA] chose" (Owen memo of February 10, 1986; Gary Webb, *Dark Alliance* [New York: Seven Stories, 1998], 238).

40. See this book, 207n93 (National City Bank). Helliwell also became involved in several Florida real estate investments with Morris Kleinman, who had come up through Cleveland's Mayfield Road gang and later the Desert Inn of Las Vegas. Alan A. Block, *Masters of Paradise* (New Brunswick, N.J.: Transaction, 1991), 189–90.

41. The postwar intelligence-narcotics connection in Asia traces back to the Kunming station of OSS, where Helliwell worked with the KMT drug/intelligence chief Tai Li and OSS payments to agents were made in opium. Stationed there were Helliwell, who later set up Civil Air Transport and Sea Supply, Inc., Lou Conein, who became the CIA's liaison to Corsican and other traffickers in Saigon, Ray Cline and John Singlaub, both part of the CIA's KMT connection and its offshoot, the drug-sponsoring Asian People's (later World) Anti-Communist League, Howard Hunt, who helped set up the Latin American section of what became the World Anti-Communist League, and Mitchell WerBell, an armorer for the CIA later indicted in an arms-for-drugs deal. WerBell was also involved in a questionable deal for the resettlement of Hmong tribesmen with the Nugan Hand Bank. Presiding over the Kunming station was George Olmsted, whose Washington bank was eventually acquired by BCCI.

42. Brewton, *Mafia*, 201.

43. Theodore Draper, *A Very Thin Line: The Iran-Contra Affairs* (New York: Hill & Wang, 1991), 200–202.

44. Cooley, *Unholy Wars*, 180.

45. *San Francisco Chronicle*, June 15, 2001. Olivier Roy once wrote in *Le Monde Diplomatique* that "when the Taliban took power in Afghanistan (1996) it was largely orchestrated by the Pakistani secret service and the oil company Unocal, with its Saudi ally Delta." Richard Labévière, *Dollars for Terror* (New York: Algora, 2000), 280. It has been pointed out to me that for Unocal to supply funds for such an operation would have violated the Foreign Anti-Corruption Act. But its partner Delta, the Saudi oil company, would have had no such inhibition.

46. Cooley, *Unholy Wars*, 157, 159.

47. Paul Findley, *They Dare to Speak Out* (Westport, Conn.: Lawrence Hill, 1985). Allegedly "it was Secretary of State John Foster Dulles' demand to talk to a single Jewish

organisation that precipitated the establishment of the AIPAC [the American Israel Public Affairs Committee]. I.L. Kenen, AIPAC's first executive director, claims that they established the organisation to counter the propaganda and the power of the 'petro-diplomatic complex,' which included oilmen, diplomats, missionaries and CIA agents. James Forrestal, Secretary of Defence, and the Arabists at the State Department were an important part of this complex" (Umut Uzer, "The Impact of the Jewish Lobby on American Foreign Policy in the Middle East" www.mfa.gov.tr/grupa/percept/VI-4/u.uzer.htm). As will be discussed below, oil and drug money are found on both sides, especially through BCCI in the pro-Arab lobby and figures like Meyer Lansky (drugs) and Marc Rich (oil plus more) in the pro-Israel lobby. See Justin Raimundo, "Marc Rich: Treason Is the Reason," www.antiwar.com/justin/j021601.html.

48. Uzer, "Impact."

49. In chapter 1, I quote at length the complaint of a former CIA officer, Robert Baer, that senior National Security Council officers in the Clinton administration were serving the ends of "the Foreign Oil Companies Group, a cover for a cartel of major petroleum companies doing business in the Caspian." Robert Baer, *See No Evil* (New York: Crown, 2002), 243–44. But Baer's complaint against the oil lobby's influence was not that of a loner. His book, which complained of CIA inaction against Iranian terrorists like Imad Mughniyah, was released in January 2002, amid a flurry of Mossad and other pro-Israel attacks pointing fingers at Mughniyah's and Iran's backing of terrorism in the Middle East. See London *Guardian*, January 12, 2002 (Baer); socrates.berkeley.edu/~pdscott/qfiran.html (pro-Israeli attacks on Mughniyah in the same week).

50. Demaris, *Dirty Business*, 191.

51. See Lawrence E. Walsh, *Iran-Contra: The Final Report* (New York: Random House/Times Books, 1994), xiv: "Independent Counsel did not charge violations of the Arms Export Control Act or Boland Amendment. Although apparent violations of these statutes provided the impetus for the cover-up, they are not criminal statutes and do not contain any enforcement provisions." It is the (various) Boland Amendments, prohibiting or restricting U.S. aid to the Contras, that apply here.

52. Allan Nairn, "Indonesia's Killers," *Nation*, March 30, 1998.

53. Consider the example of Philip Morris, "one of the few nonmilitary companies to lobby heavily on behalf of Plan Colombia." Philip Morris had an interest in Colombia because enormous quantities of cigarettes were smuggled into that country as part of a complex procedure to launder drug profits. According to Marc Schapiro, the company was thus profiting from an illegal enterprise. But its lobbying activities, though of a similar mentality to those of other companies, were also separate from them. See Mark Schapiro, "Big Tobacco," *Nation*, May 6, 2002, 11–20.

54. David Kaiser, *American Tragedy: Kennedy, Johnson, and the Origins of the Vietnam War* (Cambridge: Harvard University Press, Belknap Press, 2000), 209.

55. H. R. Haldeman, *The Haldeman Diaries: Inside the Nixon White House* (New York: Putnam, 1994), 316–17.

56. Kaiser, *American Tragedy*, 492. Immanuel Wallerstein expresses the war's cost more dramatically in economic terms: "Vietnam was not merely a military defeat or a blight on U.S. prestige. The war dealt a major blow to the United States' ability to remain the world's dominant economic power. The conflict was extremely expensive and more or less used up the U.S. gold reserves that had been so plentiful since 1945. Moreover, the

United States incurred these costs just as Western Europe and Japan experienced major economic upswings. These conditions ended U.S. preeminence in the global economy" ("The Eagle Has Crash Landed," *Foreign Policy,* July-August 2002, www.foreignpolicy.-com/issue_julyaug_2002/wallerstein.html).

57. Fredrik Logevall, *Choosing War: The Lost Chance for Peace and the Escalation of War in Vietnam* (Berkeley: University of California Press, 1996), 388.

58. Logevall, *Choosing War,* xvii.

59. This point is well made by John M. Newman, *JFK and Vietnam* (New York: Warner, 1992), 449.

60. See this book, 189–90.

61. See pages 91, 101; cf. this book, 190.

62. Michael Lind, *Vietnam: The Necessary War* (New York: Free Press, 1999); Kaiser, *American Tragedy.* Kaiser's negative assessment of the war is reinforced by Robert Mann, *A Grand Delusion* (New York: Basic, 2001).

63. Alternative sources include alternative archives. Jonathan Marshall wrote an invaluable analysis of the Chiang Kai-shek government's dependence on opium revenues before World War II, based on reports in the archives of the U.S. Federal Bureau of Narcotics: "Opium and the Politics of Gangsterism in Nationalist China, 1927–1945," *Bulletin of Concerned Asian Scholars,* July–September 1976, 19–48.

64. Arthur J. Dommen, *Conflict in Laos: The Politics of Neutralization* (New York: Praeger, 1971); Hugh Toye, *Laos: Buffer State or Battleground* (Oxford: Oxford University Press, 1968).

65. Kaiser, *American Tragedy,* 198; citing *FRUS 1961–1963,* 24, 174.

66. I invite the interested reader to compare my concise account of Laos in 1962–1964 (chapter 9 in this volume) with Kaiser's ample but more one-sided narratives that include unsupported allegations of Pathet Lao and North Vietnamese escalations (e.g., 198, 210, 316).

67. I developed close personal relationships with several members of the U.S. embassy in Warsaw, some of whom, I realized years later, were CIA officers.

68. Kaiser, *American Tragedy,* 28, 197. On page 197 Kaiser refers to "the CIA's contract airline, Air America." In fact, Air America was a CIA proprietary. Meanwhile in Logevall's book *Choosing War* (which mentions Laos more sparsely) Air America is not mentioned at all.

69. This is an issue of importance today with respect to Colombia, where the United States is again relying on quasi-autonomous "instruments" of policy, such as Southern Air and DynCorp.

70. William A. Buckingham Jr., *Operation Ranch Hand: The Air Force and Herbicides in Southeast Asia, 1961–1971* (Washington, D.C.: Office of Air Force History, United States Air Force, 1982), 133–34.

71. See this book, 170–71.

72. Among the many allegations of corruption in the U.S. Army in Vietnam, an officer in charge of defoliation was accused of secretly receiving payoffs from the company supplying the herbicide.

73. See this book, 190.

74. See this book, 7, 89.

75. Scott and Marshall, *Cocaine Politics,* 172; McCoy, *Politics of Heroin,* 16, 124;

Peter Dale Scott, *Deep Politics and the Death of JFK* (Berkeley: University of California Press, 1976), 167–76.

76. The book was Ross Y. Koen's *The China Lobby in American Politics* (New York: Macmillan, 1960). Not only did Macmillan withdraw the book in 1960, it went so far as to deny ever publishing it. Fortunately a few copies survived in libraries, including the library at UC-Berkeley. The book was eventually republished by Octagon in 1974. See this book, 193–94.

77. Scott and Marshall, *Cocaine Politics*, 172–73.

I

Afghanistan, Heroin, and Oil (2002)

1

Drugs and Oil in U.S. Asian Wars: From Indochina to Afghanistan

OIL, DRUGS, AND AMERICAN
THIRD WORLD INTERVENTIONS

In the half century since the Korean War the United States has been involved in four major wars in the Third World: in Vietnam (1961–1975), in the Persian Gulf (1990–1991), in Colombia (1991–present), and in Afghanistan (2001–2002).[1] All four wars were fought in or near significant oil-producing areas. All four involved reliance on proxies who were also major international drug traffickers.[2] The American habit of training, arming, and financing its drug-trafficking allies in order to help secure oil resources abroad has been a major factor in the huge increase in global illicit drug trafficking since World War II.

This pattern is further reinforced when we consider two of America's major indirect interventions of the same period: support for the Nicaraguan Contras (1981–1988) and the Afghan mujahedin (1979–1991). The CIA contracted for Contra support in Central America with an airline owned by a ringleader of the largest cocaine network in the region.[3] By providing funds for Gulbuddin Hekmatyar, a drug trafficker selected for support by Pakistani intelligence (the Inter-Services Intelligence Directorate, or ISI), the CIA helped propel Hekmatyar into becoming, for a while, the largest heroin trafficker in Afghanistan and perhaps the world.[4]

All empires since the Renaissance have been driven by the search for foreign resources, and nearly all—including the British, the French, and the Dutch—used drugs as a cheap way to pay for overseas expansion. When the United States decided to preserve Western influence in Southeast Asia, it inherited a social structure of former colonial regimes that had coexisted in one way or other with powerful Chinese Triads engaged in the drug traffic.[5]

27

We shall see in this chapter that the United States has become more and more committed to exclusive domination of the world oil economy, both to secure its increasing oil needs and to preclude this power from passing into the hands of anyone else. The consistent U.S. recourse to actions that have built up the global drug traffic raises an analogous question: Did the United States seek to maintain control over the global drug economy to ensure that its riches would strengthen the U.S. economy and to deny them to communist enemies?

American dependence on drug proxies can be traced to the CIA decision, in 1949–1950, to provide arms and logistic support to the residual forces of the Chinese Kuomintang in Burma. This evolved into the much larger program of support for the opium-growing Hmong tribesmen in northeastern Laos. In the wake of the domestically unpopular Vietnam War, the United States, in asserting an increasingly explicit geostrategic interest in oil reserves throughout the world, has continued to seek out local drug proxies as a supplement or an alternative to the use of U.S. armed forces.

I am not suggesting that concerns about oil and gas have dictated every U.S. policy move. On the contrary, when Clinton in 1996 was urged to recognize the Taliban by the U.S. oil company Unocal, which was eager to build a gas pipeline through the country, he declined to do so. Pressure from women's groups, appalled by the Taliban's antifeminist policies, proved decisive.[6] In general, oil is a major factor in explaining why the United States inclines toward intervention in the first place, not in determining just how or when U.S. military engagement occurred in a given area.

Over the long haul, since World War II, oil interests have dictated the general disposition of U.S. foreign policy. In Central Asia today, these interests transcend the issue of a single nation or pipeline: the goal is access to and control over the immense oil and gas fields of the Caspian basin.

I propose to show that this recurring convergence between oil and drugs is not a coincidence, but a feature of what I have called the deep politics of U.S. foreign policy—factors in policy formation that are usually repressed and not acknowledged. The role of oil in U.S. geostrategic thinking is generally acknowledged. Less recognized has been the role of drug proxies in waging and financing conflicts that would not have been adequately financed by Congress and U.S. taxpayers.

The phenomenon I am describing is sometimes characterized as blowback: the CIA's own term for unintended consequences at home of covert (and usually illegal) programs designed for abroad. But the term, by suggesting an accidental and lesser spin-off, misrepresents the dimensions and magnitude of the drug traffic that the United States helped relaunch after World War II. That drug traffic has multiplied and spread through the world like a malignant cancer. It has also branched out into other areas—notably money laundering and people smuggling—which like the drug traffic itself have contributed to the problem of terrorism we now face. Of course U.S. reliance on drug proxies, at risks that were always clear, was motivated by the desire to secure access to natural resources in the Third World—principally oil.

I prefer to characterize what is happening by a general proposition: covert operations, when they generate or reinforce autonomous political power, almost always outlast the specific purpose for which they were designed. Instead they enlarge and become part of the hostile forces the United States has to address. To put it in terms I find more precise, *parapolitics*, the exercise of power by covert means, tends to metastasize into *deep politics*, an interplay of unacknowledged forces over which the original parapolitical agent no longer has control.

The oil-drug convergence has recurred elsewhere. In 1998 the United States intervened in Kosovo, on behalf of the Kosovo Liberation Army, which earlier the U.S. State Department had described as a drug-financed terrorist force.[7] This followed talk of the Balkans as a route for a Western pipeline to transport oil from the newly exploited oil fields of Central Asia.[8]

In the 1980s, the CIA helped arrange a support network for the Nicaraguan Contras with the help of a drug cartel (the Matta Ballesteros–Caro Quintero–Félix Gallardo cartel) operating through Mexico. DEA, at the same time, had identified this cartel as a major target—accounting for a major share (perhaps a third, perhaps more than half) of all the cocaine moving between Colombia and the United States.[9] That the CIA overrode DEA's enforcement priority reflected CIA involvement with its Mexican counterpart, the DFS, and through it with the chief Mexican drug traffickers, a powerful right-wing force in oil-rich Mexico.[10]

The clearest and most important case of consequential parapolitics was the decision of the United States, in April and May 1979, to arm mujahedin guerrillas in Afghanistan, one of whom, Gulbuddin Hekmatyar, was already known as a drug trafficker with his own heroin refineries. In the subsequent years opium production soared in the Afghan-Pakistan Golden Crescent. Almost no heroin from this area reached the United States before 1979, yet according to official U.S. sources it supplied 60 percent of U.S. heroin by 1980.[11]

This scandal was kept out of the mainstream U.S. press until the CIA support was winding down. Belatedly, in 1990, the *Washington Post* reported that U.S. officials had failed to investigate drug trafficking by Pakistan's intelligence service, the ISI (Inter-Services Intelligence), and Hekmatyar, the top CIA-ISI client in Afghanistan, "because U.S. narcotics policy in Afghanistan has been subordinated to the war against Soviet influence there."[12]

OIL, GEOSTRATEGY, AND NATIONAL SECURITY

American Afghanistan policy from 1979 to 1991 was dominated by fear of the Iranian revolution, which Zbigniew Brzezinski, President Carter's national security adviser, feared in part as "a Soviet threat to Persian Gulf oil fields."[13] The

Soviet invasion a few months later aggravated this fear. *Newsweek* at the time wrote how "Control of Afghanistan would put the Russians within 350 miles of the Arabian Sea, the oil lifeline of the West and Japan. Soviet warplanes based in Afghanistan could cut the lifeline at will."[14]

Later Brzezinski wrote how the Soviet invasion precipitated a "large-scale buildup of the U.S. military presence in the Persian Gulf" and a commitment "to the defense of the Persian Gulf region."[15] This took the form of the Carter Doctrine of January 1980: "An attempt by any outside force to gain control of the Persian Gulf region will be regarded as an assault on the vital interests of the United States of America."[16] This replaced the Nixon Doctrine of relying on regional superpowers to maintain order, which had collapsed in the region with the fall of the shah of Iran to Shia fundamentalist radicals in 1979. Seen from this perspective, Brzezinski's concern about Afghanistan was rendered urgent because of the power vacuum created by the shah's fall, after the earlier British withdrawal from the Persian Gulf in 1971.

This concern is quite compatible with Brzezinski's later candid admission that he intended by meddling in Afghanistan in 1979 (*before* the Soviet invasion) precisely "to induce a Soviet military intervention."[17] The more concerned one was about a Soviet push south through Iran (from a purely geographical perspective, the easier route to the Gulf), the more attractive seemed the alternative of tying the Soviets down in a mountainous and unconquerable Afghanistan.

Brzezinski's ultimate motives in Afghanistan were geostrategic—to induce Soviet responses that would eventually weaken the Soviet Union and hasten its dissolution. His motives probably also included a desire to nullify the steps being taken by President Carter and Secretary of State Cyrus Vance toward détente with the Soviet Union, by signing the SALT II arms-reduction treaty one month earlier.[18]

But in his argument for a "Eurasian geostrategy," Brzezinski is quite clear that what makes the region of Central Asia "geopolitically significant" is above all its importance "as a potential economic prize: an enormous concentration of natural gas and oil reserves is located in the region, in addition to important minerals, including gold."[19] Brzezinski noted that these oil and gas reserves will become even more important as world demand increases by an estimated more than 50 percent in twenty years, "with the most significant increase in consumption occurring in the Far East."[20]

Many others have emphasized the strategic importance of these Central Asian energy reserves to the United States. Speaking of Azerbaijan in 1997, President Clinton said that

In a world of growing energy demand . . . our nation cannot afford to rely on any single region for our energy supplies. By working closely with Azerbaijan to tap the Caspian's resources, we not only help Azerbaijan to prosper, we also help diversify our energy supply and strengthen our nation's security.[21]

His remarks have been echoed by other authoritative sources, such as the following article from the Foreign Military Studies Office of Fort Leavenworth, which was published three months before the World Trade Center attacks:

> The Caspian Sea appears to be sitting on yet another sea—a sea of hydrocarbons. Western oilmen flocking to the area have signed multibillion-dollar deals. U.S. firms are well-represented in the negotiations, and where U.S. business goes, U.S. national interests follow. . . . The presence of these oil reserves and the possibility of their export raises new strategic concerns for the United States and other Western industrial powers. As oil companies build oil pipelines from the Caucasus and Central Asia to supply Japan and the West, these strategic concerns gain military implications. . . . The uninterrupted supply of oil to global markets will continue to be a key factor in international stability.[22]

Other authors have made it clear that oil is an underlying U.S. concern in Afghanistan today. As NSC energy expert Sheila Heslin told Congress in 1997, U.S. policy in Central Asia was "to in essence break Russia's monopoly control over the transportation of oil [and gas] from that region, and frankly, to promote Western energy security through diversification of supply."[23] The same double goal of retrieval and denial was reiterated one year later by Energy Secretary Bill Richardson: "This is about America's energy security, which depends on diversifying our sources of oil and gas worldwide. It's also about preventing strategic inroads by those who don't share our values."[24]

American oil companies (including Unocal) have since 1995 been united in a private Foreign Oil Companies group to lobby in Washington for an active U.S. policy to promote their interests in the Caspian basin.[25] Their meeting with Sheila Heslin in the summer of 1995 was followed shortly by the creation of an interagency governmental committee to formulate U.S. policy toward the Caspian.[26]

The conspicuous influence of petroleum money in the administration of oilmen George W. Bush and Dick Cheney was hardly less under their predecessors. A former CIA officer complained about the influence of the oil lobby in the Clinton administration:

> Heslin's sole job, it seemed, was to carry water for an exclusive club known as the Foreign Oil Companies Group, a cover for a cartel of major petroleum companies doing business in the Caspian. . . . Another thing I learned was that Heslin wasn't soloing. Her boss, Deputy National Security Adviser Sandy Berger, headed the interagency committee on Caspian oil policy, which made him in effect the government's ambassador to the cartel, and Berger wasn't a disinterested player. He held $90,000 worth of stock in Amoco, probably the most influential member of the cartel. . . . The deeper I got, the more Caspian oil money I found sloshing around Washington.[27]

HEROIN IN AFGHANISTAN

In the same period that U.S. interest in Afghanistan surged, Afghanistan became the world's major heroin source. Indeed one might have thought, when the United

States attacked Afghanistan in October 2001, it would be proclaimed as another chapter in the U.S. "war on drugs." Both bin Laden and the Taliban had been named abroad as financed from the drug traffic. Russia submitted a detailed report on this and other aspects of the Taliban to the UN Security Council in March 2001, but the United States, according to *Jane's Intelligence Review*, chose not to act on this information.[28]

Instead there was for a while a virtual embargo in the United States on this aspect of bin Laden's al-Qaeda network that was being widely reported in France, England, and Canada—that al-Qaeda itself earned ongoing revenues from not only a spectrum of legitimate businesses but also drug trafficking.[29] And yet, as I wrote in September 2001, I could find only one sentence on this topic in a U.S. paper, buried deep in a long story in the *Los Angeles Times*: "CIA officials say the underground network frequently crosses into gangsterism. One official cites 'ample evidence' that Bin Laden's group uses profits from the drug trade to finance its campaign. Followers also have been tied to bank robberies, holdups, credit card fraud and other crimes."[30] Gradually the reason for U.S. silence became clear: we were about to use the Northern Alliance (which had just trebled opium production in the area it controlled) as a drug proxy to defeat the Taliban (which had just enforced a total ban on opium production).

CIA collaboration with and support for Islamists like bin Laden date back at least to 1971, when the CIA joined Saudi intelligence in backing the Muslim Brotherhood and its allies in a worldwide campaign against communism.[31] During the Afghan resistance to the Soviet Union in the 1980s, bin Laden became the financier and logistics expert in Afghanistan for the Saudi-financed Makhtab al-Khidamat, the Office of Services, an organization that through the Muslim Brotherhood recruited foreign volunteers from all over the world, including the United States.[32] There are repeated allegations that the CIA, directly or through intermediaries, assisted this recruitment campaign.[33] Simon Reeve also heard from a retired CIA officer that U.S. emissaries to Pakistan "met directly with bin Laden, and that it was bin Laden, acting on advice from his friends in Saudi intelligence, who first suggested the mujaheddin should be given Stingers."[34] French and Italian newspapers have alleged a contact between bin Laden and a CIA officer as late as July 2001.[35]

It is striking that, with all the press focus on bin Laden, no newspaper to my knowledge quoted from his 1999 biography by Yossef Bodansky, director of the U.S. Congressional Task Force on Terrorism:

> An up-and-coming venue for Islamist funds is a combination of the former Soviet states of Central Asia with Germany and Eastern Europe. Access to this seemingly unrelated group of states was made possible through bin Laden's building of relations with the Russian Mafia. . . . This connection is becoming extremely important with the vast expansion of the Afghan drug trade. . . . As the sums of money available from the drug trade have increased, bin Laden and the Russian Mafia have estab-

lished yet another complex money-laundering operation. . . . These funds are used
to finance the Taliban movement and a host of Islamist terrorist operations. Bin
Laden makes a commission on the transactions, which is laundered by the Russian
Mafia in countries other than Russia and Afghanistan.[36]

Why, in this situation, did the United States and its dutiful media not proclaim
a war on drugs? Because the primary U.S. target at first was not bin Laden but
the Taliban, who by 2001 had already responded to U.S. and UN demands that
they halt opium cultivation. As *Jane's Intelligence Review* (October 22, 2001)
noted, "the ban imposed by Taliban supreme leader Mullah Mohammad Omar in
July 2000 . . . resulted in some 70% of the world's illicit opium production being
wiped out virtually at a stroke." Our drug proxy allies were the Northern Alliance, who responded to the Taliban ban on opium cultivation in 2000 by trebling
output in their sector of northeastern Afghanistan.

The United States was not waging a war *on* drugs, in short, but a war helped
by drugs. It is true that previously the Northern Alliance had controlled less than
5 percent of the Afghan opium traffic, compared to the Taliban's 75–80 percent.
But even before the onset of the U.S. bombing, that was changing. In October
2001 *Jane's Intelligence Review* (October 22, 2001) reported that while "poppy
cultivation has almost totally disappeared" from the areas of Afghanistan under
Taliban control, "a rising tide of narcotics—both opium and the heroin refined
from it" was flooding out of the northeast corner of Afghanistan under the control of the Northern Alliance.[37]

A subsequent article in the London *Observer* attributed the shift in opium supplies to the ban on cultivation enacted by the Taliban in 2000: "During the ban
the only source of poppy production was territory held by the Northern Alliance.
It tripled its production. In the high valleys of Badakhshan—an area controlled
by troops loyal to the former President Burhanuddin Rabbani—the number of
hectares planted last year jumped from 2,458 to 6,342. Alliance fields accounted
for 83 percent of total Afghan production of 185 tons of opium during the ban.
Now that the Alliance has captured such rich poppy-growing areas as Nangarhar,
production is set to rocket."[38]

In short, the U.S. military intervention in Afghanistan in 2001 was accompanied by restoration of opium for the world market, a recreation of what happened
with the earlier U.S. intervention of 1979–1980, and before that with the U.S.
intervention in Indochina after 1959, and in Southeast Asia in 1950. We can conclude once again that, as a Brookings Institution expert wrote of the U.S. intervention of 1979–1980, "drug control evidently became subordinated to larger
strategic goals."[39]

NOTES

1. There were a number of briefer military, paramilitary, and covert involvements.
What I say about drugs and/or oil can be adapted to some of these involvements, notably
Indonesia and Panama.

2. In this chapter I shall not deal at length with the Iraq war because the scheduled uprising by Kurdish proxies never really took place. They have, however, been accused of drug trafficking. Concerning them, a well-placed Washington observer (Anthony Cordesman) observed that "the only military skill the Iraqi Kurds have ever demonstrated is the ability to fight each other over smuggling rights" (*Los Angeles Times*, November 19, 1998).

3. Peter Dale Scott, *Drugs, Contras, and the CIA: Government Policies and the Cocaine Economy* (Sherman Oaks, Calif.: From the Wilderness Publications, 2000), 30. The ringleader was Juan Ramón Matta Ballesteros.

4. Alfred W. McCoy, *The Politics of Heroin: CIA Complicity in the Global Drug Trade* (Brooklyn, N.Y.: Lawrence Hill, 1991), 19.

5. See Carl A. Trocki, *Opium, Empire, and the Global Political Economy: A Study of the Asian Opium Trade, 1750–1950* (London: Routledge, 1999); Timothy Brook and Bob Tadashi Wakabayashi, eds., *Opium Regimes: China, Britain, and Japan, 1839–1952* (Berkeley: University of California Press, 2000).

6. Ahmed Rashid, *Taliban: Militant Islam, Oil, and Fundamentalism in Central Asia* (New Haven: Yale University Press, 2001), 173–75, 182.

7. *Washington Times*, May 3, 1999: "In 1998, the U.S. State Department listed the KLA—formally known as the Ushtria Clirimtare e Kosoves, or UCK—as an international terrorist organization, saying it had bankrolled its operations with proceeds from the international heroin trade and from loans from known terrorists like Osama bin Laden." The *Times* of London also reported on March 24, 1999, that the Kosovo Liberation Army (KLA) is allegedly funded by profits from narcotics trafficking.

8. *Guardian* (London), January 15, 2001: "During the 1999 Balkans war, some of the critics of Nato's intervention alleged that the western powers were seeking to secure a passage for oil from the Caspian sea. This claim was widely mocked. . . . For the past few weeks, a freelance researcher called Keith Fisher has been doggedly documenting a project which has, as far as I can discover, has been little-reported in any British, European or American newspaper. It is called the Trans-Balkan pipeline, and it's due for approval at the end of next month. Its purpose is to secure a passage for oil from the Caspian sea."

9. David McClintick, *Swordfish: A True Story of Ambition, Savagery, and Betrayal* (New York: Pantheon, 1993), 227–28; *Newsweek*, May 15, 1985; Peter Dale Scott, *Drugs, Contras, and the CIA*, 29–32.

10. Peter Dale Scott and Jonathan Marshall, *Cocaine Politics: Drugs, Armies, and the CIA in Central America* (Berkeley: University of California Press, 1998), 37–42.

11. William French Smith, "Drug Traffic Today: Challenge and Response," *Drug Enforcement*, Summer 1982, 2–3; McCoy, *Politics*, 447 (60 percent in 1980). Cf. U.S. General Accounting Office, *Drug Control: U.S. Supported Efforts in Burma, Pakistan, and Thailand*, GAO/NSIAD-88-94, February 1988, 12; Peter Dale Scott, "Honduras, the Contra Support Networks, and Cocaine," in Alfred W. McCoy and Alan A. Block, eds., *War on Drugs: Studies in the Failure of U.S. Narcotics Policy* (Boulder: Westview, 1992), 127. In a review of this book Michael Massing denigrated the Afghan heroin threat (backed by GAO statistics) by the irrelevant (and debatable) argument that most U.S. heroin "in the late 1960s" came from Turkey (*New York Review of Books*, December 3, 1992).

12. *Washington Post*, May 13, 1990; McCoy, *Politics*, 459.

13. John K. Cooley, *Unholy Wars: Afghanistan, America, and International Terrorism* (London: Pluto, 2000), 17.

14. Alexander Cockburn and Jeffrey St. Clair, *Whiteout: The CIA, Drugs, and the Press* (London: Verso, 1998), 259; cf. Daniel Yergin, *The Prize: The Epic Quest for Oil, Money, and Power* (New York: Simon & Schuster, 1991), 701.

15. Zbigniew Brzezinski, *The Grand Chessboard: American Primacy and Its Geostrategic Imperatives* (New York: Basic, 1997), 7.

16. Yergin, *The Prize*, 702.

17. It is worth recalling in detail Brzezinski's remarks to *Le Nouvel Observateur* (January 15–21, 1998): "Indeed, it was July 3, 1979 that President Carter signed the first directive for secret aid to the opponents of the pro-Soviet regime in Kabul. And that very day, I wrote a note to the president in which I explained to him that in my opinion this aid was going to induce a Soviet military intervention.

Q: Despite this risk, you were an advocate of this covert action. But perhaps you yourself desired this Soviet entry into war and looked to provoke it?

B: It isn't quite that. We didn't push the Russians to intervene, but we knowingly increased the probability that they would.

Q: When the Soviets justified their intervention by asserting that they intended to fight against a secret involvement of the United States in Afghanistan, people didn't believe them. However, there was a basis of truth. You don't regret anything today?

B: Regret what? That secret operation was an excellent idea. It had the effect of drawing the Russians into the Afghan trap and you want me to regret it? The day that the Soviets officially crossed the border, I wrote to President Carter: We now have the opportunity of giving to the USSR its Vietnam war. Indeed, for almost 10 years, Moscow had to carry on a war unsupportable by the government, a conflict that brought about the demoralization and finally the breakup of the Soviet empire.

Q: And neither do you regret having supported the Islamic fundamentalism, having given arms and advice to future terrorists?

B: What is most important to the history of the world? The Taliban or the collapse of the Soviet empire? Some stirred-up Moslems or the liberation of Central Europe and the end of the cold war?

Q: Some stirred-up Moslems? But it has been said and repeated: Islamic fundamentalism represents a world menace today.

B: Nonsense! It is said that the West had a global policy in regard to Islam. That is stupid. There isn't a global Islam. Look at Islam in a rational manner and without demagoguery or emotion. It is the leading religion of the world with 1.5 billion followers. But what is there in common among Saudi Arabian fundamentalism, moderate Morocco, Pakistan militarism, Egyptian pro-Western or Central Asian secularism? Nothing more than what unites the Christian countries."

18. Brzezinski was helped in his anti-détente maneuvers in the same month of June when "NSA and Army intelligence argued that a combination of photography, signal intelligence and a rare bit of human intelligence pointed unmistakably to the presence of a clandestine Soviet brigade" in Cuba (*Washington Post*, September 9, 1979). The existence of this so-called phantom brigade has since been widely discounted.

19. Brzezinski, *Grand Chessboard*, 124. Brzezinski's admission reveals how shallow and misleading is his dated metaphor of Eurasia as the "grand chessboard." What is espe-

cially significant now is not the enemy's pieces but the board itself, or more specifically what lies under it.

20. Brzezinski, *Grand Chessboard,* 125.

21. White House press statement of August 1, 1997; as quoted in Michael Klare, *Resource Wars: The New Landscape of Global Conflict* (New York: Metropolitan Books/ Henry Holt, 2001), 4.

22. Lester W. Grau, "Hydrocarbons and a New Strategic Region: The Caspian Sea and Central Asia," *Military Review,* May–June 2001.

23. Testimony of Sheila Heslin in Senate hearings into illegal fund-raising activities, September 17, 1997; quoted in Rashid, *Taliban,* 174.

24. Michael Klare, *Resource Wars,* 90; from *New York Times,* November 8, 1998. In 1949 the United States adopted an oil-denial strategy, with plans to blow up oil installations and plug oil fields in the Gulf States in the face of a Soviet invasion (*New York Times,* January 29, 2002).

25. Rashid, *Taliban,* 162; *Guardian* (London), January 12, 2002.

26. In 1996 a similar group was formed by Occidental, BP Amoco, Enron, and other firms to lobby for U.S. energy interests in Colombia. See below, chapter 6.

27. Robert Baer, *See No Evil: The True Story of a Ground Soldier in the CIA's War on Terrorism* (New York: Crown, 2002), 243–44.

28. *Jane's Intelligence Review,* October 5, 2001, www.janes.com/security/ international_security/news/jid/jidpromo011005.shtml.

29. See *London Daily Telegraph,* September 15, 2001, September 16, 2001; *Montreal Gazette,* September 15, 2001; *Le Monde,* September 14, 2001.

30. *Los Angeles Times,* September 15, 2001.

31. Cooley, *Unholy Wars,* 43.

32. Michael Griffin, *Reaping the Whirlwind: The Taliban Movement in Afghanistan* (London: Pluto, 2001), 133; Cooley, *Unholy Wars,* 243; Peter L. Bergen, *Holy War, Inc.: Inside the Secret World of Osama bin Laden* (New York: Free Press, 2001), 133.

33. Rashid, *Taliban,* 129; Cooley, *Unholy Wars,* 87; Yossef Bodansky, *Bin Laden: The Man Who Declared War on America* (New York: Random House/Prima, 2001), 213. Cf. Richard Labévière, *Dollars for Terror: The United States and Islam* (New York: Algora, 2000), 102–4, 223–24. According to *Der Spiegel* (October 6, 1986), a Kuwaitian trained in explosives was supplied with false Afghan papers by the CIA in Germany in 1986, and then was flown to Pakistan en route to Afghanistan.

34. Simon Reeve, *The New Jackals: Ramzi Yousef, Osama bin Laden, and the Future of Terrorism* (Boston: Northeastern University Press, 1999), 167. It is probable that these U.S. emissaries included congressmen such as Rep. Charles Wilson, an associate of the American Security Council backed by Texan defense interests. Wilson, one of the chief proponents of the Stinger program, made fourteen trips to South Asia in promoting the Afghan cause (Cooley, *Unholy Wars,* 110–11). In addition Labévière asserts direct CIA involvement with both the Makhtab and bin Laden; most U.S. authorities see CIA support mediated by Pakistani and Saudi intelligence.

35. *Guardian* (London), November 1, 2001.

36. Bodansky, *Bin Laden,* 314–15: "The annual income of the Taliban from the drug trade is estimated at $8 billion. Bin Laden administers and manages these funds— laundering them through the Russian Mafia—in return for a commission of between 10 and 15 percent, which provides an annual income of about a billion dollars."

37. See www.janes.com/security/international_security/news/jir/jir011022_3_n.sht ml. Of the Afghan leaders whom the United States considered eligible in 2001 to fill out an interim post-Taliban government, many were figures implicated in drug trafficking in the 1980s. The BBC compiled a list of these leaders in November 2001. Leading the list was President Burhanuddin Rabbani, whose home province of Badakshan became in the 1990s, while under his control, "the stepping stone for an entirely new means of conveying opiates to Europe, via Tajikistan, Uzbekistan and Russia's Central Asian railway service" (Griffin, *Reaping the Whirlwind*, 150). Veteran General Rashid Dostum, in Mazar-i-Sharif, "was suspected of earning huge profits by exporting drugs via Uzbekistan" (Cooley, *Unholy Wars*, 155). Of the seven Pashtun leaders named, three (Pir Sayed Gailani, Gulbuddin Hekmatyar, and Hazi Bashir) had been linked in the past to drug trafficking. A fourth, Younus Khalis, was a powerful figure from drug-rich Nangarhar province, and the man with whom Osama bin Laden made contact in 1996, before offering his riches to the Taliban. The restored leader of the Shura-i-Mashriqi (or Eastern Shura) in Nangarhar province, Haji Abdul Qadir, became rich in former times as the Afghan source of a drug pipeline involving in Pakistan Haji Ayub Afridi, "the lord of Khyber heroin dealing" (Griffin, *Reaping the Whirlwind*, 142–43; cf. Cockburn and St. Clair, *Whiteout*, 267). Under the headline "US turns to drug baron to rally support," *Asia Times Online* reported on December 4, 2001 that "Afridi was freed from prison in Karachi last Thursday [November 29, 2001] after serving just a few weeks of a seven-year sentence for the export of 6.5 tons of hashish."

38. *Observer*, November 25, 2001, www.observer.co.uk/Distribution/Redirect_Artifact/ 0,4678,0–605618,00.html.

39. Paul Stares, *Global Habit: The Drug Problem in a Borderless World* (Washington, D.C.: Brookings Institution); quoted in John Kerry, *The New War: The Web of Crime That Threatens America's Security* (New York: Simon & Schuster, 1997), 96.

2

Indochina, Colombia, and Afghanistan: Emerging Patterns

As in Afghanistan in the 1980s or Laos in the 1960s, our principal proxy in the 2001–2002 Afghan war was a dominant element in the regional drug traffic. In Colombia also, we are fighting a war (supposedly *on* drugs but in fact financed in part *by* drugs) with a drug proxy—the corrupt Colombian army and its even more corrupt paramilitary auxiliaries. In 2001 Colombian government sources estimated that 40 percent of Colombian cocaine exports were controlled by right-wing paramilitary warlords and their trafficking allies. Meanwhile the amount controlled by the Revolutionary Armed Forces of Colombia (FARC), the target of the U.S. "war on drugs," was estimated by the Colombian government to be 2.5 percent.[1]

The oil aspect of the Colombian conflict is also conspicuous. The origins of the current U.S. presence in Colombia can be traced back to 1984, one year after the discovery by Occidental Oil of the billion-barrel Caño Limon oilfield in 1983. A concerted U.S. propaganda campaign was mounted in 1984 against alleged drug trafficking by a conspiracy involving Nicaraguan Sandinistas, Colombian "narco-guerrillas," and traffickers in Medellín, notably Carlos Lehder and Pablo Escobar. This campaign distorted the truth in two related respects: it falsely implicated the FARC and it rewrote history to efface references to the Medellín cartel's competitors in Cali, who were closer to the army and national security apparatus. But it led to the national security decision directives of 1986 and 1989 that created a U.S. military presence in Colombia.[2]

Consider also the pattern of drugs and oil that emerged in Southeast Asia following the victory of the Chinese revolution and the exile of the Kuomintang to Taiwan. The U.S. drug proxies in Laos, including the Hmong, Laotian, and former KMT armies, were all major drug traffickers. The KMT armies were also principal agents in building up Laotian drug production, from an estimated 50 tons in 1953 to 100–150 tons in 1968.[3]

Oil, especially the offshore oil deposits of the South China Sea, helps explain the general U.S. interest in Southeast Asia. In the speeches of Americans like Nixon who defended or lobbied for an increased U.S. presence in the region, the U.S. presence in Vietnam, as in SEATO (Southeast Asia Treaty Organization) before it, was defined as the "shield" protecting anticommunist forces in Indonesia.[4] One of the most industrious of such lobbyists was William Henderson, who was simultaneously an officer of the American Friends of Vietnam and an adviser on International Affairs to Socony Mobil (a major oil investor in Indonesia). The 1970 U.S. incursion into Cambodia followed aerial surveys of Cambodian offshore waters by U.S. Navy planes, following which Union Oil of California (now Unocal), established in Thailand by 1963, acquired a concession for all onshore Cambodian oil and much offshore oil as well.[5]

THE UNDERLYING PATTERNS

Dramatic Boost to International Drug Trafficking, Including a Rise in U.S. Drug Consumption, with Each War

When the CIA began its covert involvement in Burma in the early 1950s, local opium production was in the order of eighty tons a year. Ten years later, thanks to KMT warlords supported by CIA and Civil Air Transport (later Air America), the region produced 300–400 tons a year.[6] During the Vietnam War, production at one point reached 1,200 tons a year. By 1971 there were also seven heroin labs in the region, one of which, close to the forward CIA base of Ban Houei Sai in Laos, was estimated to produce 3.6 tons of heroin a year.[7]

With the waning of the Vietnam War, opium production in the Golden Triangle also declined. In the case of Laos, it plummeted from two hundred tons in 1975 to thirty tons in 1984.[8] Heroin consumption in the United States also declined. Although the decline in Laotian production has been attributed to drought conditions, a related factor was clearly the increase in cultivation in the so-called Golden Crescent along the border between Pakistan and Afghanistan, from 400 tons in 1971 to 1,200 tons in 1978.[9] This coincided with a number of political developments in the region, including an increase in Pakistani support for Afghan Islamic resistance movements following a left-wing Afghan coup in 1973.[10]

The decline in U.S. heroin consumption also occurred in the context of an increase in other areas, notably Europe and Australia. In the case of Australia, the first major drug imports were financed by the Nugan Hand Bank, organized in part by veterans of U.S. Special Forces and CIA in Laos. The bank combined drug financing with arms deals and support for CIA covert operations in other regions such as Africa.[11] The Australian surge occurred just as Richard Nixon inaugurated a "war on drugs" to keep opium and heroin from reaching the United States.[12]

The U.S. military intervention in Colombia has also been accompanied, as I predicted in 1991, by a dramatic increase in coca production (from 3.8 to 12.3 thousand hectares between 1991 and 1999).[13] These boosts are cumulative, and up to now not permanently reversible. The U.S. Bureau of Narcotics reported in 1970 that annual illicit opium production at that time was between 1,250 and 1,400 tons, more than half of it coming from the Golden Triangle of Burma, Laos, and Thailand (which before World War II accounted for about 47 tons).[14] In 1999 the United Nations put the opium production of Afghanistan alone at 4,600 tons, or 70 percent of the world's crop.[15]

The strengthening of the global narcotics traffic has fueled other smuggling and related criminal activities, leading to the consolidation of an international criminal milieu. Chinese Triads, Japanese Yakuza, Russian gangs, and the Mafias of Italy, America, and Colombia have now combined into a "worldwide criminal consortium" that is, according to experts, "growing exponentially."[16] Delegates to a global crime conference in November 1994 were informed that organized crime generates $750 billion annually; many of these illicit dollars end up corrupting markets, institutions, businessmen, and of course politicians.[17] Writing in 1997 of his experience in exposing BCCI, Senator John Kerry concluded that "today globalized crime can rob the U.S. not only of our money but also of our way of life."[18]

We can take his words as a prophecy now fulfilled. Although al-Qaeda and the Taliban might appear on the surface to exemplify a "clash" of civilizations, their activities were paid for, as noted above, by heroin and other transactions at the very heart of this global crime milieu that transcends religious boundaries.

Accelerating U.S. Dependency on International Oil and Petrodollars in the Context of Globalization and War

At the height of the Vietnam War, with inflation threatening to wreck his domestic program for a "great society," Lyndon Johnson relaxed the import quota system that had been introduced by Eisenhower to protect domestic U.S. oil production.[19] This increased U.S. vulnerability pressure from OPEC oil boycotts in the 1970s, and that vulnerability would be further heightened after Nixon abolished quotas altogether in 1973.

The United States handled the quadrupling of oil prices in the 1970s by arranging, by means of secret agreements with the Saudis, to recycle petrodollars back into the U.S. economy. The first of these deals assured a special and ongoing Saudi stake in the health of the U.S. dollar; the second secured continuing Saudi support for the pricing of all OPEC oil in dollars.[20] These two deals assured that the U.S. economy would not be impoverished by OPEC oil price hikes. The heaviest burdens would be borne instead by the economies of less developed countries.[21]

From these developments emerged the twin phenomena underlying 9/11—triumphalist U.S. unilateralism on the one hand and global Third World indebtedness on the other. The secret deals increased U.S.-Saudi interdependence at the expense of the international comity that had been the basis of U.S. prosperity since World War II. They also increased Saudi leverage on U.S. foreign policy, as was seen in the 1979 sale of F-15 fighter planes to Saudi Arabia, against strong Israeli opposition.[22] In particular they explain why George Bush moved so swiftly in 1990 to counter the threat posed by Saddam Hussein to U.S.-Saudi security in the Persian Gulf. The threat was not just that the United States itself would lose oil from the Gulf, against which it was partially insured by the redundancy in world oil supplies. A bigger threat was that Saddam would become the dominant power in the Persian Gulf, directly controlling 20 percent of OPEC production and 25 percent of world oil reserves.[23]

The U.S.-Saudi deals also increased U.S. dependence on oil- and drug-funded Arab assets such as BCCI—the Bank of Credit and Commerce International—which in the 1980s became a chief paymaster for the anti-Soviet Afghan mujahedin and even ran arms directly to them from Karachi.[24] (The failure of the U.S. government to investigate and prosecute BCCI reflected not only the extent of BCCI penetration of U.S. ruling circles but also U.S. economic dependence on the continued influx of petrodollars and narco-dollars. As a former NSC economist commented, "[Treasury Secretary James] Baker didn't pursue BCCI because he thought a prosecution of the bank would damage the United States' reputation as a safe haven for flight capital and overseas investments."[25]

Some had expected that the successful OPEC revolt in the 1970s against Washington's and London's economic policies would presage a "new economic order" that would strengthen the South vis-à-vis the North. The secret Saudi-U.S. deals led to a different outcome: a "new world order" that saw increasing U.S. military dominance combined with increasing economic instability and occasional crises elsewhere. Statistics reveal the change in direction. Between 1960 and 1980 per capita income grew 73 percent in Latin America and 34 percent in Africa. Between 1980 and 2000 income grew less than 6 percent in Latin America, and declined by 23 percent in Africa.[26]

This loss of economic stability and momentum, combined with political impotence in the face of U.S. military hegemony, are of course root factors to be addressed in any serious effort to combat terrorism.

U.S. WARS IN THE LIGHT OF THE
INTERNATIONAL DRUG TRADE

The examples cited above, of drug factors underlying U.S. interventions, illustrate what I mean by deep politics. The point is not to suggest that the increase in drug consumption was a conscious aim of high-level U.S. planning, but that it was a direct consequence of policy decisions. There are, however, grounds for considering a different question: Did successive crises in the illicit drug traffic induce some drug-trafficking U.S. interest groups and allies to press successfully for U.S. involvement in an Asian war? This is a question asked in my book *The War Conspiracy.*[27] Although I had partly retreated from this question by the time I finished the book in 1971, conspicuous recent developments have persuaded me to revive it today.

I have no evidence that the U.S. government intervened militarily as a conscious means of maintaining control over the global drug traffic. However, conscious decisions were definitely made, time after time, to ally the United States with local drug proxies. The U.S. motives for doing so were usually to minimize the costs and exposure of direct engagement. However, the drug proxies and their associates appear to have exploited these conditions of nonaccountability with escalations to meet their own drug agendas, particularly at moments when the survival of the drug traffic was threatened.

The whole history of the United States in the Far East since World War II has involved from the beginning a drug trafficking proxy—the KMT—that from the days of the China lobby had obtained or purchased significant support within the U.S. political establishment. Although the picture is a complex one defying reduction, one can certainly see the role of the China lobby as a factor in the events leading to America's first war on the Asian mainland—the Korean War in 1950.[28] This was right after the victorious armies of Mao Tse-tung began to eliminate Chinese opium, the source of 85 percent of the world's heroin.

Furthermore, drugs from regions where the CIA has been active have tended to migrate through other countries of CIA penetration, and more importantly through and to agencies and groups that can be classified as CIA assets. In the 1950s opium from Indochina traveled through Iran and Lebanon to the Corsican Mafia in Marseilles and the Sicilian Mafia under Lucky Luciano.[29] In the 1980s mujahedin heroin was reaching the Sicilian Mafia via the Turkish Gray Wolves, who "worked in tandem with the Turkish Army's Counter-Guerrilla Organization, which functioned as the Turkish branch of the CIA's multinational 'stay behind' program."[30] The routes shifted with the politics of the times, but the CIA denominator remained constant.

The following sections examine moments in which U.S. wars were deeply intertwined with the world drug traffic, beginning with the most recent.

2001

In October 2001 a UN report confirmed that the Taliban had successfully eliminated the year's opium production in Afghanistan, which in recent years had supplied 90 percent of Europe's heroin. However, it appears that what would have been the world's largest curtailment of opium production in half a century has now been reversed. Following the defeat of the Taliban, farmers began replanting wheat fields with opium poppy; and it is now estimated that in 2002 opium harvest is about 3,700 tons (3,400 metric tons, or more than the 2000 harvest).[31]

On October 16, 2001, the United Nations Office for Drug Control and Crime Prevention released its Afghanistan annual opium poppy survey for 2001. It reported that the 2000 ban on opium imposed by the Taliban was almost universally enforced. The estimated 2001 crop of 185 metric tons was only 6 percent of Afghanistan's 2000 total of 3,276 tons, which had been more than half the world's output. Over 90 percent of the 2001 crop came from provinces under the control of America's eventual ally the Northern Alliance, where the area under cultivation radically increased. Helmand province under the Taliban, the highest cultivating area in 2000, recorded no poppy cultivation in the 2001 season.[32]

The UN ODCCP report further noted that the approximately 3,100-ton reduction in 2001 opium production in Afghanistan (compared to 2000) was not offset by increases in other countries. As *Jane's Intelligence Review* (October 22, 2001) noted, "The ban imposed by Taliban supreme leader Mullah Mohammad Omar in July 2000 . . . resulted in some 70% of the world's illicit opium production being wiped out virtually at a stroke." Those skeptical about Mullah Omar's motives for the ban speculated that the Taliban held substantial reserves of processed opium and wished to drive up prices. Nevertheless, even the U.S. State Department reported in March 2002 that the Taliban's ban had been "remarkably successful," reducing total Afghan opium production from 3,656 tons in 2000 to 74 tons in 2001. More credible explanations stress the Taliban's efforts to gain legitimacy and recognition from the United States and other nations, a policy that proved abortive. Despite the ban, Afghanistan remained (in the words of the report) "one of the world's leading opium producers by virtue of continued cultivation in its northern provinces [controlled by the Northern Alliance]."[33]

As the Taliban was ousted from province after province in 2001, starving farmers everywhere started to replant the one lucrative crop available to them, often at the behest of local commanders. The crop augured the return of warlordism to Afghanistan—regional commanders and armies, financed by the opium in their area, jealously refusing to relinquish such a lucrative income source to a central government. Thus there could be a revival of the vicious internecine feuds that took so many civilian lives in the 1990s after the Soviet withdrawal.[34]

The London *Observer* on November 25, 2001, reported that "Western and Pakistani officials fear that, within a year or two, Afghanistan could again reach its peak production figures of 60,000 hectares of poppies producing 2,800 tonnes of opium—more than half the world's output." It reported further on December 10, 2001, "With the Taliban gone, Afghanistan's farmers are going back to their old, lucrative ways. In the tribal areas of Pakistan, where most of the opium is processed, prices have plummeted in expectation of a bumper crop."

The *Financial Times* (London) reported (February 18, 2002): "The U.S. and

United Nations have ignored repeated calls by the international antidrugs community to address the increasing menace of Afghanistan's opium cultivation, threatening a rift between Europe and the U.S. as they begin to reconstruct the country."

The initial failure of the U.S. press to report or comment on these developments was an ominous sign that the U.S. government might be prepared to see its former protégés finance themselves once again through the drug traffic. More ominous was active disinformation by officials of the U.S. government. The Taliban's drastic reduction in opium cultivation was ignored, and indeed misrepresented, by CIA Director George Tenet in his report to Congress on February 7, 2001, in a speech that threatened retaliatory strikes against the Taliban: "Production in Afghanistan has been exploding, accounting for 72 percent of illicit global opium production in 2000. The drug threat is increasingly intertwined with other threats. For example, the Taliban regime in Afghanistan, which allows bin Laden and other terrorists to operate on its territory, encourages and profits from the drug trade."[35]

On January 17, 2002, Afghanistan's new leader Hamid Karzai issued a new ban on opium poppy cultivation and promised to work with donors to ensure it could be implemented. However, as the State Department reported, "Whether factions will follow a ban on poppy cultivation, issued by the Interim Authority is uncertain. The Northern Alliance, for example, has, so far as the U.S. is aware, taken no action against cultivation and trafficking in the area it controls. There have also been recent reports of farmers cultivating a second opium crop in Northern Alliance–controlled areas."[36]

As a result, drugs have continued to flow north into Tajikistan and Kyrgyzstan, where they finance Islamist radical groups. Author-journalist Ahmed Rashid has reported the conviction of Tajik officials that the main drug-financed group they faced, the Islamic Movement of Uzbekistan (IMU), was being covertly assisted by Russia "because Moscow was trying to pressure [Uzbek dictator] Karimov into accepting Russian troops and greater Russian influence in Uzbekistan. . . . Other Tajik officials claimed that the IMU was supported by Saudi Arabia and Pakistan, who were backing Islamic movements in Central Asia in order to gain leverage in the region."[37] Rashid himself confirms both Saudi funds and ISI "discreet support" for the IMU, adding that "senior ISI officials are convinced that the IMU has close intelligence links to Russia."[38]

We are still waiting for a clearer American resolve to deal with the restored drug flows it has created, for adequate funds to restore the shattered Afghan economy, and for a firm commitment to address the problem of warlordism. Until then, it can only be concluded that once again the United States is unprepared to challenge the drug politics of its proxies in the region. Perhaps there are some in the U.S. government who, like their Russian counterparts, accept the corruption of the Central Asian states through drugs as a means of increasing influence over politicians there.[39]

1979

The situation in 2001 recreated many elements of the 1980s, when, in the words of the *Washington Post* (May 13, 1990), U.S. officials ignored heroin trafficking by the mujahedin "because U.S. narcotics policy in Afghanistan has been subordinated to the war against Soviet influence there."

The consequences of that official toleration of trafficking have been summarized vividly by Michael Griffin:

> By the mid-1980s, the processing and export of heroin had created a black economy in Pakistan of about $8 billion—half the size of the official one—and Pakistan's military administration was showing signs of evolving into a fully-blown narco-government. . . . The number of Pakistani addicts, meanwhile, had spiralled from nil in 1979 to between 1.2 and 1.7 million at the end of 1988. Such a rapid rate would have been impossible without the protection or active collaboration of the ISI which, empowered by CIA funding and arms deliveries, had grown from a small military department into a modern intelligence network with a staff of 150,000 and hundreds of millions of dollars a year at its disposal. . . . The U.S. colluded in the development of this new heroin source for fear of undermining the CIA's working alliance for the *mujahedin.*[40]

Many authors besides Griffin have seen this enormous expansion of the drug trade as a by-product of the anti-Soviet war. But there are signs that opium traffickers did more than just profit from the war: they may have helped induce it. It is certain that the buildup of opium and heroin production along the Afghan-Pakistan frontier was not a consequence of the war: it preceded it. What is particularly eye-catching is that, in 1979 just as in 2001, the war helped avert what would otherwise have been an acute drop in world opium production from earlier heights.

In his important book *The Politics of Heroin,* Alfred McCoy notes that heroin from southern Asia had been insignificant in the global market until the late 1970s, when there was a two-year failure of the monsoon rains in the Burma-Laos area. It was in response to this drought that Pakistani cultivation increased and heroin labs opened in the North-West Frontier province by 1979 (a fact duly noted by the Canadian *Maclean's Magazine* of April 30, 1979).

McCoy notes the subsequent increase: "By 1980 Pakistan-Afghan opium dominated the European market and supplied 60 percent of America's illicit demand as well."[41] He also records that Gulbuddin Hekmatyar controlled a complex of six heroin laboratories in the Koh-i-Sultan district of Baluchistan, a region (we are told elsewhere) "where the ISI was in total control."[42]

This timetable raises the same question as events in 2001. What forces led the

CIA in May 1979, armed with an NSC authorization from Brzezinski one month earlier, to work with the Pakistani ISI and its protégé Hekmatyar in the context of an already burgeoning heroin trade that would come to dominate the activities of the ISI-Hekmatyar connection?[43]

Before that time the CIA had already cultivated Pakistani assets that would become an integral part of the Afghan arms pipeline. One was the Gulf Group shipping line of the Gokal brothers, a firm that was heavily involved in shipping goods to Third World countries for American aid programs.[44] Another was BCCI, the biggest financier of Gulf Group.[45] BCCI chairman Agha Hasan Abedi had been suspected of links to U.S. intelligence even before he founded BCCI in 1972.[46] BCCI's inside connection to the CIA appears to have been strengthened in 1976, when under CIA Director George Bush "the CIA strengthened its relationships with so-called friendly Arab intelligence agencies. One of the most important of these was Saudi Arabia's intelligence service [the Istakhbarat], run by Kamal Adham, Prince Turki [al-Faisal al-Saud], and Abdul-Raouf Khalil, all of whom were BCCI insiders."[47]

BCCI's links with the CIA milieu—and more specifically with CIA Director Bush and his eventual successor, William Casey, are said to have increased in 1976, after Bush's non-reappointment by Jimmy Carter. At this time the swelling ranks of ex-CIA operatives, dismissed for the sake of a downsized clandestine service, are said to have combined to create a shadow "CIA-in-exile"—an "off-the-books group made up of the old boys."[48] It has been alleged that in 1976 CIA Director Bush acted with British intelligence and with William Casey (who at the time was campaign manager for Reagan's first presidential campaign) to help set up the Cayman Island affiliate (and intelligence connection) of the BCCI.[49] The purpose was to establish BCCI as "an intelligence consortium among the British, the Americans, and the Arabs."[50]

According to this theory, the Syrian drug dealer Monzer al-Kassar, who had been recruited by British intelligence, "played a key role in this. . . . He convinced all the terrorist groups, from Abu Nidal to the Marxists, to transfer their accounts to the new BCCI branch in London. There the secret service could easily wiretap and decipher every coded transfer."[51] The Kerry-Brown Senate report on BCCI confirmed that information on the Monzer al-Kassar and Abu Nidal accounts at the London BCCI branch had been passed on to British and American intelligence by the branch manager who was apparently "a paid informant."[52] It also criticized the "casual manner" in which BCCI had been regulated in England, leading to a climax in which "the Bank of England had . . . inadvertently become partner to a cover-up of BCCI's criminality."[53]

A third firm that became part of the Afghan arms pipeline was Global International Airways of Kansas City. It had already expanded in 1979, thanks to "money borrowed from an Arabian international bank"—allegedly BCCI.[54] (Meanwhile the CIA was funding its Afghan operatives with currency purchased from the Swiss firm Shakarchi Trading, which was later revealed to have laundered profits from both Afghan heroin and Colombian cocaine.)[55]

From the outset Abedi's entry into U.S. banking was tied to the achievement of personal influence to effect national policy changes, allegedly with the help of pro-Arab elements in the CIA, extending to President Jimmy Carter, after a number of favors to Carter's embattled budget director, Bert Lance. Long after leaving the presidency, Carter continued to tour the world in Abedi's BCCI plane, allowing Abedi to profit from joint appearances with Carter in Kenya, Ghana, Pakistan, Bangladesh, China, Thailand, and the Soviet Union, "all key targets of BCCI business development."[56]

However, Abedi's efforts with Carter met with only limited success after 1979. In that year the U.S.-brokered Camp David settlement failed to satisfy a key Saudi demand: that Israel relinquish East Jerusalem and the Temple Mount.[57] In April 1979 the United States also stopped economic aid to Pakistan because of its development, financed by BCCI and by drugs, of an atomic bomb.[58] Meanwhile Saudi intelligence and BCCI continued to have better relations with some CIA personnel than with the White House.[59] BCCI's strenuous efforts to acquire an American bank in Washington, starting in 1978, were unsuccessful as long as Carter was president. However, they were unanimously approved in 1981 under the new Reagan-Bush administration.[60]

In Pakistan, meanwhile, Abedi was extremely close to General Mohammed Zia-ul-Haq, who seized power in 1977. Abedi and Zia also met frequently with Fazle Haq or Huq, the man whom Zia appointed military governor of the North-West Frontier province, and allegedly the patron of the Pakistani heroin refiners who bought the mujahedin opium.[61] Like Abedi, Fazle Haq became known as a CIA asset; he was also listed with Interpol by 1982 as an international narcotics trafficker.[62]

Drugs may have been at the heart of this relationship from the outset. A BCCI informant told U.S. authorities that Abedi's influence with Zia "benefited from the backing of a Pakistani named Fazle Haq, who was . . . heavily engaged in narcotics trafficking and moving the heroin money through the bank."[63] DEA headquarters in Washington told reporters they knew nothing about Fazle Haq. But a highly placed U.S. official explained to *Time* correspondent Jonathan Beaty that this was because Haq "was our man . . . everybody knew that Haq was also running the drug trade," and "BCCI was completely involved."[64]

We have already seen that Brzezinski subsequently claimed responsibility for the CIA-ISI intervention in Afghanistan. However, in a 1989 interview Fazle Haq maintained that it was the Pakistanis (including himself) who pressured Brzezinski to back the ISI clients in Afghanistan: "I told Brzezinski you screwed up in Vietnam and Korea; you better get it right this time."[65] In his book *Drugs in South Asia*, M. Emdad-ul Haq speculates further that Fazle Haq was the "foreign trained adviser" who, according to *The Hindustan Times*, had suggested to General Zia that he use drug money to meet the Soviet challenge.[66]

It is clear that in May 1979, months before the Soviet invasion, the ISI put the CIA in contact with Hekmatyar, the ISI protégé who would become the central figure in mujahedin drug trafficking.[67] The CIA did so at a time the international heroin trade had suffered a major drop-off in opium from the Golden Triangle and thus needed to build up a new source. After Pakistan banned opium cultivation in February 1979 and Iran followed suit in April, the absence of legal controls in the Pashtun areas of Pakistan and Afghanistan "attracted Western drug cartels and 'scientists' [including "some 'fortune-seekers' from Europe and the US"] to establish heroin processing facilities in the tribal belt."[68] All this new attention from "the international drug syndicates" apparently came *before* either the CIA active intervention in Afghanistan in August 1979 or the Soviet invasion in December.[69]

No one can doubt the importance of drug trafficking to the ISI as an asset in support of policy goals and also (for some) as a source of personal profit. Through the 1980s and 1990s, the ISI clearly allowed Hekmatyar to use drugs to increase his influence vis-à-vis other Afghan commanders over which the ISI had less control.[70]

Control of drug flows appears to have become part of the CIA-ISI strategy for carrying the Afghan war north into the Soviet Union. As a first step, Casey appears to have promoted a plan, suggested to him by Alexandre de Marenches, that the CIA supply drugs on the sly to Soviet troops.[71] Although de Marenches subsequently denied that the plan went forward, there are reports that heroin, hashish, and even cocaine from Latin America soon reached Soviet troops, and that the CIA-ISI-linked bank BCCI, along with "a few American intelligence operatives were deeply enmeshed in the drug trade" before the war was over.[72] Maureen Orth heard from Mathea Falco, head of International Narcotics Control for the State Department under Jimmy Carter, that the CIA and ISI together encouraged the mujahedin to addict the Soviet troops.[73]

But the plans went farther. In 1984, during a secret visit by CIA Director Casey to Pakistan, "Casey startled his Pakistani hosts by proposing that they take the Afghan war into enemy territory—into the Soviet Union itself. . . . Pakistani intelligence officers—partly inspired by Casey—began independently to train Afghans and funnel CIA supplies for scattered strikes against military installations, factories and storage depots within Soviet territory. . . . The attacks later alarmed U.S. officials in Washington, who saw military raids on Soviet territory as 'an incredible escalation,' according to Graham Fuller, then a senior U.S. intelligence [CIA] official who counseled against any such raids."[74]

"Thus it was," according to Pakistani Brigadier Mohammed Yousaf, "the U.S. that put in train a major escalation of the war which, over the next three years, culminated in numerous cross-border raids and sabotage missions" north of the Amu Darya.[75] According to Ahmed Rashid, "In 1986 the secret services of the United States, Great Britain, and Pakistan agreed on a plan to launch guerrilla attacks into Tajikistan and Uzbekistan."[76] The task "was given to the ISI's favorite Mujaheddin leader Gulbuddin" Hekmatyar,[77] who by this time was supplementing his CIA and Saudi income with the proceeds of his heroin labs "in the Koh-i-Sultan area [of Pakistan], where the ISI was in total control."[78] At the same time the CIA also helped ISI and Saudi Arabia distribute in the Soviet Union thousands of Korans that had been translated into Uzbek, an important contribution to the spread of Islamism in Central Asia today.[79]

Casey was an oilman, and his Central Asian initiative of 1984 was made at a time when right-wing oil interests in Texas already had their eyes on Caspian basin oil. His cross-border guerrillas, recruited from ethnic Uzbeks and Tajiks, evolved in time into heroin-financed Islamist groups like the IMU who became the scourge of Central Asia in the 1990s.[80]

There is also a second question: How far back did this use of Hekmatyar and drugs go, and who originated it? Did CIA initiate the May 1979 contact with Hekmatyar as part of Carter's and Brzezinski's national policy? Or did Abedi, Haq and company, enjoying a special relationship with pro-Saudi elements in the CIA, arrange the contact on behalf of drug interests that would soon profit handsomely?[81] Or did the CIA strengthen the drug trafficking position of its friends such as BCCI and Fazle Haq because it feared the Soviet-backed and heroin-financed intelligence activities among Muslims of men like Rifaat Assad, who controlled the drugs and laboratories of Lebanon's Bekaa valley?[82]

If that question cannot yet be definitively answered, it is clear that BCCI and its affiliated Gokal shipping interests (and possibly Global International Airways) soon formed the backbone of the CIA-ISI arms pipeline to Gulbuddin Hekmatyar. And the United States, fully conscious of Hekmatyar's drug trafficking and anti-Americanism, never exerted pressure to have the ISI deny him U.S. aid.[83] This inaction is the more striking because of Hekmatyar's conspicuous failure to contribute to the mujahedin military campaign.[84]

1959

This brings me to the original thesis of my 1972 book, *The War Conspiracy*. In 1959 drug trafficking elements in Southeast Asia, fearing the loss of their opium sources and connections, had simulated a phony war crisis in Laos. I suspected, but could not prove, that they did so in order to secure a new basis for drug operations in that country with a CIA airline the KMT partly controlled, Civil Air Transport (known after 1959 as Air America).[85] This simulation involved collusion with elements in the CIA and U.S. armed forces who shared the KMT goal of reconquering China.

Lacking certain proof, I formulated this hypothesis very tentatively in 1972, and again in the new preface I wrote to the book in early 2001.[86] However events since 9/11 embolden me to raise it again as a question. In 1959, as again in 1979 and 2001, the local drug trade was threatened by political developments; and the threat vanished after both a CIA-backed escalation and the elevation to power of drug trafficking elements.[87]

The pressures in 1959 were coming from tribesmen in northeastern Laos, from Burma, and from Thailand. For years KMT drugs had been routinely "seized" by Thai border police and then sold locally or to Hong Kong traffickers, to the profit of the CIA's puppet in Thailand, Phao Sriyanon.[88] This came to an abrupt end in 1959, when

> Field Marshal Sarit [Thanarat of Thailand] unleashed a full military assault on the opium trade. At one minute after midnight on July 1, 1959, Sarit's forces swept the country, raiding opium dens, seizing their stocks, and confiscating opium pipes. . . . Speaking to his people, Sarit declared that "1 July 1959 can be considered a date of historical significance because it began the first chapter of a new age in the history of the Thai nation."[89]

I recount in part III how a new chapter in the history of Laos began with a conspiratorial "crisis" only two weeks later, on July 16, 1959. Since 1958, KMT forces, under pressure in Burma, had begun relocating to towns like Ban Houei Sai and Nam Tha in northwestern Laos that would soon become opium centers and CIA bases. By March 1959 they were being supplied in Laos by what Bernard Fall called "an airlift of 'unknown planes'"—almost certainly from the Taiwanese airline Civil Air Transport (CAT), which fronted for the CIA proprietary known since 1959 as Air America.[90] The CIA owned 40 percent of the company; KMT bankers owned 60 percent.[91] The planes had been supplying the KMT opium bases continuously since 1951.

The result of the phony Laotian crisis of July–August 1959 was to give official White House sanction to a continuous Air America airlift to Laos.[92] Air America planes soon began the major airlift to Hmong (Meo) camps in northeast Laos as well. By 1965 they became the primary means of exporting the Hmong's traditional cash crop, opium, and by 1968 were also carrying heroin. Apparently most of this ended up in traditional KMT networks through Hong Kong to the United States.

The 1959 "crisis" was the first of a series that between 1961 and 1964 would lead to greater and greater U.S. involvement in first Laos and then Vietnam. Air America's support for a drug trafficking rebel Laotian leader, Phoumi Nosavan, contributed to these crises. Clearly the "crises" combined stimulus from outside the U.S. government with high-level support inside it. We know now that a plan for a KMT reinvasion of South China, a plan first authorized by Truman in 1951, continued to be supported long after the Korean War by some high-level generals and CIA officials. These ranged from extremists like Air Force General Curtis LeMay, who wrote privately about "nuking the chinks," to CIA Deputy Director Ray Cline, who had served as CIA station chief in Taipei.[93] The plan was revived by right-wing oppositionists in the 1959–1962 period, when to the old McCarthyite question, Who lost China? was added a new one, Who lost Cuba?[94]

Perhaps the most vocal advocate of the plan from 1959 to 1965 was the KMT-sponsored Asian People's Anti-Communist League (after 1966 the World Anti-Communist League), whose member agency at its Taiwan headquarters also sponsored the airlift to the KMT opium camps of western Laos.[95]

The KMT's stake in the CAT airlift to its troops in the "fertile triangle" became obvious in 1961, when Fang Chih, a member of the KMT Central Supervisory Committee and secretary-general of the Free China Relief Agency (FCRA), admitted responsibility for an unlisted CAT plane that had just been shot down over Thailand by the Burmese Air Force. . . . The unpublicized visit to Laos of Fang Chih, in the weeks immediately preceding the phony Laos "invasion" of 1959, suggests that the narcotics traffic, as well as Pathet Lao activity, may have been a reason why CAT's planes inaugurated their flights in that year into the opium-growing Meo areas of Sam Neua province.[96]

But KMT machinations fomenting a phony Laos crisis in 1959 would have gone unheeded had it not been for support from the local CIA station, and higher.[97] A key role was played by the influential CIA ally Joseph Alsop, an old China hand and columnist whose inflammatory reports from Laos helped trigger the U.S. authorization for charter Air America airlift.[98]

We should not be surprised that the CIA and its friends took steps to protect and strengthen the KMT drug traffic in 1959, at a time when that traffic was being challenged. For a decade the CIA and its part-owned proprietary CAT had played a key role in building up the traffic, as the most dependable CIA asset in East and Southeast Asia. The origins of that collaboration merit closer study.

NOTES

1. *Newsweek*, May 21, 2001: "Colombian intelligence sources now estimate that 40 percent of the country's total cocaine exports are controlled by these right-wing warlords and their allies in the narcotics underworld." *San Francisco Chronicle*, June 21, 2001: "The Colombian government's planning department estimates that the FARC earns $290 million yearly from the drug trade. That represents less than 2.5 percent of the value of Colombia's estimated annual cocaine output of 580 tons."

2. Scott and Marshall, *Cocaine Politics*, 96–103.

3. Alfred W. McCoy, *The Politics of Heroin: CIA Complicity in the Global Trade* (New York: Lawrence Hill, 1991), 299.

4. Richard Nixon, "Asia after Vietnam," *Foreign Affairs,* October 1967, 111. Other examples in Peter Dale Scott, "Exporting Military-Economic Development," in Malcolm Caldwell, ed., *Ten Years' Military Terror in Indonesia* (Nottingham, U.K.: Spokesman, 1975), 215–17.

5. Peter Dale Scott, *The War Conspiracy: The Secret Road to the Second Indochina War* (Indianapolis: Bobbs-Merrill, 1972), 154–67.

6. McCoy, *Politics*, 162.

7. McCoy, *Politics*, 286–87.

8. Peter Dale Scott, "Honduras, the Contra Support Networks, and Cocaine: How the U.S. Government Has Augmented America's Drug Crisis," in Alfred W. McCoy and Alan A. Block, eds., *War on Drugs: Studies in the Failure of U.S. Narcotics Policy* (Boulder, Colo.: Westview, 1992), 126–27.

9. McCoy, *Politics*, 446.

10. M. Emdad-ul Haq, *Drugs in South Asia: From the Opium Trade to the Present Day* (New York: St. Martin's, 2000), 175–86; Rashid, *Taliban*, 12–13.

11. Jonathan Marshall, Peter Dale Scott, and Jane Hunter, *The Iran-Contra Connection: Secret Teams and Covert Operations in the Reagan Era* (Boston: South End, 1987), 36–40; McCoy, *Politics*, 461–79; Jonathan Marshall, *Drug Wars: Corruption, Counterinsurgency, and Covert Operations in the Third World* (Forestville, Calif.: Cohan & Cohen, 1991), 55–56; Jonathan Kwitny, *The Crimes of Patriots* (New York: Simon & Schuster, 1987).

12. Among the unanswered questions about Nugan Hand: Why was its regional branch in Chiangmai, Thailand, located down the hall from the local DEA office? Why did so many CIA veterans become Nugan Hand bank officers, despite their lack of training? Why, when Australian officials asked for FBI help when prosecuting the bank, were their requests for Nugan Hand bank documents turned down by the United States on grounds of "national security"?

13. Scott, "Honduras, the Contra Support Networks, and Cocaine," 126–27.

14. McCoy, *Politics*, 191, and sources therein cited.

15. John K. Cooley, *Unholy Wars: Afghanistan, America, and International Terrorism* (London: Pluto, 2000), 139.

16. Claire Sterling, *Thieves' World: The Threat of the New Global Network of Organized Crime* (New York: Simon & Schuster, 1994), 44; citing lecture of November 1990 by Italian Judge Giovanni Falcone.

17. Antonio Nicaso and Lee Lamothe, *Global Mafia: The New World Order of Organized Crime* (Toronto: Macmillan Canada, 1995), xiii.

18. Kerry, *New War*, 18.

19. Yergin, *The Prize,* 538–39.

20. David E. Spiro, *The Hidden Hand of American Hegemony: Petrodollar Recycling and International Markets* (Ithaca, N.Y.: Cornell University Press, 1999), x: "In 1974 [Treasury Secretary William] Simon negotiated a secret deal so the Saudi central bank could buy U.S. Treasury securities outside of the normal auction. A few years later, Treasury Secretary Michael Blumenthal cut a secret deal with the Saudis so that OPEC would continue to price oil in dollars. These deals were secret because the United States had promised other industrialized democracies that it would not pursue such unilateral policies." Cf. 103–12.

21. "So long as OPEC oil was priced in U.S. dollars, and so long as OPEC invested the dollars in U.S. government instruments, the U.S. government enjoyed a double loan. The first part of the loan was for oil. The government could print dollars to pay for oil, and the American economy did not have to produce goods and services in exchange for the oil until OPEC used the dollars for goods and services. Obviously, the strategy could not work if dollars were not a means of exchange for oil. The second part of the loan was from all other economies that had to pay dollars for oil but could not print currency. Those

economies had to trade their goods and services for dollars in order to pay OPEC" (Spiro, *Hidden Hand,* 121).

22. John Loftus and Mark Aarons, *The Secret War against the Jews* (New York: St. Martin's, 1994), 343, who do not mention the two secret financial deals with the Saudis, offer a different and I think one-sided account of the sale of the F-15s; cf. Spiro, *Hidden Hand,* 123–24.

23. Yergin, *The Prize,* 772.

24. Cooley, *Unholy Wars,* 116–17.

25. Jonathan Beaty and S. C. Gwynne, *The Outlaw Bank: A Wild Ride into the Heart of BCCI* (New York: Random House, 1993), 357.

26. Greg Palast, *The Best Democracy Money Can Buy* (London: Pluto, 2002), 48. Palast supplies examples of how the IMF, created at Bretton Woods in 1944 to promote economic stabilization and growth, has since 1980 promoted the opposite by policies that contract economies to preserve debt payments. Cf. Nobel-winning economist Joseph Stiglitz, formerly of the World Bank, on the IMF response to the Asian crisis of 1997: "It went to the countries and told them to be more contractionary than they wanted, to increase interest rates enormously. It was just the opposite of the economic analysis that was the basis of the founding of the IMF. Why? In order to make sure that creditors got repaid" (Joseph Stiglitz, interview by Lucy Komisar, *Progressive,* June 2000, 34).

27. See this book, 194–95.

28. Bruce Cumings, *The Origins of the Korean War.* Vol. 2, *The Roaring of the Cataract, 1947–1950* (Princeton: Princeton University Press, 1990), 106–17, 599–602 (especially 601), and passim.

29. For the CIA connections to the Luciano and Corsican Mafias, see Peter Dale Scott, foreword to Henrik Krüger, *The Great Heroin Coup* (Boston: South End, 1980), 3, 14–15.

30. Martin A. Lee, *The Beast Reawakens* (Boston: Little, Brown, 1997), 202.

31. *Washington Post,* December 10, 2001; *San Francisco Chronicle,* December 21, 2001 (replanting); *New York Times,* October 28, 2002 (3,700 tons). A metric ton is 1.1 tons.

32. United Nations Office for Drug Control and Crime Prevention, *Afghanistan Annual Opium Poppy Survey, 2001.*

33. U.S. Department of State, *International Narcotics Strategy Report, 2001,* www .state.gov/g/inl/rls/nrcrpt/2001/rpt/8482.htm.

34. Thus the revival of the Afghan opium economy is good news for Islamist terrorists from Kosovo to Kashmir, who have depended on it since the connection was established with ISI encouragement in the 1980s.

35. Statement by director of Central Intelligence George J. Tenet before the Senate Select Committee on Intelligence, February 7, 2001, www.cia.gov/cia/public_affairs/ speeches/archives/2001/UNCLASWWT_02072 001.html.

36. U.S. Department of State, *International Narcotics Strategy Report, 2001.*

37. Ahmed Rashid, *Jihad: The Rise of Militant Islam in Central Asia* (New Haven: Yale University Press, 2002), 178.

38. Rashid, *Jihad,* 214–16.

39. In Peter Dale Scott, *Deep Politics and the Death of JFK* (Berkeley: University of California Press, 1996), 203, I reported how a U.S. oil company employed a major Sicilian Mafia figure as managing director of a subsidiary, prior to that subsidiary's securing oil

leases in Tunisia. I commented that "it is normal, not unusual, for the entry of major U.S. firms into Third World countries to be facilitated and sustained, indeed made possible, by corruption." Rashid's book *Jihad* corroborates how Western oil company investments are "creating an extremely wealthy, corrupt minority class" in the Central Asian states, thereby "breeding even greater social discontent" (p. 237). Olivier Roy has written that "it is the Americans who have made inroads in Central Asia, primarily because of the oil and gas interests. Chevron and Unocal are political actors who talk as equals with the States (that is, with the presidents). The oil companies have come to play a greater and greater role in the area" (quoted in Richard Labévière, *Dollars for Terror: The United States and Islam* (New York: Algora, 2000), 280; Labévière gives no citation, but Roy has confirmed to me that he wrote these words for *Le Monde Diplomatique*).

40. Michael Griffin, *Reaping the Whirlwind: The Taliban Movement in Afghanistan* (London: Pluto, 2001), 145–46. Cf. Christina Lamb, *Waiting for Allah: Pakistan's Struggle for Democracy* (New York: Viking, 1991), 195: "The Afghan war had made Pakistan the world's largest supplier of heroin, and by 1989 drugs were bringing in at least $4 billion a year—more foreign exchange than all Pakistan's legal exports combined." Lamb cites Pakistan Narcotics Control Board figures; also Melvyn Levitsky, U.S. assistant secretary of state for international narcotics, before a House committee, Washington, January 8, 1989. Giovanni Quaglia, the chief of operations for the UN Office of Drug Control, has estimated that the total contraband economy in Pakistan now amounts to $15 billion (Orth, *Vanity Fair*, March 2002, 178).

41. McCoy, *Politics*, 447; cf. 446. For his production figures in Pakistan, Afghanistan, and Iran, McCoy cites U.S. State Department statistics. But according to other sources, including a 1986 U.S. congressional report, these statistics were politically manipulated to show a drop in Pakistan-Afghan production in the 1980s, accompanied by an increase in Iranian production. (The State Department actually "claimed that due to climatic conditions opium production in Pakistan and Afghanistan dropped in the 1980s.") The reverse was almost certainly true: see M. Emdad-ul Haq, *Drugs in South Asia*, 194–95.

42. McCoy, *Politics*, 458; Griffin, *Reaping the Whirlwind*, 148 (labs); Emdad-ul Haq, *Drugs in South Asia*, 189 (ISI).

43. Lawrence Lifschultz, "Pakistan: The Empire of Heroin," in *War on Drugs*, 451.

44. Peter Truell and Larry Gurwin, *False Profits: The Inside Story of BCCI, the World's Most Corrupt Financial Empire* (Boston: Houghton Mifflin, 1992), 123.

45. Kerry-Brown Report: U.S. Congress, Senate, Committee on Foreign Relations, *The BCCI Affair*, by Senator John Kerry and Senator Hank Brown (Washington, D.C.: GPO, 1992), 27–28.

46. Truell and Gurwin, *False Profits*, 123.

47. Truell and Gurwin, *False Profits*, 130.

48. Joseph J. Trento, *The Secret History of the CIA* (New York: Forum/Crown/Random House, 2001), 410, 467.

49. Loftus and Aarons, *Secret War*, 395. The Cayman Islands affiliate was an inner bank, International Credit and Investment Company Ltd. (ICIC). The law firm that established ICIC for BCCI, Bruce Campbell & Company, also acted as registered agent for the CIA-related Australian drug bank, Nugan Hand. Nugan Hand and BCCI also used the same auditors, Price Waterhouse (Truell and Gurwin, *False Profits*, 125).

50. This theory correlates with the widely held observation that CIA officers let go by Carter's DCI, Admiral Stansfield Turner, regrouped as a "shadow" agency with outside

backing and funding: "The CIA did not like President Jimmy Carter. . . . The wolves in Clandestine Services went for the president's jugular, and eventually destroyed his presidency. . . . [The] non-hiring of George Bush [as DCI] gave momentum to the creation of a CIA in exile. This was a group of out-of-work agents. . . . By the time Reagan and Bush took office, they had a choice of two CIA's they could do business with—one that required oversight by Congress, and another off-the-books group made up of the old boys" (Trento, *Secret History*, 466–67).

51. Loftus and Aarons, *Secret War*, 395. Loftus and Aarons refer to various news stories leaked later by Mossad, such as the following: "The CIA had a covert relationship with BCCI in 1976. At the very same time, George Bush was director of the CIA. We are told the late William Casey . . . met secretly and regularly with the BCCI bank's founder, Aga Hassan Abedi" (Arnold Fine, *Jewish Press*, March 6, 1992).

52. Kerry-Brown Report, 68; cf. 611.

53. Kerry-Brown Report, 361–63. For a more severe account of British passivity in the BCCI case, see Beaty and Gwynne, *Outlaw Bank*, 105–7.

54. Quotation from Stephen Pizzo, Mary Fricker, and Paul Muolo, *Inside Job: The Looting of America's Savings and Loans* (New York: McGraw-Hill, 1989), 89.

55. Marshall, *Drug Wars*, 52; Robert I. Friedman, *Red Mafiya* (Boston: Little, Brown, 2000), 226–27; *Independent* (London), February 18, 1990.

56. Beaty and Gwynne, *Outlaw Bank*, 195–96. In the end Carter took millions from Abedi, "including $1.5 million long after BCCI was indicted and convicted for laundering drug money" (Beaty and Gwynne, *Outlaw Bank*, 63).

57. Robert Lacey, *The Kingdom: Arabia and the House of Sa'ud* (New York: Avon, 1981), 451–55.

58. *New York Times*, July 16, 1980, April 16, 1979; *Washington Post*, April 18, 1979 (aid cutoff); Beaty and Gwynne, *Outlaw Bank*, 238, 255, 272–77 (BCCI).

59. Kerry-Brown Report, 300, citing *New York Times*, December 6, 1981: "While Adham was still in place as the CIA's liaison [to the Istakhbarat] in 1977, the CIA station chief for Saudi Arabia, Raymond H. Close, chose to go to work for Adham upon leaving the CIA. . . . As Jeff Gerth of the New York Times reported in 1981 . . . 'some think Mr. Close may still be working for the CIA in some capacity, although he officially retired in 1977. They add that a further complicating factor is that some Saudis privately share the same perception.' The Times account describes how Close had actually given approval to weapons sales from Saudi Arabia to Pakistan in the early 1970's, in contravention to the 'official policy' enunciated by the American ambassador." Cf. Cooley, *Unholy Wars*, 112–13.

60. James Ring Adams and Douglas Frantz, *A Full Service Bank* (New York: Pocket Books, 1992), 64–72. Until 1977 Financial General had been controlled by General George Olmsted, the head of OSS China during World War II.

61. Truell and Gurwin, *False Profits*, 160–61; McCoy, *Politics*, 454; Lawrence Lifschultz, "Pakistan: The Empire of Heroin," in *War on Drugs*, 342. Zia's role in appointing Fazle Haq is reported by Alain Labrousse, *La drogue, l'argent et les armes* (Paris: Fayard, 1991), 110.

62. Beaty and Gwynne, *Outlaw Bank*, 52 (CIA); Lifschultz, "Pakistan," 342 (Interpol).

63. Beaty and Gwynne, *Outlaw Bank*, 48. The informant, named here as "Mirza," is identified by Adams (p. 257) and the Kerry-Brown Report (p. 348, cf. p. 226) as Amir Lodhi.

64. Beaty and Gwynne, *Outlaw Bank*, 52.

65. General Fazle Haq (on Pakistan's confidence that Washington would back their decision to support the Afghan resistance); quoted in Christina Lamb [Haq's interviewer], *Waiting for Allah*, 222 (cf. 206); cited in M. Emdad-ul Haq, *Drugs in South Asia*, 185.

66. M. Emdad-ul Haq, *Drugs in South Asia*, 187; citing *Hindustan Times*, October 1, 1994. Fazle Haq's story (that the U.S. backing of the mujahedin was in response to a Pakistani initiative) is corroborated by Robert Gates of the CIA. His memoir speaks of "an approach by a senior Pakistani official to an Agency officer" in March 1979, four months before Carter "signed the first finding to help the Mujahedin covertly." Robert M. Gates, *From the Shadows* (New York: Simon & Schuster, 1996), 144, 146. Haq's suggestion might explain the CIA-backed ISI decision to focus aid on Gulbuddin Hekmatyar, whose Hizb-i-Islami faction was allegedly ignored and "almost non-existent" during the formation of the first organized Afghan resistance in Pakistan in mid-1978. See M. Emdad-ul Haq, *Drugs in South Asia*, 187 (cf. 185); citing Hamidullah Amin and Gordon B. Schiltz, *A Geography of Afghanistan* (Kabul: Centre for Afghanistan Studies, 1984), 381. Cf. Larry Goodson, *Afghanistan's Endless War: State Failure, Regional Politics, and the Rise of the Taliban* (Seattle: University of Washington Press, 2001), 56; Cooley, *Unholy Wars*, 64.

67. McCoy, *Politics*, 451; Lifschultz, "Pakistan," 321–23, 326.

68. M. Emdad-ul Haq, *Drugs in South Asia*, 188. The transnational drug presence in Afghanistan was even clearer by the 1990s, when a French journalist learned "that 'the Pakistanis'—presumably the ISI's clandestine operators . . . had actually provided seed grains of a new and more productive species of poppy . . . said to have come from Burma . . . and Africa, probably Kenya" (Stephane Allix, *La petite cuillère de Schéhérazade, sur la route de l'héroïne* [Paris: Editions Ramsay, 1998], 33–34; Cooley, *Unholy Wars*, 150; cf. Griffin, *Reaping the Whirlwind*, 148).

69. According to a contemporary account, Americans and Europeans started becoming involved in drug smuggling out of Afghanistan from the early 1970s; see Catherine Lamour and Michel R. Lamberti, *The International Connection: Opium from Growers to Pushers* (New York: Pantheon, 1974), 190–92.

70. Cf. Maureen Orth, *Vanity Fair*, March 2002, 170. As late as 2001, one ISI general was convicted in Pakistan for having "assets disproportionate to his known sources of income" (Orth, *Vanity Fair*, 152).

71. Cooley, *Unholy Wars*, 128–29; Beaty and Gwynne, *Outlaw Bank*, 305–6.

72. Beaty and Gwynne, *Outlaw Bank*, 306, 82; also Allix, *La petite cuillère*, 35, 95.

73. Maureen Orth, *Vanity Fair*, March 2002, 170–71. A Tajik sociologist added that she knew "drugs were massively distributed at that time," and that she often heard how Russian soldiers were "invited to taste."

74. *Washington Post*, July 19, 1992.

75. Mohammed Yousaf and Mark Adkin, *Afghanistan—Bear Trap: The Defeat of a Superpower* (Havertown, Penn.: Casemate, 2001), 189.

76. Rashid, *Jihad*, 43.

77. Rashid, *Taliban*, 129.

78. M. Emdad-ul Haq, *Drugs in South Asia*, 189.

79. Yousaf, *Bear Trap*, 193; Rashid, *Jihad*, 223.

80. Allix, *La petite cuillère*, 100.

81. For BCCI and drugs, see, for example, Kerry-Brown Report, 49–51; Truell and Gurwin, *False Profits,* 160.

82. Loftus and Aarons, *Secret War,* 381–82.

83. Bergen, *Holy War Inc.,* 67.

84. Bergen, *Holy War Inc.,* 70.

85. See this book, 142n52; also 188–94.

86. See this book, xvi–xvii, cf. 188–89.

87. See this book, 128–32. In 1970, following Arthur Schlesinger, I treated the 1960 CIA station chief in Laos, Gordon Jorgensen, as an opponent of local KMT plotting. I soon realized that he was removed in 1962 because of his backing for the right-wing anti-neutralist Phoumi Nosavan (Peter Dale Scott, "Vietnamization and the Drama of the Pentagon Papers," in *The Pentagon Papers,* Senator Gravel ed. [Boston: Beacon, 1972], 5:231; cf. McCoy, *Politics,* 300).

88. McCoy, *Politics,* 162, 184–86; Scott, this book, 192–93.

89. McCoy, *Politics,* 190. This statement indicated a reorganization of the drug trade, not an abolition. The legal opium monopoly in Thailand ended in 1959, as did that of Laos two years later. The traffic continued to prosper and consolidate under the new conditions.

90. Bernard Fall, *Anatomy of a Crisis* (Garden City, N.Y.: Doubleday, 1969), 99; this book, 195.

91. See this book, 194–95.

92. Two key authorizations for the CAT/Air America airlift to Laos, on September 4, 1959, and again in mid-December 1960, were made on presidential authority at a time when Eisenhower was in fact not in his office, and Vice President Richard Nixon may have acted on his behalf. I was first drawn to the possibility of an ongoing conspiratorial CAT-Nixon connection by events just before the 1968 election, when undeniably Nixon conspired (there is no other word) with Anna Chennault, the Chinese wife of CAT founder Claire Chennault. The two managed to induce South Vietnamese President Thieu to reject the plans announced by Lyndon Johnson for peace talks. Thieu's announcement was made on November 2, only three days before the election.

93. Scott, *War Conspiracy,* 64 (Cline); Cumings, *Origins,* 102 (LeMay). LeMay's remark was made in the 1960s in a note to his friend Whiting Willauer (one of the founders of CAT).

94. See Anthony Kubek, *How the Far East Was Lost* (Chicago: Henry Regnery, 1963); discussed in Scott, *Deep Politics,* 292–93.

95. In April 1971 the French learned that a long-time APACL delegate, Prince Sopsaisana of Laos, had arrived at Orly with a suitcase of heroin "worth $13.5 million on the streets of New York" (McCoy, *Politics,* 283–84).

96. See this book, 194. Today I would discount the "Pathet Lao activity" even more than I did in 1972.

97. The CIA station chief in 1959, Henry Hecksher, went on to be the CIA station chief in Chile in 1970, when he played a key role acting behind the ambassador's back in the anti-Allende coup plot that led to the murder of General René Schneider. See Seymour Hersh, *The Price of Power* (New York: Summit Books/Simon & Schuster, 1983), 267–68, 288–89, 293, passim.

98. A mutual friend later told me that Alsop admitted to him he had written these columns in the belief that he was "helping out."

3

The Origins of the Drug Proxy Strategy: The KMT, Burma, and U.S. Organized Crime

After World War II it should have been possible to contain the global opium traffic, which had been severely weakened by the interruption of maritime commerce. The expulsion of the Kuomintang from mainland China in 1949 and the founding of the People's Republic were followed by the elimination of the opium crops in Yunnan and Sichuan that had been perhaps the chief source of world supply, as well as a source of local income for the KMT regime.[1]

But even before the outbreak of the Korean War in June 1950, there was support in Washington for strengthening the remnant KMT armies in Burma. On April 10, 1950, the Joint Chiefs of Staff proposed a program to exploit the "renewed vitality" of the Chinese Nationalist Force.[2] Under the program, the Office of Policy Coordination (OPC) worked under private cover to supply the Chinese Nationalist forces of Li Mi in Burma, who was working for the CIA by May 1950 if not earlier.[3] The true author of the plan, as noted previously (p. 2), was General Claire Chennault, whose airline CAT became the OPC-Li Mi supply line.

General Li Mi's army soon proved itself to be no threat to the new Chinese People's Republic. Its two attempted invasions in 1951 and 1952 were easily repulsed by Yunnanese militia, after advances of only sixty miles.[4] As a force to restore the supply of opium to the KMT, however, Li Mi and his army were so successful that Burma's total annual harvest of opium increased from fewer than forty tons before World War II to between three hundred and four hundred tons by 1962. "By the end of the 1950s, Burma, Laos, and Thailand together had

I regret that when I wrote this chapter, I had not seen Sterling Seagrave's useful but tendentious *Lords of the Rim: The Invisible Empire of the Overseas Chinese* (New York: Putnam's, 1995), especially chapter 10. Seagrave argues that the postwar opium polity linking the KMT 93rd Division and Thailand had its roots in secret 1944 meetings in Yunnan between the KMT, the Thais, and a Japanese officer, Tsuji Masanobu, who was close to Chinese General Tai Li (this book, 61).

become a massive producer, and the source of more than half the world's present illicit supply of 1,250 to 1,400 tons annually."[5]

OPC, later merged into the CIA, was vital to this surge in production. Starting in February 1951, airplanes of the CIA-refinanced airline CAT supplied the troops with arms from another CIA proprietary, Sea Supply, at an OPC-built airbase, Mong Hsat. "After delivering the arms to the KMT in Burma, an unknown number of CAT's American pilots were loading the KMT's opium for the return flight to Bangkok. One of these, a U.S. China veteran named Jack Killam, was murdered in 1951 after an opium deal went wrong and was buried in an unmarked grave by CIA [actually OPC] agent Sherman Joost."[6] But after being flown south, most of the KMT opium was sold to Thai police chief Phao Sriyanon, who by what McCoy calls a "coincidence" was "the CIA's man in Thailand."[7] (The coincidence was deeper than this, because the same proprietary, Sea Supply, Inc., supplied both the KMT and the Thai border police.)

Continuing CIA support for the KMT opium enterprise in Burma can be at least partly explained by the U.S. desire to (in McCoy's words) "combat the growing popularity of the People's Republic among the wealthy, influential overseas Chinese community throughout Southeast Asia."[8] The KMT reached these communities through Triads and other secret societies that had traditionally been involved in the opium traffic. Thus the restoration of an opium supply in Burma to replace that lost in Yunnan had the result of sustaining a social fabric that was traditional, albeit corrupt.[9] It also financed the KMT sabotage and opposition to the People's Republic.

This explanation assumes that the OPC and CIA were using the KMT and organized crime. But one can also ask the deep political question whether the opposite was not also true. In other words, did forces determined to restore the prewar opium trade manipulate postwar U.S. government policies in order to restore that traffic?

We have to look, first of all, at what Bruce Cumings, following Nietzsche, calls the *historia abscondita* or concealed history of the Korean War ("the worst of American postwar interventions, the most destructive, far more genocidal than Vietnam").[10] Powerful forces built up toward its outbreak in June 1950 from both the Soviet and the American side. On the American side, lobbying by Chiang Kai-shek, Chennault, and others helped lead to the Korean War and the CAT role in it; this in turn led to the CAT airlift to the KMT troops in Burma.[11]

These events were marked by extraordinary intrigues that drew, at the time, multiple charges of diverse and opposing conspiracies.[12] According to Cumings, the definitive chronicler of these complex intrigues, "The China Lobby infiltrated the CIA, and vice versa;" and insiders knew by mid-1950 that the war would soon be coming.[13] It was in this context that, in mid-June 1950, Whiting Willauer of CAT flew to Washington to negotiate the final takeover of the airline by the U.S. government's Office of Policy Coordination (OPC). "Probably before the outbreak of the Korean War on June 25," Frank Wisner of OPC decided "to acquire the airline,"[14] and on June 28, 1950, CIA director Hillenkoetter formally approved the OPC/CIA takeover.[15] This was three days after the outbreak of the war that would generate 15,000 missions for CAT.[16] Recall, however, that General Li Mi, whose survival in Burma would depend on the same airline, was reportedly already "working for the CIA by May 1950, if not earlier."[17]

Meanwhile, in June 1950, a debate arose in Washington (much like that after the events of 9/11 in 2001) as to whether or not there had been an "intelligence failure." It still continues. Cumings summarizes the anomalies trenchantly:

> The CIA predicts, on June 14, a capability for invasion at any time. No one disputes that. Five days later, it predicts an impending invasion. Some dispute that judgment, but the report is [still] missing. Kennan says that no one paid attention to Korea— except to worry about the South attacking—and Acheson says we had only MacArthur's intelligence, when there were fifteen committees collecting intelligence on Korea. . . . Now, Corson also says that the June 14 report leaked out to "informed circles," and thus it was feared that administration critics in Congress might publicly raise the issue. In consequence, a White House decision of sorts was made to brief Congress that "all was well in Korea." . . . Would it not be the expectation that Congress would be told that all was *not* well in Korea? That is, unless a surprised and outraged Congress is one's goal.[18]

With this and much more evidence, Cumings suggests that the war suited people in high places, not only in Taipei and Seoul but also in Washington.

However, it is symptomatic of what might be called Cumings's archivalist inclination that he does not mention Paul Helliwell, the man who first arranged in 1949 for Chennault to meet with Wisner and seek support for his plan.[19] Helliwell was obviously a key figure. A veteran of the OSS Kunming station, which worked with opium warlords in World War II and regularly made payments in opium, Helliwell dealt with Tai Li, the KMT police chief whose bureau was composed largely of Green Gang drug traffickers. and like Tai Li he went on to become the architect of a governmental intelligence-drug connection. As an OPC official Helliwell not only arranged for the creation of CAT Inc. (Civil Air Transport, later Air America) but also formed Sea Supply, Inc., the proprietary which supplied arms to Chiang despite State Department disapproval.[20] After 1949 Sea Supply shipped arms to both the KMT drug forces in Burma and the Thai border police of Phao Sriyanon—the two main arms of the KMT-Burma-Thai drug connection.[21]

But for years Helliwell was also counsel to Meyer Lansky's bank in Miami, and he invested in real estate while representing Thailand, at a time when KMT money from Thailand and Burma came via Hong Kong to be washed through Lansky-related property firms."[22] Still later, he helped establish the Castle Bank in the Bahamas, which laundered funds for both the CIA and organized crime.[23] Castle Bank was only one of a series of banks in this double role; it had complex links to both the Nugan Hand Bank in Australia and to the Washington banker

(George Olmsted) whose firm (Financial General Bankshares) was eventually taken over by BCCI.[24]

Helliwell's career is symptomatic of a web of extragovernmental connections centered on the business and laundering activities of organized crime. With respect to these extragovernmental intrigues, Cumings's archival history has less to say than I do. This can be seen right away from his index, which (although far more extensive than my own) contains no entries for Helliwell, tongs, Triads, Mafia, or opium.[25] Far more surprising, in a book containing 102 pages of references to Chiang Kai-shek and fifteen to the China lobby, is his failure to mention what I consider the key to their power in U.S. politics. I mean the charge made by Ross Koen in 1960:

> There is . . . considerable evidence that a number of [Nationalist] Chinese officials engaged in the illegal smuggling of narcotics into the United States with the full knowledge and connivance of the Nationalist Chinese Government. The evidence indicates that several prominent Americans have participated in and profited from these transactions. It indicates further that the narcotics business has been an important factor in the activities and permutations of the China Lobby.[26]

This silence is in keeping with Cumings's failure to explore the tongs, secret societies, and Triads that were the true sociological underpinnings of the KMT and the China lobby—in China, in Southeast Asia, and above all in America. He speaks narrowly of "China Lobby types who were fixated on Taiwan" (p. 515), ignoring the real power of those whose existence depended only marginally on Taiwan, or even mainland China, but had everything to do with the preservation and restoration *of the opium traffic itself.*[27]

These secret societies were older by far than the KMT and have continued to function until the present, long after the KMT has ceased to be historically important. We now know from a number of excellent histories of the opium trade that in Southeast Asia since the middle of the nineteenth century "the opium farms were almost always connected to the secret societies that flourished in Chinese communities."[28] It is now also generally recognized how Chiang Kai-shek's seizure of both the KMT and China was achieved with the help of the opium-trafficking Green Gang of Tu Yueh-sheng, to the mutual profit of both.[29] By the mid-1930s China was producing seven-eighths of the world's opium supply, and some of it came to Chinese tongs in the United States and their organized crime contacts like Meyer Lansky and Lucky Luciano.[30]

These contacts with the U.S. mob were apparently not wholly broken by World War II.[31] They were clearly renewed after 1949, when Tu Yueh-sheng and the remnants of the Green Gang fled to Hong Kong along with a rival secret society.[32] An unconfirmed report says that Fang Chih, who visited Laos for the KMT in 1959, had been with Tu Yueh-sheng in Shanghai in the 1930s. It is certain that a high-level drug bust in 1959 in San Francisco involved the same Hip Sing tong as an earlier organized crime drug bust in 1930. Significantly, U.S. officials arranged for the ringleader Chung Wing Fong, an official of the San Francisco Anti-Communist League (a KMT front), to escape to Taiwan before local arrests were made. A subsequent U.S. report to the United Nations on the incident noted that the tong's activities possibly paralleled "the operations of the Triad societies in Hong Kong."[33]

The Hip Sing's dope and other criminal activities, like those of the On Leong, Bing Kong, and other American tongs, predated and outlasted by far the KMT linkup with the Green Gang in 1927. The 1905–1906 tong war in New York City was between the Hip Sing tong and their chief rivals the On Leong tong. Ninety years later the organized crime of New York's Chinatown was still dominated by three tongs, two of which were the Hip Sing and the On Leong.[34] In 1996, long after the decline of the KMT as a political force in Taiwan, the Hip Sing tong was involved in yet another major San Francisco drug bust.[35] The KMT has faded, but the tongs and their drug connections are still, thanks largely to OPC in 1949–1951, very much with us.

These continuities lend a coherence to the intrigues leading up to the Korean War that would otherwise be missing. For example, Cumings notes how Satiris "Sonny" Fassoulis, a minor mob player who went on to major organized crime swindles in stolen securities, supplied half a million dollars as part of a China lobby campaign to support Chiang Kai-shek (with army backing but against State Department opposition).[36] Fassoulis was tapped by "one Col. Williams from the Army" to be part of the campaign. Almost certainly this was Colonel Garland Williams, the creator of the U.S. Army Counterintelligence Corps. After the war Williams continued his intelligence career in the Federal Bureau of Narcotics, as one of a small group of FBN officials who used their knowledge of the drug world to recruit mobsters for intelligence purposes.[37] A key example was Williams's former subordinate George White, who with the aid of Meyer Lansky recruited Lucky Luciano during World War II for the OSS-ONI Project Underworld and in 1959 arranged for the escape of Chung Wing Fong in the Hip Sing tong drug bust.[38]

In other words, the political efforts of the China lobby were inseparable from their connections to the American mob, which had a bigger stake in the future of the drug traffic than in the outcome of Chinese politics. And these figures in turn could play a role because of their deep political connections to U.S. intelligence. No one was better located in this respect than Meyer Lansky, who by the 1960s enjoyed protection and virtual immunity from prosecution, both in the FBI and in the CIA.[39] If we look at these deep underpinnings to the intrigues of postwar U.S. politics in the Far East, it helps us understand how these could have led to the restoration of the world's chief opium source, just at the point when its prewar source of supply was about to be eliminated.[40]

Let me be clear here about what I am not saying. I am not suggesting that anyone in the highest levels of U.S. government made a conscious decision to restore and/or expand the global opium traffic. However, it is clear that elements in the U.S. government were prepared to work with KMT troops long after their drug activities were obvious. In 1949 even the relatively moderate and cautious Dean Rusk argued at a State Department meeting that the United States "should employ whatever means were indicated . . . arms here, opium there, bribery and propaganda in the third place."[41] Such advice was perhaps only to be expected: as the United States took up the role in Asia of the colonial powers before it, the easiest line was to exert influence through the opium Triads that had helped in earlier years to support the colonies of the British and French.[42] And those outside government with the requisite skills to organize the global drug traffic knew very well that one of the most important of these requisites was the ability, which on occasion they clearly possessed, to manipulate governments.

CONCLUSION

It is too early to diagnose whether the de facto restoration of the opium traffic in 2001 was the result of such manipulation. But as we look back in time to the U.S. interventions of 1979, 1959, and finally 1949, evidence of such manipulation becomes clearer and clearer. Clearest of all is the role of these interventions in fostering the opium traffic as a major international force.

The drug traffic today is bigger and more powerful than ever before. At the same time we can expect the U.S. presence in the region to increase as well. As Paul Rogers has pointed out, U.S. oil reserves have declined to 2.8 percent of the world total whereas the Gulf states now have 66.5 percent. Meanwhile U.S. oil dependency continues to increase: in 1990, the United States imported 42 percent of its total oil requirements; ten years later this had risen to 60 percent.[43] And the national debate on foreign policy is increasingly dominated by geostrategists from both parties who link unilateral control of the world to control of its oil-producing areas.

These two factors—drugs and oil—virtually guarantee that the United States will be confronted with new crises in this region, where the traditions of liberal democracy carry little weight and so many live in abject poverty in sight of enormous fortunes gained from drugs and oil. This is especially true of the drug-ridden nations of Central Asia. For a decade after the breakup of the Soviet Union, Russia used dirty tricks to pressure its former dependencies and maintain Russian control of all pipelines bringing oil and gas out of the Caspian basin. As we have seen, many Asian observers believe that these dirty tricks included "close intelligence links" with the heroin-trafficking IMU.[44]

Unquestionably the United States has done much in the past few years to combat Islamism in Central Asia, especially after reports that bin Laden would try to hit U.S. embassies and oil company offices there.[45] Yet it is reasonable to ask if the CIA, or at least the U.S. multinational oil companies, would not have the same ambivalent motives as the Russians to coexist with the IMU. The IMU's drug flows threaten the Uzbek regime and corrupt its officials. In this way they make it easier for the U.S. government to secure military agreements, and for U.S. corporations, working through middlemen, to secure access to the region's energy resources.

What is true of Uzbekistan and its sister states is true of Russia itself. There have been allegations that drug money has helped fund the privatization of Russian oil and other assets, thus opening up Russia and Central Asia to penetration by major U.S. oil corporations. (According to Maureen Orth in the March 2002 *Vanity Fair*, the Russian Council on Foreign and Defense Policies estimated that in 1996 more than $180 million in drug profits had been invested in Russian privatization, mostly in the energy and telecommunications industries.)

Finally there is the question of the extent to which U.S. and European banks profit from laundering the proceeds from the Afghan drug traffic. (The high-end profits are of course realized in the countries of destination, not where the opium originates.) The scholar Alain Labrousse, formerly editor of the respected *Geopolitical Drug Dispatch*, has estimated that 80 percent of the profits from drug trafficking ends up in the banks of the wealthy countries or their branches in the underdeveloped countries where there is weaker legal control.[46] We have already seen the extent to which the current U.S. dependency on foreign oil has required a favorable flow of petro- and narco-dollars.

Today it seems increasingly clear that in the current decade the Bush administration is exerting its own pressures, from Georgia to Uzbekistan and Kyrgyzstan, to neutralize Russian influence. The United States has already stationed one hundred troops in Georgia, one thousand troops in Uzbekistan, and three hundred close to the Chinese border in Kyrgyzstan, with more scheduled to arrive.

One can argue that this U.S. presence on Russia's borders should benefit both the region and the United States by increasing the new nations' autonomy from Russia and facilitating the export of their oil and gas. But these states, especially the dictatorship of Uzbekistan, are so oppressive and corrupt that armed opposition to them is virtually inevitable. The influx of U.S. military aid and corporate investment tended up to now, in the eyes of observers like Pakistani journalist Ahmed Rashid, to benefit only those at the top. On the one hand, "military aid has not been accompanied by large-scale economic incentives." On the other, "Western oil company investments, by creating an extremely wealthy, corrupt minority class, are breeding even greater social discontent."[47]

The State Department has seemed determined to ignore this problem, proclaiming on its website that "the United States . . . values Uzbekistan as a stable, moderate force in a turbulent region."[48] This recalls the absurd claims made once by the State Department about Diem's Republic of Vietnam. If in truth the United States has learned nothing since that war, one can predict confidently that U.S. troops will once again be shot at.

The American people must work to find better approaches to the social problems of the area, in which the mistakes of the past will not be repeated.

NOTES

1. Carl A. Trocki, *Opium, Empire, and the Global Political Economy: A Study of the Asian Opium Trade, 1750–1950* (London: Routledge, 1999), 134.

2. Peter Dale Scott, "Vietnamization and the Drama of the Pentagon Papers," in *The Pentagon Papers,* Senator Gravel ed. (Boston: Beacon, 1972), 1:366; quoted in Alfred W. McCoy, *The Politics of Heroin: CIA Complicity in the Global Drug Trade* (Brooklyn, N.Y.: Lawrence Hill, 1991), 165.

3. Joseph Burkholder Smith, *Portrait of a Cold Warrior* (New York: Ballantine, 1976), 66–67; Cumings, *Origins,* 2:533, 872.

4. McCoy, *Politics,* 170, 177.

5. McCoy, *Politics,* 191, citing a 1970 report from the U.S. Bureau of Narcotics and Dangerous Drugs.

6. McCoy, *Politics,* 178, citing William R. Corson, *The Armies of Ignorance: The Rise of the American Intelligence Empire* (New York: Dial, 1977), 320–22. In the wake of such scandals, a resulting "Thailand flap" led to a decision to abolish OPC and merge it with CIA. The result, however, was to expand the OPC style inside CIA rather than contain it (McCoy, *Politics,* 177–78).

7. McCoy, *Politics,* 173, 178.

8. McCoy, *Politics,* 185. McCoy then quotes from a 1954 NSC position paper in support of encouraging anticommunist activity in the overseas Chinese communities (*Pentagon Papers,* Senator Gravel ed., 1:438).

9. See this book, 192.

10. Cumings, *Origins,* 2:770.

11. As Bruce Cumings notes (*Origins,* 2:600), Chiang Kai-shek "may have found the fulcrum on the Korean peninsula, the provocation of a war that saved his regime for two more decades, and bid fair to bring Nationalist troops back to the mainland."

12. For example, Cumings, *Origins,* 2:65 (General Hodge to Preston Goodfellow, January 15, 1947): "Either [Syngman] Rhee doesn't know developments here or he is guilty of heinous conspiracy against American efforts. I believe the latter" (Goodfellow Papers, Hoover Institution Archives, Stanford, Calif., Box 1).

13. "On Taiwan, the CIA funded pro-Chiang rollbackers. The brother of T.V. Soong mounted a corner on the soybean market timed for the outbreak of some unexpected event on the weekend of June 25, 1950; Joe McCarthy was reportedly a beneficiary" (Cumings, *Origins,* 2:123). Cf. this book, 189, 197, 202.

14. Leary, *Perilous Missions,* 110. The CIA denied Leary access to its official history of the airline. The notes of a lawyer who did see it, on which Leary's statement is based, did not supply a more precise date.

15. Leary, *Perilous Missions,* 110.

16. Byrd, *Chennault,* 343.

17. Cumings, *Origins,* 2:872.

18. Cumings, *Origins,* 2:611, 613; citing Corson, *Armies of Ignorance,* 315–21. Cumings quotes further from Dean Rusk's testimony to Congress on June 20: "We see no

present indication that the people across the border have any intention of fighting a major war for that purpose" (taking over South Korea).

19. McCoy, *Politics*, 167; cf. Scott, *Deep Politics*, 165–66. Also involved in negotiating with Chennault's lawyer Tommy Corcoran was Richard G. Stilwell; see Burton Hersh, *The Old Boys: The American Elite and the Origins of the CIA* (New York: Scribner's, 1992), 299.

20. McCoy, *Politics*, 167–68, 268. For more on the drug-related postwar careers of the six known officers of the OSS Kunming station, see Marshall, Scott, and Hunter, *Iran-Contra*, 64–65. Two of them, Ray Cline and Howard Hunt, are said to have helped create branches of the Asian People's Anti-Communist League.

21. McCoy, *Politics*, 168–70; see this book, 187, 196, 198.

22. Penny Lernoux, *In Banks We Trust* (Garden City, N.Y.: Anchor Doubleday, 1984), 42–44, 84 (Lansky): R. T. Naylor, *Hot Money and the Politics of Debt* (New York: Simon & Schuster, 1987), 292.

23. *Wall Street Journal*, April 18, 1980; Lernoux, *In Banks We Trust,* 82–88. Among those who had trust accounts at Castle Bank were Chiang Kai-shek's daughter and her husband (Lernoux, *In Banks,* 86). Another may have been Richard Nixon (Summers, *Arrogance of Power*, 253–57).

24. Scott and Marshall, *Cocaine Politics,* 92–93 (Nugan Hand); Lernoux, *In Banks,* 87 (Olmsted). Lernoux writes that Olmsted "had known Helliwell when he ran the OSS China section."

25. There are in fact references to the Mafia (p. 133) and opium (p. 533) in his text, but not in ways he considered central to his title, *The Origins of the Korean War.*

26. Ross Y. Koen, *The China Lobby in American Politics* (New York: Macmillan, 1960), ix. See this book, 193–94. This paragraph, when contested, led Macmillan to withdraw the book.

27. Cumings, *Origins,* 2:515. The role of Triads in preserving the KMT on Taiwan is noted in a book based largely on U.S. and foreign law enforcement sources: "When China, sinking under addiction, banned opium in nearly all its forms . . . the Triads had a luxuriant black market in heroin all to themselves. When China fell to the communists after World War II, the Triads had the foresight to help a Triad brother named Generalissimo Chiang Kai-shek [a Green Gang member] flee to Formosa (now Taiwan), taking along much of China's movable wealth" (Sterling, *Thieves' World*, 45).

28. Trocki, *Opium*, 149. Cf. Brook and Wakabayashi, eds., *Opium Regimes*, 83, 92, 94, 97, 305, 309; John Butcher and Howard Dick, eds., *The Rise and Fall of Revenue Farming* (New York: St. Martin's, 1993), 90–91, 168–69, 179–80, 251–55, etc.

29. McCoy, *Politics*, 262–68; Trocki, *Opium*, 133, Brook and Wakabayashi, *Opium Regimes*, 278, 327; see this book, 193.

30. Trocki, *Opium,* 133; citing Jonathan Marshall, "Opium and the Politics of Gangsterism in Nationalist China, 1927–1945," *Bulletin of Concerned Asia Scholars*, July–September 1976, 29–30; see this book, 193.

31. The American pilots of Chennault's wartime Flying Tigers, suspected of drug trafficking on the side, would meet regularly with a mysterious Madame Chung in San Francisco, who in turn would meet with Bugsy Siegel's mistress. See Peter Dale Scott, "Opium and Empire: McCoy on Heroin in Southeast Asia," *Bulletin of Concerned Asian Scholars*, September 1973, 49–56. This is a review of Alfred W. McCoy et al., *The Politics of Heroin in Southeast Asia.*

68 Chapter 3

32. McCoy, *Politics*, 270; see this book, 193.
33. Scott, *Deep Politics*, 167; see this book, 193.
34. *New York Times*, June 2, 1995, A1, A16. Claire Sterling estimated in 1994 that the "Triads were bringing in three-quarters of America's heroin" (*Thieves' World*, 43).
35. *San Francisco Chronicle*, February 6, 1996; February 7, 1996.
36. Cumings, *Origins*, 2:511–12. As another example of such coherence, Cumings notes that the point man for the KMT support for which Fassoulis worked was William Pawley. He records Pawley's role in setting up the Flying Tigers with Genera; Chennault, and his "many sensitive missions for the CIA in the early 1950s." He then adds that "rumors linked [Pawley] to Mafia leaders" (p. 133), but he does not relate this fact (more than a rumor) to his narrative in which drugs are barely mentioned. Cumings's cited source identifies the chief Mafia leader as John Martino. Martino was an operative of the international drug trafficker Santos Trafficante who also performed many sensitive operations in Central America for the CIA.
37. Alan A. Block, "Failures at Home and Abroad: Studies in the Implementation of U.S. Drug Policy," in *War on Drugs*, 41; Alan A. Block and John McWilliams, "On the Origins of American Counterintelligence: Building a Clandestine Network," *Journal of Policy History*, 1989.
38. Scott, *Deep Politics*, 165–67.
39. Curt Gentry, *J. Edgar Hoover: The Man and the Secrets* (New York: Penguin, 1991), 531–32 (FBI); Scott, *Deep Politics*, 145–46 (FBI); Sally Denton and Roger Morris, *The Money and the Power* (New York: Alfred A. Knopf, 2001), 254, 424 n. (cf. 28), (CIA); Peter Dale Scott, *Minding the Darkness: A Poem for the Year 2000* (New York: New Directions, 2000), 178–79 (FBI, CIA).
40. Oil did not play a conspicuous role in the intrigues of 1949–1951, although some American capitalists were clearly interested in Korean gold and tungsten (Cumings, *Origins*, 2:62, 123, 143, 803, etc.). But "Texas oil people" did for some reason participate in the Fassoulis-Williams intrigues (Cumings, *Origins*, 2:512). Cumings speculates that these included H. L. Hunt.
41. Cumings, *Origins*, 2:872 n. 93.
42. For this, see McCoy, *Politics*, 89–96; see this book, 192.
43. Paul Rogers, "Oil and the 'War on Terrorism': Why Is the United States in the Gulf?" January 9, 2002, www.opendemocracy.net/forum/document_details.asp?Cat ID = 103&DocID = 969: "Moreover, the rate of discovery of new reserves in the United States was not keeping pace with demand, whereas discovery of reserves in the Gulf region was exceeding production."
44. Rashid, *Jihad*, 216; cf. 178.
45. Rashid, *Jihad*, 166, 191–92.
46. Alain Labrousse, interview with *Pulso* (Bolivia), www.narconews.com/pressbriefing 21september.html.
Labrousse also agreed "absolutely" with the statement by Carlos Fuentes that for each dollar earned in the business of drugs, two-thirds stays in the banks of United States. *Pulso* further observed that the *Geopolitical Drug Dispatch* "is currently closed for lack of financing, difficult to obtain because they realized such direct criticisms against governments and established power structures."
47. Rashid, *Jihad*, 236–37.
48. www.state.gov/r/pa/bgn/2924.htm.

II

Colombia, Cocaine, and Oil (2001)

4

The United States and Oil in Colombia

Current U.S. involvement in Colombia has escalated by stages since the original commitment to a counterinsurgency program under the Kennedy administration. Key stages since then have been

- a CIA and Special Forces program in 1962 for training police and paramilitary groups *(autodefensas)* in counterinsurgency techniques, including sabotage and terror
- National Security Decision Directive 221 of April 1986, which for the first time defined drug trafficking as a national security matter, allowing in 1991 for the use of U.S. troops in Colombia in alliance with the CIA
- Clinton's $1.3 billion aid program in 2000 in support of Plan Colombia
- George W. Bush's measures since 2001 to expand the U.S. role beyond counternarcotics, including a program to underwrite Colombian army security for oil pipelines.

In 2002, as this book is being written, it seems certain that the violence in Colombia, already exacerbated by decades of ill-advised U.S. interference, will escalate still further. The new president, Alvaro Uribe Vélez, is himself a product and an exponent of the paramilitary counterrevolutionary system the United States helped install in Colombia.

As *Business Week* reported in February 2002,

Uribe Velez claims that if elected President, he will take a firmer line with the rebels. That's just what he did between 1995 and 1997 when he was governor of Antioquia, Colombia's second-largest province and onetime home to the infamous Medellin drug cartel. There, Uribe Velez promoted the creation of the controversial Convivirs. Styled as self-defense patrols, these armed militias supplied intelligence to the armed forces and helped police combat crime. It wasn't long before some of the local militias, which eventually numbered 67 in Antioquia and 400 nationwide, morphed into deadly paramilitary squads that targeted not only guerrillas but also suspected civilian sympathizers. That led the Colombian government to strip the Convivirs of most of their power in 1997.

Business Week predicted that Uribe's promise to further such policies on the national level "could well drag Colombia deeper into a conflict that has claimed 30,000 lives in the past decade."[1] Efforts to reform the Colombian army's records have shown meager results; and we now know that the CIA in 1998 predicted that military-paramilitary ties "are likely to continue and perhaps even increase."[2] Others foresee that the conflict, which has already expanded into Venezuela and Ecuador, will blend still further into the social disturbances of neighboring countries, including Peru and Brazil.

With the passage of time FARC (Revolutionary Armed Forces of Colombia) has, under U.S. pressure, become more and more like the drug-financed operation that government propagandists have depicted it as for almost two decades. In 2002 FARC used conventional mortars and battle tactics to reclaim a large area of northern Colombia, possibly (as some U.S. analysts claim) because of the area's importance for drug trafficking routes. A new factor of increasing importance is the role of powerful Russian Mafia elements in both Colombian drug trafficking and the supply of arms, possibly to both sides.

Not all the news on the Colombian front is equally dismal. In September 2001 Secretary of State Colin Powell finally placed the right-wing paramilitary AUC (Autodefensas Unidas de Colombia) on the list of foreign terrorist organizations. Recognizing the AUC's role in both rural violence and drug trafficking, General Gary Speer, acting head of U.S. Southern Command, called it "the most critical long-term threat" to Colombian democracy.[3] But the State Department's sanctions against AUC (suspending visas of AUC members and putting other names on a visa watch list) are unlikely to do much to curb the AUC's terror campaign. Nor is the United States likely to prevent U.S. corporations in Colombia from working with AUC to secure their assets there. As of now all indications are that the United States in Colombia will remain focused on FARC (which the Colombian government in 2001 called responsible for 2.5 percent of Colombia's coca production), rather than FARC's enemy the AUC (said to be responsible for 40 percent).

A more candid explanation for the U.S. military effort in Colombia would be the U.S. oil companies and their pipelines, which revolutionary armies like FARC attack but AUC defends. As will be discussed below, the current U.S. interest in Colombia began one year after Occidental Oil discovered the billion-barrel Caño Limon oilfield in 1983. It led to the national security decision directives of 1986 and 1989 that authorized a U.S. military presence.

In this chapter I argue that, at every stage, U.S. programs have aggravated the problem they are attempting to deal with. Here there is a strong analogy with

Vietnam: U.S. activities have aggravated the conflict in an already divided country. And this aggravation presents successive U.S. administrations with the unhappy choices of continuing with unsuccessful programs, escalating to a new level that will make matters even worse, or getting out.

PLAN COLOMBIA: A PROGRAM DEEMED WRONG EVEN BY ITS ORIGINAL PROMOTERS

The American press has called the current U.S. aid program "Plan Colombia." This is a misnomer, a wolf in sheep's clothing. Plan Colombia was originally a white paper put forward by Colombian President Andrés Pastrana after he took office in 1998, to reduce the social turmoil in his country. It proposed a much more ambitious, $7.5 billion program with a balanced mix of economic, social, and military components. This was intended not just to achieve a reduction in the Colombian drug traffic but more importantly to establish a peace process for his troubled country.

As developed under Clinton, the U.S. Plan Colombia was, like so many so-called U.S. aid programs in the past, 90 percent military. Originally it was meant to complement economic aid from the European Union, but the EU pulled back because it disapproved of the U.S. military approach.[4] This was after a coalition of thirty-seven Colombian human rights and other NGO groups signed a statement rejecting the plan's funds for development and appealed to Europe to withhold support.[5]

In response to these criticisms, the incoming Bush administration announced at a Quebec City summit in April 2001 that it would supplement Plan Colombia with its new Andean Regional Initiative, designed "to bolster economic growth and prosperity in the Andes." To this end President Bush proposed giving $882 million for democratic institution building, of which half would be allocated to Colombia.[6]

In May 2001 the State Department announced further that it would supplement existing aid with funds earmarked for economic development, child survival, and health.[7] But the new funds, although they have silenced the vocal opposition of leaders like Hugo Chávez in Venezuela, are not enough to correct the destabilizing imbalance between U.S. social and military allocations. Thus the effect of the new funds remains cosmetic. One is reminded of the well-intentioned programs that were similarly designated for Vietnam during the Vietnam War but were prevented from coming to proper fruition by the tragic realities of that war.[8]

The heart of the U.S. plan remains on the surface less a plan than a boondoggle. Without any coherent objective for Colombia, it is a godsend for the usual suppliers of munitions, herbicides, and helicopters (a $234 million contract for Sikorsky Aircraft alone).[9] The Pentagon is also using the occasion to establish new bases such as Manta in Ecuador, from which it hopes to continue (after the

loss of key bases in Panama) to dominate the entire oil-rich region. The petroleum industry, although not vocal, clearly hopes to see an end to the tactics in
which the ELN (National Liberation Army, the second-largest revolutionary
force) blow up the oil companies' pipelines. Most importantly, as will be developed below, the Pentagon is using Plan Colombia to steer fat contracts and profits
to outsourced parts of its infrastructure that it needs to sustain: notably in the
areas of military air transport and private military forces (DynCorp and MPRI).

There has been a surprising consensus among disinterested students of Colombia, both in this country and abroad, that present U.S. plans will aggravate that
country's problems. Perhaps the most eloquent testimony comes from former
proponents, committed antirevolutionaries who were at the heart of the Reagan
efforts in Central America. One of these is Andrew Messing, former commander
of Green Beret Special Forces in El Salvador under Reagan:

> Well, first of all, if we're going to provide aid, it should be two-part aid. One-fourth
> of the aid should be military aid, three-quarters of it should be economic aid. That's
> the formula of success that we used in El Salvador, and that's what we have to do.[10]

Representative Benjamin Gilman (R-New York), chairman of the House International Relations Committee, was formerly one of the plan's strongest advocates.
Along with Messing, he withdrew his support, saying U.S. aid should be directed
to the Colombian national police and not the armed forces.[11]

If the United States were serious about its stated goal of fighting drugs, one
might expect it to number among its targets the Colombian military and their
paramilitary allies. These have been directly involved in drug trafficking, as
opposed to FARC guerrillas who until recently merely taxed the trade. In November 1998, for example, a Colombian air force plane landed at Fort Lauderdale–
Hollywood International Airport with a hidden cargo: sixteen hundred pounds of
cocaine.[12] The plane had been continuously in the hands of the Colombian air
force.

Even more involved are the vicious paramilitary death squads, who in many
parts of Colombia work hand in hand with the military, and who every year
account for from 70 to 80 percent of noncombat killings in the country. A recent
Colombian government investigation collected compelling evidence that through
the years 1997 to 1999 "Army officers worked intimately with paramilitaries
under the command of Carlos Castaño," Colombia's chief paramilitary leader,
who is from a family of drug traffickers.[13]

In a rare television interview, Castaño stated that 70 percent of the income for
his group, the United Self-Defense Forces of Colombia (AUC), came from drugs.
In July 2000 Colombian police made one seizure of over thirty-two hundred
pounds of cocaine (worth $53 million in the United States). The police attributed
the drug shipment to the AUC.[14] Colombian intelligence sources estimated in

2001 that 40 percent of Colombian cocaine exports were controlled by right-wing paramilitary warlords and their trafficking allies.[15]

No less an authority than the DEA has linked Castaño closely to the powerful Henao-Montoya drug trafficking network:

> The Henao-Montoya organization is the most powerful of the various independent trafficking groups that comprise the North Valle drug mafia. . . . This organization has a well-deserved reputation for violence and is closely linked to the brutal paramilitary groups run by Carlos Castaño.[16]

Donnie Marshall, who became Clinton's administrator of the Drug Enforcement Administration, told Congress in 1997 that the major North Valle drug Mafia organizations, of which the Henao-Montoyas run the most powerful, "are poised to become among the most powerful drug trafficking groups in Colombia."[17]

In the U.S. press, one does not often see the official Colombian estimates as to the percentage of the drug trade controlled by the paramilitaries, as compared to FARC. According to Colombian government estimates in 2001, as reported by *Newsweek* and the *San Francisco Chronicle* respectively, these figures were 40 percent for the paramilitaries, 2.5 percent for FARC.[18] Nevertheless Plan Colombia's eradication program is focused primarily on the Amazon region controlled by FARC, not on the drug areas controlled by warlords like Castaño and the Henao-Montoya group.

This narrow focus on Colombia's leading left-wing insurgency is consistent with the Pentagon's sustained policies in Colombia since 1962. In fact a brief survey of that history provides an object lesson in what is wrong with a militarized approach to economic and social problems in the Third World. It is fair to say that the United States itself has played a significant role in generating the three major problems that are now devastating Colombia: FARC (and other revolutionary movements), the paramilitaries, and most recently the Colombian drug economy.

The customary defense of U.S. eradication efforts is to claim that, even if only 10 percent of the total quantity of drugs is stopped, this represents an improvement of the situation. But the opposite is the case. No one should be surprised that, after a decade of increased U.S. military efforts, drug production in Colombia and Colombian drug imports into the United States are both at all-time highs. Drug trafficking thrives in times of conflict; and by now it is obvious that U.S. military interventions in drug areas have been, and will be, accompanied by significantly increased drug flows into this country. The new highs are more because of U.S. efforts than despite them.

More than ten years ago I noted (1) how opium production had soared over two decades of CIA-KMT meddling in Burma and Laos, then plummeted in 1975 after U.S. withdrawal from the region and (2) how heroin from the Afghan-

Pakistan border, after five years of CIA intervention there, climbed by U.S. official figures to 52 percent of the heroin consumed in the United States in 1984 (from zero in 1979).[19] I noted a comparable explosion in cocaine imports during the U.S. intervention in Central America in the 1980s. (Only later did we learn that a major figure in the CIA's Contra support network, Honduran trafficker Juan Ramón Matta Ballesteros, was linked by DEA to a major share—perhaps a third, perhaps more than half—of the cocaine moving between Colombia and the United States.)[20]

I warned then that Bush's Andean initiative "seems designed to open analogous new windows of opportunity [for drug trafficking] in cocaine's countries of origin."[21] U.S. official statistics in the subsequent decade amply confirm my gloomy warning. They demonstrate that despite increased eradication efforts, coca production in Colombia tripled between 1991 and 1999 (from 3.8 to 12.3 thousand hectares), while the cultivation of opium poppy increased by a multiple of 5.8 (from .13 to .75 thousand hectares).[22]

U.S. MILITARY INVOLVEMENT
IN COLOMBIA, 1962–2001

As is often pointed out, Colombia had a violent history long before U.S. intervention. This violence reflects an almost feudal social structure, in which a wealthy overclass has long used brutal tactics to displace peasants and oppress plantation workers. But America's arrival in 1962 with counterinsurgency techniques made matters worse: it forced small bands of revolutionaries to coalesce into an organized national movement. (Here too is an analogy with Vietnam, where the National Liberation Front was formed in 1960 in response to U.S.-assisted extermination of former Viet Minh cadres.)[23]

In February 1962 a U.S. Special Warfare team, headed by General William Yarborough, visited the country for two weeks. The era of systematic counterterror, inflicted by professionally trained paramilitary units, dates from that visit, which reflected the Kennedy administration's predilection for counterinsurgency and unconventional warfare. Fearing that Castro might soon try to establish his brand of revolution on the South American continent, the Special Warfare experts at Fort Bragg rushed to instruct the Colombian army in the same counterinsurgency techniques being introduced at that time into Vietnam. Yarborough's trip report to the Joint Chiefs of Staff recommended development of "a civil and military structure . . . to perform counter-agent and counter-propaganda functions and as necessary execute paramilitary, sabotage, and/or terrorist activities against known communist proponents. It should be backed by the United States."[24]

In the wake of Yarborough's visit, a series of training teams arrived, contributing to the Colombian army's Plan Lazo, a comprehensive counterinsurgency plan implemented between 1962 and 1965. It was in response to this systematic campaign in reinforcement of class repression, rather than any outside assistance from Castro, that FARC and ELN were first organized in 1964. As Michael McClintock has observed, "The banditry of the early 1960s . . . was transformed into organized revolutionary guerrilla warfare after 1965, which has continued to date."[25]

An important ingredient in the Fort Bragg approach to counterinsurgency, as reflected in its training manuals, was the organization of "self-defense units" and other paramilitary groups, including "hunter-killer teams."[26] The thinking and nomenclature of these field manuals were translated and cited in the Colombian army's counterguerrilla manual, *Reglamento de Combate de Contraguerrillas*. It defined the self-defense group *(junta de auto-defensa)* as "an organization of a military nature made up of select civilian personnel from the combat zone who are trained and equipped to carry out actions against groups of guerrillas."[27] The *autodefensas* (as the paramilitaries are now called in Colombia) have been a scourge ever since.

In the 1970s the CIA offered further training to Colombian and other Latin American police officers at its so-called bomb school in Los Fresnos, Texas. There AID, under CIA's so-called Public Safety Program, taught a curriculum including "Terrorist Concepts; Terrorist Devices; Fabrication and Functioning of Devices; Improvised Triggering Devices; Incendiaries," and "Assassination Weapons: A discussion of various weapons which may be used by the assassin." During congressional hearings, AID officials admitted that the so-called bomb school offered lessons not in bomb disposal but in bomb making.[28]

Trained terrorist counterrevolutionaries thus became assets of the Colombian state security apparatus. They were also employed by U.S. corporations anxious to protect their workforces from unionization, as well as in antiunion campaigns by Colombian suppliers to large U.S. corporations.[29] Oil companies in particular have been part of the state-coordinated campaign against left-wing guerrillas. In June 2001 a Colombian court heard how a U.S. security firm working for Occidental Petroleum had played a fatal role in an ill-starred army raid against FARC, "directing helicopter gunships that mistakenly killed 18 civilians."[30]

Many accounts of the Colombian conflict ignore the early U.S. input into paramilitary organization and date the army-paramilitary alliance from 1981. This was the year in which the country's major drug traffickers, collaborating with the Colombian army, established a training school for a nationwide counterterrorist network, Muerte a Sequestradores (Death to Kidnappers, or MAS).[31] The traffickers put up the money and the generals contracted for Israeli and British mercenaries to come to Colombia to run the death squad school. A leading graduate was Carlos Castaño.

Although the stated purpose of the network was to combat kidnapping (a preferred fund-raising technique of FARC), MAS played an overtly political role as a criminal extension of the army. Most notably it enabled the army to frustrate the peace agreement negotiated with FARC by President Betancur in the 1980s, by murdering over seven hundred FARC members who entered the constitutional political process as members of a political party, the Unión Patriótica.[32] There is no sign that the Reagan administration, which disapproved of Betancur and his peace plan, exerted any pressure on the army to stop these killings.

The *autodefensas* operated with impunity until 1989, when their activities were outlawed. But Human Rights Watch, in a detailed report, has documented how in 1991 U.S. military and CIA personnel collaborated with the Colombian army to institute a new system of civilian intelligence units. Despite express prohibitions in the army's grounding document, Order 200–05/91, some of these units continued to act as paramilitaries and were armed, sometimes with U.S. equipment, by the Colombian army.[33]

In a new report in 2000, Human Rights Watch continued to document the involvement of senior army commanders in the planning and execution of paramilitary massacres. According to the report, "Evidence . . . links half of Colombia's eighteen brigade-level army units to paramilitary activity." The report also describes a process, called *legalización*, whereby paramilitaries bring civilian corpses to army barracks and exchange them for weapons. The officers then claim that the corpses were guerrillas killed in battle.[34]

The intent of these U.S.-backed strategies has been to drive FARC out of the oil-bearing northern and central Colombia into the Amazon region southeast of the cordillera, in a remote zone that since 1998 has been virtually conceded to it by the central government. There the former guerrilla force is now in effect a governing one, administering and taxing the regions it controls.

Incredibly, the result of another U.S. policy, drug eradication, has been to turn this region into a major coca-producing area. This might have been predicted when the U.S. vigorously pursued vigorous coca eradication programs in nearby Bolivia and Peru. Despite the spectacular reductions in these countries, "there was no large decline in the total area under cultivation: coca cultivation expanded in Colombia to take up the slack."[35] Politically, however, the situation is now very different. Coca production is now concentrated in an area under the ongoing control of a revolutionary force, in a region where the central government cannot normally operate.

Thus the end result of considerable U.S. effort has been to create a U.S. nightmare: the narco-guerrilla. The term "narco-guerrilla" was mocked by experts when it was coined in the Casey-Bush years of the Reagan administration, and shown to be the deceptive rhetoric of right-wing intelligence agents in Latin America who were themselves involved with drug traffickers.[36] Even when Clinton's drug czar, General Barry McCaffrey, renewed the war cry against narco-guerrillas in 1997, the *New York Times* pointed out that the term had been publicly disputed by the American ambassador to Colombia, Myles R. Frechette.[37] But today after so much effort the narco-guerrilla exists, and the Pentagon is finally engaged in a struggle that Congress will support. Aid to the Colombian army, cut off by Congress in 1994 because of human rights violations, has now been restored through Plan Colombia.

American policies in Colombia, despite their stated objectives, have clearly contributed to the breakdown of social order in that country. Colombia is indeed the largest and clearest example of a pattern seen elsewhere in the world and particularly in Central and South America. By giving unbalanced aid and assistance to the military, the United States has strengthened the role and autonomy of the armed forces in Colombian society, to the point that they can operate oppressively while ignoring the restraints imposed on them by successive presidents and legislatures.

There is no doubt that some U.S. planners desired and encouraged this outcome. As I have written elsewhere, in 1959 RAND sponsored a conference on "The Role of the Military in Underdeveloped Countries," attended by military officers from nations such as Brazil, Burma, and Indonesia. At this conference, CIA-linked U.S. academics challenged the Western "bias" against "militaristic societies" and urged officer corps to play a more active political role. The following remarks by Professor Lucian Pye of MIT were far from the most extreme:

> Military leaders are often far less suspicious of the West than civilian leaders because they themselves are more emotionally secure. . . . Military rule itself can become sterile if it does not lead to an interest in total national development. . . . This leads U.S. to the conclusion that the military in the underdeveloped countries can make a major contribution to strengthening essentially administrative functions.[38]

Within six years, military officers of Burma, Brazil, and Indonesia (some of whom had attended the RAND conference) staged successful military coups in their home countries.

At the same conference, recently deposed Colombian dictator General Rojas Pinilla was classed as one of Latin America's "new-type, reform-minded leaders," "making a substantial contribution toward democracy."[39] His downfall in 1957 was attributed to his lack of schooling in administration and to having "stubbornly followed mistaken civilian advice." Thus "public opposition reached the point where his military colleagues had to unseat him."[40]

Colombia, since 1957, has been one of the few Latin American countries that has not seen a U.S.-sponsored military coup. But the army, conscious of Pentagon support, has behaved as an autonomous authority; until recently it was permitted by law to try in its own courts (and almost always exonerate) officers and troops accused of human rights crimes. In May 2001 the Colombian legislature was debating an antiterrorism bill that would restore this immunity to the army.[41]

Summing up, it is not too much to say that U.S. policies of the last four decades have contributed disastrously to social conflict in Colombia. FARC, the paramilitaries, and the phenomenon of drug-financed revolution all can be seen as more the result of U.S. destabilizing policies than the cause of them.

Even the U.S. campaign against drugs in Colombia, which we consider in the next chapter, has contributed to the institutionalization and government acceptance of drug cartels, to the increase in Colombia of cartel-instigated violence, and above all to a significant increase in the total production of drugs.

NOTES

1. *Business Week*, February 12, 2001, online issue, www.businessweek.com/2001/01_07/b3719158.htm. Uribe, the son of a narco-trafficker, arose to political eminence in Antioquia province at a time that it was completely dominated by the wealth and influence of Pablo Escobar. His campaign manager and longtime aide from that era, Pedro Juan Moreno Villa, owns a chemical company that was a recipient for precursor chemicals that were briefly seized by the DEA in California and then released. See Al Giordano, "Narco-Candidate in Colombia: Uribe's Rise from Medellin: Precursor to a Narco-State," *Narco-News*, March 19, 2002, www.narconews.com/narcocandidate1.html.

2. Declassified CIA report of August 1998, www.gwu.edu/~nsarchiv/NSAEBB/NSAEBB69/part3.html#doc64.

3. Quoted in testimony of José Miguel Vivanco, executive director, Americas Division, Human Rights Watch, before the Senate Foreign Relations Committee, Subcommittee on Western Hemisphere, Peace Corps, and Narcotics Affairs, April 24, 2002.

4. On February 1, 2001, the European Parliament adopted, by a vote of 474–1, a resolution sharply critical of the U.S. emphasis in Plan Colombia on military measures and crop-spraying (*Nation*, March 19, 2001; Transnational Institute, "Drugs and Democracy," February 1, 2001, www.tni.org/drugs).

5. Ana Carrigan, *Irish Times*, August 23, 2000.

6. State Department release, April 21, 2001, ea.usa.or.th/mirror/usinfo.state.gov/topical/global/drugs/01042116.htm. In response, the European Union pledged almost $300 million in funding for Colombia. But in so doing they made it clear that they want no part of the U.S.-financed military assault on Colombia's drug industry (*St. Petersburg Times*, May 3, 2001).

7. State Department, briefing on Andean Initiative, May 16, 2001.

8. Even those who defend the U.S. role in Vietnam concede that the war prevented U.S. social reforms there from achieving their expected long-range effects. See, for example, Guenter Lewy, *America in Vietnam* (New York: Oxford University Press, 1978), 185–86. Lewy points approvingly to the fact that AID provided funds for the construction of nine new hospitals in Vietnam (p. 301)—small compensation for the death of perhaps 3 million Vietnamese.

9. It is not generally recognized that Monsanto, the supplier of Agent Orange in Vietnam, is the major provider of the herbicide glyphosate for Plan Colombia. Once again defoliants promised as safe are proving to have toxic effects on animals and possibly humans. See Jeremy Bigwood, "Toxic Drift: Monsanto and the Drug War in Colombia," www.alternet.org/story.html?StoryID=11088. Greenpeace reports that "in California, glyphosate is the third most commonly-reported cause of pesticide related illness among agricultural workers. Glyphosate is the most frequent cause of complaints to the UK's

Health and Safety Executive's Pesticides Incident Appraisal Panel" (Glyphosate fact sheet, greenpeaceusa.org/media/factsheets/glyphosate.htm).

10. Center for Defense Information, *Show Transcript: Colombia in Crisis*, www.cdi .org/adm/1315/transcript.html. Another skeptic about the U.S. "Plan Colombia" is Cresencio Arcos, a former Reagan ambassador in Central America who under Clinton was a member of the president's Foreign Intelligence Advisory Board (*Houston Chronicle*, July 16, 2000).

11. *Washington Post*, December 10, 2000.

12. *Miami Herald*, November 11, 1998.

13. Human Rights Watch, *COLOMBIA: The Ties That Bind: Colombia and Military-Paramilitary Links*, www.hrw.org/reports/2000/colombia/#COLOMBIA AND MILITARY-PARAMILITARY. On September 24, 2002, paramilitary leader Carlos Castaño and two other leaders of the United Self-Defense Forces of Colombia (AUC) were indicted by the United States Department of Justice and charged with trafficking over seventeen tons of cocaine since 1997.

14. *St. Louis Post-Dispatch*, July 5, 2000, A10.

15. *Newsweek International*, May 21, 2001.

16. Drug Enforcement Administration, *Traffickers from Colombia*, www.usdoj.gov/ dea/traffickers/colombia.htm.

17. www.usdoj.gov/dea/pubs/cngrtest/ct970709.htm. Cf. *Los Angeles Times,* September 30, 1997. Another example of an AUC associate involved in drug trafficking is Hernán Giraldo. "Giraldo is wanted for drug trafficking and the formation of paramilitary groups. *Newsweek* describes him as one of the top five traffickers in Colombia (May 21, 2001) and says that Colombian police estimate that he heads a burgeoning drug syndicate that accounts for $1.2 billion in annual shipments to the United States and Europe, putting him among the country's top five cocaine traffickers" (Vivanco testimony, April 24, 2002).

18. *Newsweek*, May 21, 2001: "Colombian intelligence sources now estimate that 40 percent of the country's total cocaine exports are controlled by these right-wing warlords and their allies in the narcotics underworld." *San Francisco Chronicle*, June 21, 2001: "The Colombian government's planning department estimates that FARC earns $290 million yearly from the drug trade. That represents less than 2.5 percent of the value of Colombia's estimated annual cocaine output of 580 tons."

19. Peter Dale Scott, "Honduras, the Contra Support Networks, and Cocaine: How the U.S. Government Has Augmented America's Drug Crisis," in Alfred W. McCoy and Alan A. Block, eds., *War on Drugs: Studies in the Failure of U.S. Narcotic Policy* (Boulder: Westview, 1992), 126–27. I presented these remarks at a conference in 1990.

20. David McClintock, *Swordfish* (New York: Pantheon, 1993), 228; Peter Dale Scott, *Drugs, Contras, and the CIA* (Sherman Oaks, Calif.: From the Wilderness Publications, 2000), 7.

21. Scott, "Honduras," 161.

22. *International Narcotics Control Strategy Report, 1999*. Released by the Bureau for International Narcotics and Law Enforcement Affairs, U.S. Department of State, Washington, D.C., March 2000, www.state.gov/www/global/narcotics_law/1999_narc_report.

23. Joseph Buttinger, *Vietnam: A Political History* (New York: Praeger, 1968), 456–60.

24. U.S. Army Special Warfare School, "Subject: Visit to Colombia, February 26, 1962," Carrollton Press, Declassified Documents Reference Series (1976:154D); Michael

McClintock, *Instruments of Statecraft: U.S. Guerrilla Warfare, Counterinsurgency, and Counterterrorism* (New York: Pantheon, 1992), 222. In 1959, even before Kennedy was elected, the United States dispatched to Colombia Colonel Charles Bohannan, a veteran of the bloody Philippine counterinsurgency after World War II (McClintock, *Instruments,* 143).

25. McClintock, *Instruments,* 223. In the same way, the military insurgency of the Vietnamese National Liberation Front can be traced to Ngo Dinh Diem's repressive campaign in the late 1950s against the followers of Ho Chi Minh, who until then had been waiting for an internationally supervised election that they expected to win.

26. 1963 *Field Manual on U.S. Army Counterinsurgency Forces* (FM 31–22), 82–84; quoted in McClintock, *Instruments,* 252.

27. *Reglamento de Combate,* 317; quoted in McClintock, *Instruments,* 252; cf. 223.

28. McClintock, *Instruments,* 193; citing Office of Public Safety, International Police Academy, syllabus for Course no. 6. Nineteen Colombians took the course, the largest group from any single country.

29. The revolutionary group M-19 evolved from a group of nonviolent student activists whose efforts to organize the employees of U.S. firms led to some of their group being murdered. See Ana Carrigan, *The Palace of Justice: A Colombian Tragedy* (New York: Four Walls Eight Windows, 1993). We need to know more about corporate paramilitary connections, particularly whether U.S. oil companies in Colombia, as alleged, have used drug trafficking gangs for their security assets. For another U.S. oil company's use of a major international mafia figure, see Peter Dale Scott, *Deep Politics and the Death of JFK* (Berkeley: University of California Press, 1996), 202–4.

30. *San Francisco Chronicle,* June 15, 2001. It is common for oil companies abroad to become involved with local security forces who then commit atrocities in which the oil companies are implicated. In Aceh, Indonesia, Exxon-Mobil has maintained what Bloomberg.com has called a "less than arms-length detachment from the military" ("a long-term miscalculation"), which has tortured civilians on or near to company facilities (Bloomberg.com, March 25, 2001, cited in Robert Jereski, "The Conflict in Aceh," www.preventconflict.org/portal/main/research/jereski.htm). In September 2002 victims of Myanmar military atrocities committed in connection with security for a Unocal pipeline won the right to sue for damages in a U.S. court (*Los Angeles Times,* September 19, 2002).

31. Scott and Marshall, *Cocaine Politics,* 89.

32. Human Rights Watch, *State of War: Political Violence and Counterinsurgency in Colombia,* www.hrw.org/reports/1993/stateofwar1.htm.

33. Human Rights Watch, *Colombia's Killer Networks: The Military-Paramilitary Partnership and the United States,* 1996, www.hrw.org/hrw/reports/1996/killer1.htm; cf. Frank Smyth, *Progressive,* June 1998: "Take Colombia. In the name of fighting drugs, the CIA financed new military intelligence networks there in 1991. But the new networks did little to stop drug traffickers. Instead, they incorporated illegal paramilitary groups into their ranks and fostered death squads. These death squads killed trade unionists, peasant leaders, human-rights workers, journalists, and other suspected 'subversives.' The evidence, including secret Colombian military documents, suggests that the CIA may be more interested in fighting a leftist resistance movement than in combating drugs."

34. Human Rights Watch, *The Ties That Bind: Colombia and Military-Paramilitary Links,* 2000, www.hrw.org/reports/2000/colombia; Alma Guillermoprieto, "Our New War in Colombia," *New York Review of Books,* April 13, 2000.

35. Guillermoprieto, "Our New War": "In 1995, according to a recent report by the U.S. State Department, Bolivia had 48,600 hectares of coca under cultivation. In 1999 there were only 21,800. Even more dramatic are the figures for Peru, where production peaked at 115,300 hectares in 1995, and shrank four years later to barely 38,700. But if one takes the total combined figures for hectares of coca under cultivation in Colombia, Bolivia, and Peru in 1995, and again in 1999, the picture is somewhat different. In 1995 the estimated total was 214,800 hectares. In 1999 it was 183,000." Cf. *Chicago Sun-Times*, January 21, 2001: "Peru and Bolivia began major anti-coca efforts of this type in the 1990s. Peru's coca cultivation is down 66 percent in the last four years (helped in part by a fungus that attacked Peru's coca bushes). Bolivia's has fallen 55 percent in 2½ years. Colombia's coca production rose rapidly at the same time, but not as much as these drops, meaning there was a net reduction in the total amount of coca grown. Or so the authorities thought. Further analysis showed that Colombian cocaine productivity was 2½ times higher than previously believed. It's impossible to say for how long the United States has been underestimating South American cocaine production. Once the 1998 and 1999 figures for Colombia were adjusted accordingly, the major drop in cocaine production vanished."

36. Scott and Marshall, *Cocaine Politics*, 81–84.

37. *New York Times*, October 25, 1997.

38. Lucian R.W. Pye, "Armies in the Process of Political Modernization," in *The Role of the Military in Underdeveloped Countries*, ed. John J. Johnson (Princeton: Princeton University Press, 1962), 87–89. At the same conference Guy Pauker of RAND urged Indonesian officers present to "strike, sweep their house clean" (p. 224); quoted in Peter Dale Scott, "The United States and the Overthrow of Sukarno, 1965–1967," *Pacific Affairs* (Vancouver, B.C.), Summer 1985, 239–64. Some of those present played important roles in the subsequent Indonesian coup of 1965.

39. Edwin Lieuwen, "Militarism and Politics in Latin America"; in Johnson, *Role of the Military*, 138, 147.

40. Johnson, *Role of the Military*, 153–54.

41. *New York Times*, May 28, 2001.

5

The CIA and Drug Traffickers in Colombia

Comparatively little is known of the CIA's role in Colombia. As noted above, the CIA undertook in the 1960s to train Colombian police officers in sabotage and other terror tactics. The resulting involvement with paramilitaries in Colombia has survived into the CIA's present mission in Colombia—to fight drugs.

In the early 1990s, according to Human Rights Watch,

> a U.S. Defense Department and Central Intelligence Agency (CIA) team worked with Colombian military officers on the 1991 intelligence reorganization that resulted in the creation of killer networks that identified and killed civilians suspected of supporting guerrillas.[1]

Former U.S. military attaché Colonel James Roach, who worked on the reorganization, has said since his retirement that the CIA was the major partner in the reorganization and even financed the new networks directly.[2]

Drug trafficking and right-wing terrorist activity have been linked in Colombia for at least thirty years. The evidence suggests that the Colombian state security apparatus, in conjunction with the CIA, has had continuing contact with this right-wing nexus and may even have played an organizing role. The story goes back to the Alianza Anticomunista Americana in the 1970s, an international network centered in Argentina that targeted revolutionaries with the assistance of CIA-trained Cuban American terrorists.[3] Left-wing sources have claimed that the AAA operated in Colombia as part of the state security apparatus, and with CIA assistance.[4]

It seems clear that the CIA has had an ongoing relationship to some paramilitary units, dating back at least to the creation of the Muerte a Sequestradores (MAS) in 1981. In the 1980s MAS functioned as a working coalition between the army and the drug cartels against FARC (and its political arm, the Unión Patriótica), and there are signs that the CIA endorsed this alliance.[5] One is that Santiago Ocampo, then head of the Cali cartel (and president of MAS), was able to travel into and out of the United States without difficulty, to the frustration of DEA officers who had him targeted.[6] Another is that the same Israeli instructors who worked for Ocampo and MAS in Colombia worked for the U.S.-backed Contras in Honduras, as well as the Guatemalan army.[7] This work drew the comment from a general in the Israeli Knesset that "Israel is the 'dirty work' contractor for the U.S. Administration. Israel is acting as an accomplice and arm of the United States."[8] And Ocampo's drug ally in Honduras, Juan Ramón Matta Ballesteros, was untouchable until the U.S. Contra support effort was closed down in 1988. The CIA, and in its wake the U.S. State Department, had contracted all air support business for the Contras in Honduras to Matta's airline, SETCO.[9]

It is relevant that in the 1980s cocaine from Colombia was helping to finance nearly all of the competing factions of the CIA-supported Contras in Central America.[10] It was indeed a long-established practice for the CIA to allow its client armies to supplement their income through drug trafficking, sometimes with Agency assistance: from Burma and Laos in the 1950s and 1960s to the Hizb-i-Islami guerrilla army of Gulbuddin Hekmatyar in the 1980s.[11] Thanks in part to CIA assistance and protection, Hekmatyar became for a while one of the leading heroin suppliers in the world.[12] With alleged encouragement from CIA Director Casey, Colombian cocaine also began in this period to enter the Soviet Union via Hekmatyar's mujahedin in Afghanistan, the apparent precursor of today's massive cocaine trade linking Colombian cartels to Russia's so-called Red Mafiya.[13]

The U.S. government did not merely condone the drug trafficking of most Contra factions, it favored known drug traffickers with government contracts and intervened to prevent incipient drug cases from being prosecuted.[14] Active in the latter role was a chief assistant U.S. attorney in Miami by the name of Richard Gregorie, the man later responsible for the indictment of Manuel Noriega.[15] Gregorie was backed in his efforts by the number three Justice official in Washington, Mark Richard.[16] In the crucial year 1986 Richard was given an award by the CIA for "protection of national security during criminal prosecutions."[17]

This U.S. government's protection of the Contras affected U.S. drug policy overall, and particularly in Colombia. A concerted U.S. propaganda campaign was mounted in 1984 against alleged drug trafficking by a conspiracy involving Nicaraguan Sandinistas, Colombian narco-guerrillas, and traffickers in Medellín, notably Carlos Lehder and Pablo Escobar.[18] This campaign distorted the truth in two related respects: it falsely implicated FARC and it rewrote history to efface references to the Medellín cartel's competitors in Cali. For example, the major Tranquilandia cocaine plant raided in 1984 was said by U.S. authorities to have been "guarded by Communist [FARC] guerrillas" and planned by the Medellín cartel.[19] In fact the plant had been protected by the Colombian army and planned at a joint meeting in Cali.[20] Major drug traffickers and shipments that had once been linked to Cali were now, like MAS itself, reattributed by the U.S. government to the Medellín cartel.[21] Thus the vigorous prosecution of the Medellín cartel both abetted and protected the ongoing continuity of interest linking anti-FARC terrorists, the Cali cartel, and the CIA.

Many of the 1984 charges of a Sandinista-Medellín-FARC alliance came from the U.S. ambassador in Bogotá, Lewis Tambs. Tambs was an unusually ideological political appointee who on drug matters took direction not from the State Department but by back channels from William Clark, Reagan's national security adviser.[22] But Tambs's charges were supported by official testimony before congressional committees, and above all by the U.S. Department of Justice.

In 1984 the same Richard Gregorie who would bury the Contra-support drug case linked the Nicaraguan Sandinistas to drug trafficking by bringing the first of two indictments against Lehder, Escobar, and a Sandinista official. For this he relied on the testimony and controversial photographs of former CIA contract pilot Barry Seal, the photos having been taken from a CIA-equipped plane.[23] Thus the indictments named, in addition to five traffickers in Medellín (the Ochoa brothers, Pablo Escobar, and Carlos Lehder), Federico Vaughan, an alleged assistant to Tomás Borge, the Nicaraguan minister of the interior. The second indictment against the Medellín cartel and the Sandinistas was released by Gregorie to the press on November 18, 1986, one day before President Reagan's disastrous press conference about the breaking Iran-Contra scandal.[24]

After DEA administrator Lawn himself expressed doubts about the involvement of Borge, the United States focused more particularly on Lehder, who was accused of links both to the revolutionary M-19 movement and to Fidel Castro.[25] In February 1987 Lehder was captured and extradited to the United States, having been betrayed by Escobar in connection with a deal he had proposed to the U.S. attorney general, Ed Meese.[26] This was the first in a series of dramatic drug busts of U.S. targets in Colombia, busts abetted not just by law enforcement but by competing traffickers.

This unlikely alliance with M-19 was used by then Vice President George Bush to justify National Security Decision Directive 221 of April 1986. For the first time it defined drug trafficking as a national security matter, allowing for the use of U.S. troops in Colombia in alliance with the CIA.[27] In retrospect, NSDD 221, and a follow-up NSDD signed by Bush in the summer of 1989, has proven to be an executive equivalent of the Tonkin Gulf Resolution of 1964, leading to the direct involvement of the U.S. military in another nation's civil war.

Like the Tonkin Gulf Resolution, NSDD 221 was justified by allegedly hard intelligence data that have since been discredited. When Vice President Bush announced it in July 1986, he

charged the Sandinista government in Nicaragua with using money from illegal drugs to finance international terror, blamed Cuban President Fidel Castro for harboring airplanes used in drug smuggling and . . . alleged that there was a drug connection behind the 1985 assault on Colombia's Palace of Justice by M19 guerrillas, in which 100 people were killed, including 12 Supreme Court justices. He said Colombian authorities discovered after the siege that the rebels had destroyed all U.S. extradition requests for Colombia's major drug traffickers.[28]

History has validated DEA's coolness at the time to these ideological claims, especially the last.[29] (It was almost certainly the army's counterattack against the M-19 that killed the justices and destroyed the files.)[30]

The enlarged U.S. presence in Colombia, following NSDD 221, produced not order but a major escalation of Medellín cartel violence. This reached a peak in 1989, when a Colombian commercial airliner was blown up, killing all 110 passengers (but not the presidential candidate who had been the target). In September the new Bush administration, treating such violence as a national security matter, launched the Andean initiative with a new NSDD, authorizing an expanded role for the U.S. military in the Latin American drug war. At the same time the CIA station in Bogotá grew to a size of nearly one hundred, making it the largest CIA station in the world.[31]

Although the new U.S. interagency presence brought the latest technology to the pursuit of targeted drug traffickers, a key role continued to be played by alliances with other traffickers, notably the Cali cartel. It is not disputed that in 1993, while working for the Cali cartel, AUC leader Carlos Castaño "collaborated with the CIA and the Colombian police to bring down the fugitive drug baron, Pablo Escobar."[32] Carlos Castaño and his brother were leaders of a death squad, Los Pepes, that tracked down and killed members of Escobar's organization. They did so on the basis of information from the CIA, which was transmitted via a special squad of the Colombian National Police, on good terms with the Cali cartel.[33] The U.S. embassy had intelligence reports that in fact Los Pepes "had been created by the Cali Cartel," yet the Los Pepes killers fraternized with at least two DEA agents and gave one of them a gold watch.[34]

Escobar's ability to run his drug operations while nominally in prison ended only with his death. It seemed for a while that the traffic would be dominated by the more accommodating Cali cartel, whose style was to work through governments rather than against them. But events changed in June 1994, with the release of tapes of an intercepted phone call, suggesting strongly that the Cali cartel had put $3.5 million into the electoral campaign of the eventual winner, Ernesto Samper.[35] The revelations allowed the U.S. government to take stern measures with the weakened Samper government, and by August 1995 the three major leaders of the Cali cartel had been arrested.[36] Apparently the Cali leaders, like Escobar before them, continue to oversee their drug trafficking from prison.[37]

According to the DEA, the drug trade in Colombia has become more decentralized with the breakup of the Cali cartel.[38] A Colombian expert has a different perspective: he estimates (and the DEA appears to agree) that with the effective dismantling of the two big cartels an increasing share of Colombian drug exports is now controlled by cartels in Mexico.[39] According to the DEA, one of the principal suppliers to the Mexican cartels is the Henao-Montoya organization with which Carlos Castaño is affiliated.[40]

Some in the United States may not be unhappy at this Mexican shift. Twice in the last two decades Mexico has threatened to default on repayments to U.S. banks, crises averted only by the issuance of emergency U.S. government loans. Drug profits contribute significantly to the foreign exchange earnings of Mexico, and they generated more than half of the foreign exchange earnings needed to repay these loans. Before the first loan was issued in 1982, the U.S. government had already ascertained from DEA and CIA that the profits from drug exports for Colombia and Mexico "probably represent 75 percent of source-country export earnings."[41]

To sum up: the CIA can (and does) point to its role in the arrest or elimination of a number of major Colombian traffickers. These arrests have not diminished the actual flow of cocaine into the United States, which on the contrary reached a new high in 2000. But they have institutionalized the relationship of law enforcement to rival cartels and visibly contributed to the increase of urban cartel violence.

The true purpose of most of these campaigns, like the current Plan Colombia, has not been the hopeless ideal of eradication. It has been to alter market share: to target specific enemies and thus ensure that the drug traffic remains under the control of those traffickers who are allies of the Colombian state security apparatus and/or the CIA.[42] This confirms the judgment of Senate investigator Jack Blum a decade ago, that America, instead of battling a narcotics conspiracy, has "in a subtle way . . . become part of that conspiracy."[43]

DRUG ALLEGATIONS CONCERNING CIA AIRLINES

In Colombia as in the Far East, the CIA's proprietary and contract airlines have been accused of more direct involvement in drug trafficking. The U.S. airline Southern Air Transport has been flying to Colombia and Venezuela since at least 1960, when it became for a while a CIA proprietary company.[44] A series of reports, none of them proven, have linked the airline since then to cocaine. In January 1987, during the first phase of the Iran-Contra revelations, newspapers reported that the Justice Department had recently suppressed a DEA investigation of Southern Air Transport for drug trafficking:

> The suspicions, which are vigorously denied, are causing alarm. Officials of the Federal Drug Enforcement Agency are revealing that they reported an arms-for-drugs air ferrying operation involving Southern Air Transport—the former CIA owned airline at the heart of the Irangate shipments—as long ago as last September, only to have their evidence discounted by the Justice Department.[45]

The *New York Times* reported at the time that the accusations "will be studied again" as part of the Iran-Contra investigation. Predictably, they were not. Yet allegations continued. According to a recent report by the CIA inspector general,

> a 1991 DEA cable to CIA reported that SAT was "of record" in DEA's database from January 1985-September 1990 for alleged involvement in cocaine trafficking. An August 1990 entry in DEA's database reportedly alleged that $2 million was delivered to the firm's business sites, and several of the firm's pilots and executives were suspected of smuggling "narcotics currency."[46]

This claim corroborates one made in 1986 by an FBI informant, Wanda Palacio, who was the wife of a Colombian trafficker. Palacio told investigators for the Kerry Senate subcommittee investigating Contra drug trafficking that in 1983 she had seen Southern Air Transport planes in Barranquilla, Colombia, unloading guns and being loaded with cocaine.[47]

Two subsequent events lent substance to Palacio's story. First, when a Southern Air Transport plane was shot down in Nicaragua on October 5, 1986, flight plans found in its wreckage showed that the pilot had flown an SAT transport plane to Barranquilla in 1985.[48] Second, the U.S. government responded in an interesting way when Senator Kerry and his aide Jonathan Winer took an eleven-page proffer based on Palacio's statement to Justice Department official William Weld. Winer later wrote a memo describing the meeting:

> Weld read about half a page and chuckled. I asked him why. He said this isn't the first time today I've seen allegations about CIA agent involvement in drugs. . . . he stated several times in reading Wanda's statement that while he couldn't vouch for every line in it . . . there was nothing in it which didn't appear true to him, or inconsistent with what he already knew.[49]

(The proffer was eventually referred by Justice to Richard Gregorie in Miami, who dismissed it, claiming that Palacio was "as wacky as they come.")[50]

At least one of the firms that was enmeshed with SAT in controversial Contra support operations is doing contract work today for Plan Colombia. This is EAST, Inc., alias Eagle Aviation Services and Technology, Inc., a subcontractor with Dyncorp in the operations to spray coca plantations with herbicide.[51] EAST was founded in 1982 by retired air force officer Richard Gadd, who was pushed by Oliver North into Contra support operations despite a CIA officer's warning that his background check set off "shyster alarms."[52] Accused by another ex-CIA operative of "big profit" and "rip-off," Gadd through his firm EAST received $550,000 for covert Contra support work. In 1999 and 2000, EAST received more than $30 million under several Defense Department contracts. This is in addition to its unknown share of DynCorp's five-year, $170 million contract in Colombia with the State Department.[53]

Gadd received immunity for his Iran-Contra testimony and was never indicted.

There were, however, a number of rumors linking drugs to the airstrip that EAST built for the Oliver North Enterprise on the Santa Elena peninsula in Costa Rica.[54]

Jet Avia is another small airline, now defunct, suspected of both flying under contract for the CIA in Colombia and involvement in drug trafficking. According to authors Sally Denton and Roger Morris, "federal law enforcement officials . . . were aware that Jet Avia had been used by the CIA since the company's inception." In 1977 Jet Avia Lear landed in Colombia with Jimmy Chagra, a major Texan drug trafficker; the plane was owned by Danny Ray Lasater, "a Las Vegas high roller who was soon to be under investigation for ties to organized crime and eventually convicted for cocaine distribution."[55]

Lasater was not only a gambler and drug dealer, he was also alleged to have made major cash contributions to the campaigns of both Arkansas Governor Bill Clinton and Kentucky Governor John Y. Brown, Jr.[56] Like the complex story of Afghan heroin and BCCI in Washington, so also the story of Colombian cocaine and Las Vegas, if further studied, will cast light on the deep politics of not just the Third World but also the United States.

NOTES

1. Human Rights Watch, *Colombia's Killer Networks: The Military-Paramilitary Partnership and the United States*, 1996, www.hrw.org/hrw/reports/1996/killer1.htm.

2. Frank Smyth, *Progressive*, June 1998.

3. Jonathan Marshall, Peter Dale Scott, and Jane Hunter, *The Iran-Contra Connection: Secret Teams and Covert Operations in the Reagan Era* (Boston: South End, 1987), 70–71.

4. See, for example, "Paramilitarismo como política contrainsurgente de estado," home3.swipnet.se/~w-34817/FARC/990120-para-militar-documento.htm.

5. Peter Dale Scott and Jonathan Marshall, *Cocaine Politics: Drugs, Armies, and the CIA in Central America* (Berkeley: University of California Press, 1998), 89; citing Rensselaer W. Lee III, *The White Labyrinth* (New Brunswick, N.J.: Transaction, 1988), 117–18.

6. Scott and Marshall, *Cocaine Politics*, 88; citing James Mills, *The Underground Empire* (New York: Dell, 1986), 882.

7. Three thousand Kalashnikov rifles from a police stockpile in Nicaragua were delivered by Israeli arms dealers to the paramilitary United Self-Defense Forces of Colombia (AUC) in November 2001 (Associated Press, May 9, 2002).

8. Andrew Cockburn and Leslie Cockburn, *Dangerous Liaison: The Inside Story of the U.S.-Israeli Covert Relationship* (New York: HarperCollins, 1991), 214–18. Israeli Colonel Yair Klein remarked of his death-squad training for Medellín Cartel leader José Gonzalo Rodríguez Gacha: "'We are positive that what we are doing is within the interests of the Americans, and so far it was always like that.' They would have heard about it, said Klein, if it was not" (p. 215). Klein went on to sell arms in Sierra Leone from the Ukraine and Belarus; arrest warrants are still outstanding for him in Colombia and the United States (*Washington Post*, October 16, 1999; *Jerusalem Post*, September 21, 1999).

9. Scott and Marshall, *Cocaine Politics*, 56–64. The Ocampo-Matta connection in Mexico, Miguel Angel Félix Gallardo, also supported the Contras and for a while enjoyed protection (Scott and Marshall, *Cocaine Politics*, 41–42). Peter Dale Scott, *Drugs, Contras, and the CIA* (Sherman Oaks, Calif.: From the Wilderness Publications, 2000), 7–8.

10. Scott and Marshall, *Cocaine Politics*, 54–64, 101–21; Scott, *Drugs, Contras, and the CIA*, 7–37.

11. Alfred W. McCoy, *The Politics of Heroin* (Brooklyn, N.Y.: Lawrence Hill, 1991), xiv–xv, 162–78, 284–92, 448–60, passim.

12. In March 1982 the Reagan administration drafted a secret memo of understanding between the CIA and the Justice Department, exempting CIA officials from their previous obligation to report to Justice the drug trafficking activities of their agents, assets, and contractors: U.S. Central Intelligence Agency, Office of Inspector General [Frederick Hitz], Investigations Staff, *Report of Investigation concerning Allegations between CIA and the Contras in Trafficking Cocaine to the United States*, 96-0143-IG, vol. 2, *The Contra Story*, paras. 23–30, 57–71; Scott, *Drugs, Contras, and the CIA*, 12.

13. Compare chapter 2 in this volume; Stephen Handelman, *Comrade Criminal: Russia's New Mafiya* (New Haven: Yale University Press, 1995), 195–204. Casey's so-called Operation Mosquito deserves to be investigated, as does the CIA use at this time of currency from Shakarchi Trading, a Swiss firm later accused of laundering funds from both Afghan heroin and Colombian cocaine.

14. Scott and Marshall, *Cocaine Politics*, 10–12, 132–50.

15. Scott and Marshall, *Cocaine Politics*, 149. See also David Harris, *Shooting the Moon* (Boston: Little, Brown, 2001), 157–59.

16. Scott and Marshall, *Cocaine Politics*, 133–34, 149–50, 154.

17. Gary Webb, *Dark Alliance* (New York: Seven Stories Press, 1998), 332.

18. As noted below, this propaganda campaign from the White House and CIA began one year after the discovery by Occidental Oil of the billion-barrel Caño Limon oilfield in 1983. It led to the National Security decision directives of 1986 and 1989 that created a U.S. military presence in Colombia.

19. *New York Times*, March 21, 1984 ("guerrillas"); Mark Bowden, *Killing Pablo* (New York: Atlantic Monthly Press, 2001), 44 ("Medellín Cartel"). The charge that FARC protected the Tranquilandia lab seems to have derived from the discovery of a FARC uniform nearby, which may well have been planted.

20. Scott and Marshall, *Cocaine Politics*, 97–98.

21. For examples, see Scott and Marshall, *Cocaine Politics*, 94.

22. Martha Honey, *Hostile Acts: U.S. Policy in Costa Rica in the 1980s* (Gainesville: University Press of Florida, 1994), 412.

23. The indictments would be used to counter allegations against supporters of the CIA's Contras. Thus Reagan charged that "top Nicaraguan government officials are deeply involved in drug trafficking" on March 16, 1986. This was a few hours after the *San Francisco Examiner*, in a front page story, had revealed the involvement of Contra leaders and supporters in a local drug bust three years earlier (Scott and Marshall, *Cocaine Politics*, 172–73).

24. There has been great disagreement as to which traffickers are seen in the murky photos (see Scott and Marshall, *Cocaine Politics*, 99–103).

25. At the time Lehder was accused of coordinating an attack with the leftist group

M-19 and the Nicaraguan Sandinistas against the Colombian Palace of Justice. This charge was used by George Bush to promote NSDD 221. It has since been discredited by DEA officials and experts such as Rensselaer Lee (Scott and Marshall, *Cocaine Politics*, 95–96, 102).

26. Bowden, *Killing Pablo*, 54.

27. Scott and Marshall, *Cocaine Politics*, 102; Bowden, *Killing Pablo*, 54.

28. *Los Angeles Times*, June 8, 1986. It is worth recalling that Barry Seal, the former CIA contract pilot who was the government's source for the Sandinista allegations, was put in touch with DEA by a military representative on Vice President Bush's South Florida Task Force (Harris, *Shooting the Moon*, 18). He allegedly told the DEA at his first meeting that he would implicate the Sandinistas, a detail at odds with later USG-inspired accounts of his story (*Wall Street Journal*, April 22, 1987; cf. Elaine Shannon, *Desperados* [New York: Viking, 1988], 150).

29. Lee, *White Labyrinth*, 172–75, 179–81; Shannon, *Desperados*, 142–43, 173–76; Scott and Marshall, *Cocaine Politics*, 95–96, 102.

30. Carrigan, *Palace of Justice,* passim.

31. Bowden, *Killing Pablo*, 159.

32. Ana Carrigan, *Irish Times*, August 23, 2000. By late 1989, the Cali Cartel had become "the principal source of information to the [Colombian] security agencies" (Patrick Clawson and Rensselaer W. Lee III, *The Andean Cocaine Industry* [New York: St. Martin's, 1996], 57).

33. Bowden, *Killing Pablo*, 184–225. In April 2001 Amnesty International USA filed a lawsuit to obtain CIA records on Los Pepes. AIUSA alleged that its investigation pointed to "an extremely suspect relationship between the U.S. government and the Castaño family—at a time when the U.S. government was well aware of that family's involvement in paramilitary violence and narcotics trafficking" (Amnesty International USA press release, April 25, 2001; www.amnestyusa.org/news/2001/colombia04252001_2.html).

34. *Washington Post*, July 21, 1996 (reports); Bowden, *Killing Pablo,* 186, 263, 268 (fraternized). According to the respected Colombian writer Ana Carrigan, the DEA in 2000 still regarded Castaño as a potential ally: "Serious allegations have emerged that agents of the U.S. Drug Enforcement Agency (DEA) have offered to subsidise the 'paramilitary' leader, Carlos Castaño, in return for his support in combating the traffickers. Speaking on national television from his northern fiefdom, Castaño said he did not know whether a request for his help reflected U.S. policy or came from agents acting on their own initiative. A DEA informant, who says he acted as translator at meetings between DEA agents, traffickers and members of Castaño's paramilitaries, claims it was agreed that U.S. officials should meet Castaño to conclude a deal" (Ana Carrigan, *Irish Times*, August 23, 2000). Carrigan believed that Castaño intended by sustained military activity to divert middle-class hopes away from the peace process and toward a military-civilian "national unity government," with himself at its head.

35. The tapes were released by the eventual loser, Andrés Pastrana, who would win four years later. "On the tape, Rodríguez Orejuela seems to suggest Pastrana's campaign accepted other drug money, but Pastrana denied it" (*Los Angeles Times*, June 23, 1994). U.S. sources imply that the once-secret tapes were made public in September 1994 by the retiring Bogotá DEA chief, Joe Toft (Bowden, *Killing Pablo*, 272; cf. *Washington Post*, July 21, 1996). What Toft released was a cleaned-up tape with the reference to Pastrana

deleted. The tapes were first released in June 1994 by Pastrana himself (e.g., *Montreal Gazette*, June 28, 1994).

36. *Washington Post*, August 28, 1995. The three were Gilberto Rodríguez Orejuela, his brother Miguel, and José Santacruz Londono. A fourth leader, Helmer Herrera Buitrago, was murdered in prison in 1998.

37. Clawson and Lee, *Andean Cocaine Industry*, 61; *Boston Globe*, November 11, 1999. An indicted drug trafficker, Fernando José Flores, made a dozen visits to Cali leaders Gilberto and Miguel Rodríguez Orejuela in prison.

38. DEA, "Traffickers from Colombia," www.usdoj.gov/dea/traffickers/colombia.htm.

39. Ricardo Rocha, "The Colombian Economy after 25 Years of Drug Trafficking," www.odccp.org:80/colombia/rocha.html.

40. www.usdoj.gov/dea/briefingbook/page34-48.htm.

41. Mills, *Underground Empire*, 1135, 1181; Peter Dale Scott, *Minding the Darkness: A Poem for the Year 2000* (New York: New Directions, 2000), 153–57.

42. In the Mapiripan massacre of July 14–20, 1997, paramilitaries were helped by the Colombian military to take over the capital of a coca-growing region. According to a senior journalist of the Colombian daily *El Espectador*, U.S. Green Beret trainers were nearby. "It was as if the army were using Mapiripan as a test in conducting operations" (*San Francisco Chronicle*, April 22, 2001). For this massacre the responsible general was eventually convicted by a military tribunal and given a forty-month sentence (*New York Times*, February 14, 2001).

43. Paul Eddy, *The Cocaine Wars* (New York: Norton, 1988), 342.

44. See information at www.airlines2.freeuk.com/417.htm. In 1972 Southern Air was "sold" to its president. The 1976 Church Committee Final Report (1:239) noted that the sales of other such "proprietary" companies were usually conditioned on "an agreement that the proprietary would continue to provide goods or services to the CIA" (Marshall, Scott, and Hunter, *Iran-Contra Connection,* 17).

45. *Guardian* (London), January 21, 1987. Cf. *New York Times*, January 20, 1987; Scott and Marshall, *Cocaine Politics*, 166. Southern Air Transport turned up as a creditor after the bankruptcy of Farhad Azima's Global International Airways, apparently because Southern Air performed maintenance work on Global's planes when they were in Miami. See Pete Brewton, *The Mafia, CIA, and George Bush* (New York: S.P.I. Books, 1992), 206.

46. Central Intelligence Agency, Office of Inspector General, Investigations Staff, *Report of Investigation concerning Allegations of Connections between CIA and the Contras in Cocaine Trafficking to the United States*, 96–0143-IG, vol. 2, para. 907. Discussed in Scott, *Drugs, Contras, and the CIA*, 36.

47. Webb, *Dark Alliance*, 254; Scott and Marshall, *Cocaine Politics*, 18; *New York Times*, August 23, 1987. In assessing these and other charges of improper CIA involvement in drug trafficking, it should be remembered that the CIA authorized the import of at least one ton of cocaine (and possibly much more) from nearby Venezuela into the United States (*Wall Street Journal*, November 22, 1996; *New York Times*, November 23, 1996; Scott and Marshall, *Cocaine Politics*, vii [1998 ed.]).

48. Scott and Marshall, *Cocaine Politics*, 17–18; Webb, *Dark Alliance*, 254.

49. Jonathan Winer, memorandum to file re: Meeting with William Weld, September 26, 1986, in Webb, *Dark Alliance*, 254. Nevertheless, the Justice Department had a quite

different response when Palacio's story reached the press a month later: "Initial disclosure of the witness' claim was made on October 30 [1986]. That day, Associate Attorney General Stephen Trott, acting at the behest of Attorney General Edwin Meese, told FBI Director William Webster to delay the bureau's investigation of Southern Air. The request for a delay came initially from Vice Admiral John Poindexter, then national security adviser, to Meese" (*San Francisco Chronicle*, January 20, 1987; Scott and Marshall, *Cocaine Politics*, 18; cf. U.S. Congress, *Iran-Contra Affair, Report of the Committees Investigating the Iran-Contra Affair,* House Report 100–433, Senate Report 100–216 [Washington: Government Printing Office, 1987], 288).

50. Harris, *Shooting the Moon*, 158.

51. Ken Guggenheim, Associated Press, June 5, 2001.

52. Cockburn and Cockburn, *Dangerous Liaison*, 218. The CIA officer was Alan Fiers. Another ex-CIA operative, Felix Rodriguez, accused Gadd (Walsh, *Iran-Contra: The Final Report* [New York: Times Books, 1994], 495).

53. Associated Press, June 5, 2001.

54. Martha Honey, *Hostile Acts: U.S. Policy in Costa Rica in the 1980s* (Gainesville: University Press of Florida, 1994), 406–9.

55. Sally Denton and Roger Morris, *The Money and the Power* (New York: Knopf, 2001), 327–29.

56. Roger Morris, *Partners in Power: The Clintons and Their America* (New York: Holt, 1996).

6

The Need to Disengage from Colombia

THE REAL U.S. INTEREST IN COLOMBIA: PEACE AND STABILITY

The true national interests of the United States (and also of Colombia) must be distinguished sharply from those of cowboy operatives in the Pentagon and the CIA, who now have four decades of failed efforts to account for. Like gamblers who have lost more than they can afford, they seem committed to compounding their mistakes by expanding rather than ending them. There is a strong analogy here with Vietnam, to which the same bureaucracies committed the United States more and more blindly, without any rational prospect of success.

The democratic interest of the United States, in contrast, is for a democratic Colombia on a democratic continent. In practical terms this means, as President Pastrana saw so clearly when he was first elected, commitment to the Colombian peace process and extrication from the conflict that now prevails.

In theory the U.S. government is committed to precisely these objectives. In its fact sheet explaining Plan Colombia, the U.S. State Department wrote that "the proposed U.S. assistance package will help Colombia address the breadth of the challenges it faces—its efforts to fight the illicit drug trade, to increase the rule of law, to protect human rights, to expand economic development, to institute judicial reform, and to foster peace."[1]

But the same fact sheet made it clear that the proposed human rights assistance would amount to $93 million over a two-year period, or under 5 percent of the $1.6 billion total U.S. proposal. As for the peace process, the fact sheet asserted that "the U.S. Government is hopeful that the peace negotiations now going on between the Colombian government and the FARC guerrilla group and the Colombian government and the ELN guerrilla group prove successful." However, not one penny was allocated to implement these hopes, and not one sentence addressed the fact that the U.S. effort was now a major obstacle to negotiations with FARC.[2]

This epitomizes what has always been wrong with U.S. aid packages in Colombia or elsewhere, which use a human rights veneer to mask a military reality. Let me quote Ambassador Robert White, who was our ambassador in Colombia under Jimmy Carter:

> Tell me where you put your money, and I'll tell you what your foreign policy is. If you put over 90 cents of your foreign policy dollar into the Pentagon and the CIA, then your policy is going to emphasize a military approach, a secretive, under the [table] approach, to the problems. For example, the budget for the White House Drug Office, this office of Narcotics Control, is greater than the State Department and the Commerce Department put together. Now what possible sense can that make? You are starving diplomacy, you are exalting a military approach to problems. And frankly, all the experience we've had is that these anti- or counter-narcotics programs do not work. During the lifetime of the program in Colombia, the last three years, this intensive counter-narcotics program, exports to the United States have more than doubled.[3]

It is no accident that, as the U.S. involvement with the Colombian armed forces has grown over the last decade, the flow of drugs into the United States has increased. As increasing numbers of planes flow back and forth, opportunities to smuggle also expand. One could have predicted the dramatic drug seizure of November 1998 in Fort Lauderdale airport: sixteen hundred pounds of cocaine in a Colombian air force plane that had never been in the hands of anyone else. A U.S. officer in Colombia and his wife have also been busted for money laundering and for smuggling heroin and cocaine.[4] We may see a repeat of the narcotics scourge accompanying the Vietnam War, when drugs were smuggled in the corpses of U.S. soldiers.

Today the paramilitaries are still the chief stumbling block to the Pastrana peace process. FARC is often represented in the U.S. press as refusing to negotiate; but in fact, mindful of its disastrous experience in the 1980s, FARC is insisting as a condition for negotiations that the *autodefensas* be brought under government control. Though Pastrana lacks the power, and the army the will, to achieve this, FARC's position is understandable.

It is increasingly dangerous for anyone in Colombia to speak out against the spiraling violence. Castaño's organization, which has hacked people to death with chain saws, has issued "threats against members of human rights groups and non-governmental organizations, by declaring them *un objetivo militar*—a military target—and by affirming its intention to abduct these individuals."[5] It has similarly threatened and abducted members of the peace movement in Colombia. More than twenty-five such individuals have been killed or "disappeared" since the beginning of 1997.[6] American peace workers in Peace Brigades International were also declared *un objetivo militar* in early 2001.[7]

Far from being marginalized by the increased U.S. presence, the paramilitary death squads work in conjunction with it, killing and terrorizing in the coca fields so that U.S. planes can then spray at low levels with impunity.[8]

Meanwhile the number of displaced people in Colombia continues to escalate dramatically. In 1998 approximately 300,000 were driven from their homes (according to the State Department), largely by paramilitary activity. Now some estimate the total to be 1.5–2.0 million.[9] Most of the recent victims are fleeing from the aerial crop spraying, which kills coca, legitimate crops, and fish in fish farms; it also sickens peasants and their livestock.[10]

COLOMBIA AS VIETNAM

If this nightmare program is to be stopped, the change of direction must come from the United States. But the situation is paradoxical. Plan Colombia has lost its original key planners and proponents, such as Major Andrew Messing and Congressman Gilman. The opinions offered in most news stories on Plan Colombia continue to range from mild criticism to moral outrage; the plan currently seems to have no vocal defenders outside the Washington bureaucracy.

Should the critics take heart from this consensus? I think not. Plan Colombia's proponents originally projected a "successful" campaign on the model of El Salvador—a dirty war in which Washington delegated the killing of insurgents to U.S.-trained local forces. Today more and more observers are seeing analogies with America's failed adventure in Vietnam. The tactics are eerily similar: from military advisers, high-tech listening posts, defoliation programs, river boats, and helicopters, to assaults on the countryside that displace hundreds of thousands of civilians.[11]

Equally similar are the interests and lobbies: the helicopter and herbicide industries, the oil companies, and the Pentagon seeking new bases in the area. One hears the same geopolitical rhetoric about sea lanes and natural resources. Professional think tanks, such as RAND and FPRI, are reinforcing the madness in Washington, with their proposals on how to make an ill-starred policy even worse.[12] And there is the same ominous background of deep-rooted links to local drug kingpins—as in Afghanistan, Peru, Haiti, Honduras, and Kosovo.

All of the analogies with Vietnam—and there are many—derive from one fundamental similarity: demands from major U.S. oil corporations for increased security have led the U.S. government still further into a de facto alliance with local right-wing forces involved in drug trafficking.[13] (The 1960s threat to U.S. oil companies came in Indonesia, not Vietnam, but it is clear that U.S. strategic thinking for Southeast Asia, as epitomized in the so-called domino theory, arose from a concern about losing oil assets in Indonesia.)[14] In thus pointing at the deep politics of oil and drugs, I do not mean to suggest that other interests and lobbies are irrelevant. But drugs and oil have this in common: they exert powerful influences over a broad spectrum, often beneath the surface.

Insufficiently recognized in the furor about Plan Colombia is the role of U.S. oil companies in lobbying for an increased U.S. military commitment to the area. Since Bush launched the Andean initiative in 1989, Colombian oil production has risen almost 80 percent. Most of the exports have gone to the United States, making Colombia the eighth-largest supplier of foreign crude oil to the United States.[15]

I have written elsewhere how in 1963 an employee of the Socony Mobil oil company, William Henderson, made a concerted public appeal for a "final commitment" to Southeast Asia, meaning "that we must be prepared to fight . . . at a minimum."[16] In like manner U.S. oil corporations have waged a concerted campaign for U.S. engagement in Colombia since at least the mid-1990s.

In 1996, BP Amoco and Occidental joined Enron Corporation, a Houston-based energy firm, and other corporations to form the U.S.-Colombia Business Partnership. Since then, backed by hefty oil-industry donations to political candidates, the partnership has lobbied hard for increased aid. Lawrence P. Meriage, Occidental's public-affairs vice president, not only pushed for Plan Colombia last year but urged a House subcommittee to extend military aid to the nations north to augment security for oil development operations.[17]

Thus the ultimate concern of some is to protect what is on the ground for as long as possible, even if there is no hope of winning. In Colombia as once in Vietnam we see again a prevailing consensus among experts that what is now being done is doomed to fail and cannot possibly meet its proclaimed objectives. From the perspective of government the pattern is the same: a large bureaucracy, unable to change direction, continuing for years to supplement a failed policy with supplemental efforts which those in charge know are unlikely to succeed.[18] We have seen that large-scale dysfunctional policies, like the so-called war on drugs, are not amenable to rational criticism. They tend instead to metastasize from a policy into a bureaucratic habit: a habit in which failure, predictably, becomes a case for escalation.

Six months into the 2000 Bush administration we heard again the warnings that used to predate successive escalations in Vietnam. According to the RAND Corporation, "The United States is confronting a deteriorating military situation in Colombia that could present the Bush administration with the choice of retreat or much deeper involvement." Conceding that crop-eradication efforts have not prevented a spike in cocaine efforts, the RAND report called on the United States to expand its focus from antinarcotics to antiguerrilla operations. Failure would present the United States with what the report called "an unpalatable choice. . . . It could escalate its commitment, to include perhaps an operational role for U.S. forces in Colombia, or scale it down, which could involve some significant costs, including a serious loss of credibility."[19]

Another similarity is the apparent management of U.S. news reporting out of Colombia. Until September 1998 it was normal in the North American press to refer to Colombia as a narco-democracy: my Lexis-Nexis index cites sixty-nine uses of the term between 1992 and September 1998 (including seven in 1998).[20] This is only appropriate for a country where for twenty years the drug cartels have contributed to the electoral campaigns of presidential candidates, and frequently (as in 1978, 1982, and perhaps 1994) to all of them.[21] Since the introduction of Plan Colombia, however, the term "narco-democracy" has vanished from the North American press. Colombia is still presented as a state under siege, but the enemy now (as in the 1970s) is presented as the revolutionary FARC (or what the press now, following General McCaffrey, called narco-guerrillas).

Still another similarity is the endlessly repeated promise that, no matter what happens, the U.S. role in the field will remain an advisory one. This is being said even as the United States is supplementing its official advisory deployment of from 250 to 500 persons with additional personnel in two "private" corporations enjoying DOD contracts, DynCorp and MPRI (Military Professional Resources, Inc.).[22] This practice of "outsourcing" sensitive work to these same corporations was practiced earlier in Croatia, Bosnia, and Kosovo. The personnel are in fact drawn from the U.S. armed services, and it is reported that employees can return with their contract years counting toward their seniority in government service.

There is another analogy here too, with the case of Air America pilots in Indochina.[23] One neglected reason for the bureaucratic inertia in Vietnam that led to repeated escalations was precisely the motive to supply business for underutilized support services, notably military air transport.[24] Then and now, the Pentagon's strategic posture requires the maintenance of contractual ties to private air transport lines that can switch from civilian to military air freight when needed. An otherwise foolish escalation in Laos by the CIA and Pentagon in 1959 makes more bureaucratic sense when seen against contemporary threats by the main air carrier to the Far East (Pan Am) to scale back its international operations "if traffic—other than normal civil traffic—doesn't become available." Pan Am's crisis was quickly solved by the ensuing Laotian airlift.[25]

Plan Colombia has played a similar role in restructuring Southern Air Transport, which declared bankruptcy in September 1998.[26] SAT had realized considerable profits from the Persian Gulf War in 1990 but was unable to survive from civilian business thereafter: "According to bankruptcy-court records, the air-cargo division of Southern Air was bleeding red ink in the mid-90s. It lost $24.9 million in 1995. . . . In 1997, Southern Air's air-cargo division lost money every month—more than $39 million for the year."[27]

But 1999 saw two other air cargo lines competing with SAT's successor, Southern Air, to gain access to SAT's designated U.S.-Colombia all-cargo scheduled service.[28] The tempo is clearly changing:

> Air cargo executives from around the globe have been invoking Latin America like
> a mantra for the past two years as one of the most promising areas for their industry.

The optimism was muted at times due to the volatile situation in some countries but overall, it has steadily gathered momentum. Today, with traditionally buoyant routes across the Pacific showing deteriorating yields, the region is even more regarded as the emerging El Dorado for air freight.[29]

Plan Colombia has been a similar bonanza for the Pentagon's outsourced training teams from the firms DynCorp and MPRI. Both corporations have a history of airlift and training contracts for the U.S. government from Korea to Croatia, Bosnia, and Kosovo. With the decline of U.S. engagement in the Balkans, Colombia has become a focus of their endeavors (although their elaborate websites do not show this). DynCorp's five-year contract with the State Department for Colombia amounts to $170 million.[30]

Those who remember Vietnam in the 1960s know that the muted contract requirements of the war business will outweigh vocal warnings in newspaper op-eds in determining the future of foreign commitments. We have also learned from Vietnam that the risks of unilateral U.S. escalation increase when there are real prospects for negotiated solutions—such as we have seen with the renewal of talks between President Pastrana and FARC. Thirty-five years ago I called this phenomenon "the politics of escalation." Already a cogently argued article has depicted an analogous pattern in the U.S. buildup in Colombia.[31]

Since 1950 the United States has extricated itself without pain from only two unwinnable situations—Somalia and Lebanon—and in neither case did the Pentagon risk its credibility. After forty years of active involvement in Colombia, it is hard to think what would make the United States voluntarily pull back. Overwhelming common sense has clearly proven insufficient. The increasing tide of international disapproval, from Europe to Brazil, has had no effect. The alienation of nearby governments and publics, notably in Ecuador and Venezuela, has been overridden.[32] Nor have the cautious admonitions of pundits and editorials been heeded.

This escalating disaster is likely sooner or later to produce one more analogy with Vietnam: the growing disaffection and opposition of Americans. Even the Pentagon should have no interest in seeing a reemergence of that widespread social alienation, the Vietnam syndrome. Yet it is clear by now that the United States cannot over a long period involve itself in warfare and terrorism abroad without threatening its peace and security at home.

It is fair to argue that international drug trafficking networks, in Colombia and elsewhere, present a significant threat to U.S. security. As exports have noted, drug trafficking routes "can be harnessed to more lethal purposes, such as transporting teams of contract assassins across international boundaries or smuggling missiles . . . and atomic mines and warheads to terrorist nations and groups."[33]

With the passage of time, we see more and more evidence of collaboration between the Colombian and Venezuelan traffickers, the Italian and Turkish Mafias, and smugglers in the Far East and former Soviet Union.[34] There are reports from time to time of global summit meetings to coordinate not only drug and cash flows, but the smuggling of illegal immigrants, prostitutes, and counterfeit money. Unfortunately in Colombia we have not targeted the largest enemy. Though its role has increased, FARC is still more marginal to this international threat than right-wing former CIA assets and their successors that are central to it.[35] This country's perception of the problem has been perverted by five decades of false U.S. propaganda about communist drug trafficking, propaganda designed to veil U.S. assistance and protection to a world of right-wing anticommunist traffickers.[36] The new onslaught of hype about the narco-guerrilla menace is only the latest effort from those who have not outgrown the worst habits of the Cold War. To resist them will take concerted efforts from groups outside the U.S. government.

NOTES

1. U.S. Department of State, "United States Support for Colombia: Fact Sheet Released by the Bureau of Western Hemisphere Affairs," March 28, 2000, www.state.gov/www/regions/wha/colombia/fs_000328_plancolombia.html.
2. The U.S. State Department did play a role in initiating the peace process at a preliminary meeting in Costa Rica. However, the United States withdrew from the talks after FARC acknowledged that one of its leaders was responsible for the unauthorized killing of three American activists working with the U'wa Indians.
3. Center for Defense Information, *Show Transcript: Colombia in Crisis*. N.d.
4. *Washington Post*, November 7, 2000.
5. Reuters, November 17, 1998 (chainsaws); Amnesty International, "Enough Is Enough!" *Amnesty International Report* AMR 23/48/99 (threats).
6. Amnesty International, "Enough Is Enough!" In June 2001 Castaño resigned from the post of AUC military chief, allegedly "to oversee the group's political wing" (*New York Times*, June 7, 2001). Some saw in this move a split inside the AUC; others that Castaño was positioning himself for a larger role in Colombia's political future.
7. *San Francisco Chronicle*, February 12, 2001.
8. Jeremy Bigwood, "DynCorp in Colombia: Outsourcing the Drug War," www.corpwatch.org.
9. *San Francisco Chronicle*, December 19, 2000.
10. See, for example, *Baltimore Sun*, June 1, 2000; *New York Times*, January 21, 2001; *Toronto Star*, January 12, 2001.
11. See, for example, Tad Szulc, "The Ghost of Vietnam Haunts 'Plan Colombia,'" *Los Angeles Times*, August 20, 2000.
12. The fallacies of "objective" quantification in Vietnam are repeating themselves, as in the following: "Ordinary Colombians . . . openly support the AUC. In fact, opinion polls suggest that AUC leader Carlos Castaño has at least twice the approval of FARC supreme [commander] Manuel Marulanda" (Michael Radu, "Colombia: A Trip Report," June 1, 2001; available from FPRI).

13. When Occidental Oil discovered the billion-barrel Caño Limon oil field in 1983, this transformed Colombia from a net importer of crude oil "into a major oil-exporting nation" (testimony of Lawrence P. Meriage, vice president, Occidental Oil and Gas Corporation, House Government Reform Subcommittee on Criminal Justice, Drug Policy, and Human Resources, February 15, 2000, www.ciponline.org/colombia/021507.htm). The White House and CIA escalation against imaginary "narco-guerrillas" began the next year, in 1984, and led to NSDD 221 in 1986.

14. Peter Dale Scott, "The United States and the Overthrow of Sukarno, 1965–1967," www.pir.org/scott.html.

15. Testimony of Lawrence P. Meriage, February 15, 2000; Thad Dunning and Leslie Wirpsa, "Oil Rigged: There's Something Slippery about the U.S. Drug War in Colombia," www.americas.org, February 2001.

16. William Henderson, Asia Society Conference of May 10–11, 1963; quoted in Peter Dale Scott, "The Vietnam War and the CIA-Financial Establishment," in Mark Selden, ed., *Remaking Asia* (New York: Pantheon, 1974), 127. In addition to being an adviser on international affairs to Socony Mobil, Henderson was an officer of American Friends of Vietnam. See chapter 2 in this volume.

17. Dunning and Wirpsa, "Oil Rigged": "The firms have allies in the U.S. national-security apparatus. In 1998, Gen. Charles Wilhelm, then head of the U.S. Southern Command, told Congress that oil discoveries had increased Colombia's strategic importance. Last April, Sen. Bob Graham (D-Florida) and former National Security Adviser Brent Scowcroft warned in a Los Angeles Times editorial that Colombia's reserves would remain untapped unless stability is restored."

18. See, for example, David Kaiser, *American Tragedy: Kennedy, Johnson, and the Origins of the Vietnam War* (Cambridge: Harvard University Press, Belknap Press, 2000), 488–93; Larry Berman, *Lyndon Johnson's War: The Road to Stalemate in Vietnam* (New York: Norton, 1989). The clearest statement of this conclusion is in Daniel Ellsberg, *Papers on the War* (New York: Simon & Schuster, 1972).

19. *Chicago Tribune*, June 10, 2001. At the same time, Michael Radu, researcher for the formerly CIA-subsidized Foreign Policy Research Institute, has written that the solution to Colombian political violence is to "arm the civilian population" (i.e., the AUC and Castaño): "It is time for the United States to see Andres Pastrana as . . . a disastrous failure and, more relevant, a lame duck" (Michael Radu, "Colombia: A Trip Report," distributed by fpri.org, June 1, 2001).

20. A characteristic passage is the following from the *Toronto Star*, August 21, 1998: "Colombia is a chaotic 'narco-democracy' where powerful drug barons, major landowners, the army, the guerrillas and private armies (who tax the drug industry, when they're not dabbling in it) all have a vested interest in preserving both the war, and the country's status as the world's leading cocaine producer. A fair chunk of Colombia's $100 billion economy—the World Bank reckons $7 billion—flows from the drug trade. El Tiempo, the country's leading newspaper, puts the cost of the war at $8 billion."

21. Mark Bowden, *Killing Pablo* (New York: Atlantic Monthly Press, 2001), 30, 33, 35, passim.

22. *Dallas Morning News*, August 19, 1898: "One U.S. reporter who attempted to talk to Dyncorp pilots at San José del Guaviare said he was threatened with banishment from the U.S. Embassy if he ever attempted to approach Dyncorp personnel again. Another

reporter said he was banned from embassy-sponsored briefings after the reporter quoted a guerrilla leader as saying that U.S. military advisers would now be targeted for attack."

23. For contracting out of U.S. policy in the Iran-Contra era to quasi-private corporations (including Southern Air Transport), see Jonathan Marshall, Peter Dale Scott, and Jane Hunter, *The Iran-Contra Connection: Secret Teams and Covert Operations in the Reagan Era* (Boston: South End, 1987), 7–17.

24. Concern about the danger of entrusting outside contractors with command positions has been voiced inside the Pentagon establishment. "Three years ago a paper written at the Army War College by a Colonel Bruce Grant warned: 'Foreign policy is (being) made by default (by) private military consultants motivated by bottom-line profits'" (*Guardian* [London], June 2, 2001).

25. Peter Dale Scott, *The War Conspiracy: The Secret Road to the Second Indochina War* (Indianapolis: Bobbs-Merrill, 1972), 197–99.

26. *Columbus Dispatch*, August 25, 1999.

27. *Columbus Dispatch*, April 4, 1999. In the 1990s (just as twenty years before) SAT claimed to have severed its CIA ties. But intrigues persisted: bankruptcy examiners found that $32 million of SAT assets had been moved before bankruptcy into the personal bank account of the wife of the owner, a former CIA lawyer.

28. See Department of Transport Docket OST-96–1153, www.airlineinfo.com/ost-html2/347.htm. The airlines competing with Southern Air are Polar Air Cargo and Kitty Hawk Aircargo, Inc. Also in the Latin America air cargo picture is Taiwan's EVA Air, apparently a successor to the former CIA proprietary Evergreen Air.

29. *Journal of Commerce*, July 8, 1996.

30. Associated Press, June 5, 2001.

31. Franz Schurmann, Peter Dale Scott, and Reginald Zelnik, *The Politics of Escalation in Vietnam* (Boston: Beacon, 1967); Mark Cook, "Colombia: The Politics of Escalation," *Covert Action Quarterly*, Fall–Winter 1999.

32. Tad Szulc, *International Herald Tribune*, December 29, 2000. More than one Ecuadorean high official has expressed fear that "if Colombia is going to be another Vietnam, as everyone keeps saying, then Ecuador is going to become the Cambodia of this war" (*New York Times*, January 8, 2001; cf. *Gazette* [Montreal], February 9, 2001).

33. Patrick Clawson and Rensselaer W. Lee III, *The Andean Cocaine Industry* (New York: St. Martin's, 1996), 89.

34. Claire Sterling, *Thieves' World* (New York: Simon & Schuster, 1994); John Kerry, *The New War* (New York: Simon & Schuster, 1997).

35. As part of its growing institutionalization, FARC has developed its own connections to the international drug milieu. In November 2000 the Mexican government announced that FARC was sending drugs to Mexican traffickers in exchange for arms, and a drug shipment seized in May 2001 (on the ship *Svesda Maru,* whose crew were Russians and Ukrainians) was attributed to this connection (*Singapore Straits Times*, May 18, 2001). Escalation of the anti-FARC war by the Bush administration is, in my view, likely to increase FARC involvement in the international drugs and arms markets.

36. For concrete examples, see Peter Dale Scott, *Deep Politics and the Death of JFK* (Berkeley: University of California Press), 166–77.

III

Indochina, Opium, and Oil (from
The War Conspiracy, 1972)

7

Overview: Public, Private, and Covert Political Power

In my book The War Conspiracy, *I examined forces that helped lead the United States into the Vietnam War. Many of these factors involved not only deceptions but repeated contraventions of authority, civilian control, and even the law. For this reason I grouped them together under the admittedly awkward term "war conspiracy," even as I made it clear that I was not pointing to some single group of guilty plotters, but to sustained patterns of collusion and deceit involving different players.[1]*

Like all the following chapters except chapter 11, this one was written before the first authoritative story in the New York Times *on June 6, 1971, about heroin reaching the United States from labs in Laos under the control of the Royal Laotian Army.[2] Thus it discusses the relationship between oil, lobbying, and U.S. foreign policy; but it is silent about the problem of drug trafficking discussed in chapter 11.*

In terms of what we know now, the analysis in this chapter is unduly limited to deception and manipulation by lower officials, whereas in many key manipulations (notably the alleged second Tonkin Gulf incident), we can now see the controlling hand of the White House. However, I believe that in broad outline both the facts and the analysis presented here are still worth considering today.

Consider the unauthorized activity in Taiwan, discussed below, of Admiral Charles M. Cooke in 1950. Cooke headed a private military mission for which his ally William Pawley tried but failed in 1949 to secure from Secretary of State Acheson the authorization he had secured earlier for Chennault's Flying Tigers during World War II.[3] In this expansion of U.S. involvement by the China lobby, of which Cooke was a well-connected member, Cooke was also supported by other influential circles. The firm set up for the mission, Commerce International China, was a subsidiary of William Donovan's World Commerce Corporation, a firm backed by leading capitalists like Nelson Rockefeller, with its own agenda for promoting capitalism in the postwar era. The firm was run by S. G. (Sonny) Fassoulis, who a few years later would be indicted in connection with manipulations of securities by organized crime. Fassoulis was apparently picked for the job by a "Col. Williams of the Army," presumably the Colonel Garland Williams who performed many intelligence functions through his work with the Federal Bureau of Narcotics. "Texas oil people" were also in the background.[4]

What is instructive here is the way official reluctance was overcome by those with influential crime connections below, backed by influential financial interests above, with an intelligence officer serving as go-between. As I recount in my book Deep Politics, *this is a recurring pattern. Thus I am now reprinting what I wrote in 1971, with only minimal corrections. I have not even deleted the book's recurring appeals for congressional or judicial redress, although such appeals would appear to have far less chance today than in 1971–1972. In these last five chapters I have, however, updated my 1971 text with new information relevant to this book's major themes of drugs, oil, and war.*

In the two decades after 1950, the year of the Korean War and the China lobby, there was never a genuine U.S. deescalation in Southeast Asia. Every apparent deescalation of the fighting, such as in Vietnam in 1954 and Laos in 1961–1962, was balanced by an escalation, often unnoticed at the time, whose long-range result increased America's war effort. In 1954, for example, America's direct involvement in the first Indochina war was limited to a few dozen USAF planes and pilots "on loan" to Chennault's airline, Civil Air Transport (CAT), plus two hundred USAF technicians to service them. Though Dulles, Radford, and Nixon failed to implement their proposals for U.S. air strikes and/or troop intervention, Dulles was able to substitute for the discarded plan for immediate intervention a "proposal for creating a Southeast Asia Treaty Organization."[5] SEATO soon became a cover for U.S. "limited war" games in Southeast Asia, which in turn grew into the first covert U.S. military involvement in Laos in 1959—the start of the second Indochina war.

In early 1961 Kennedy resisted energetic pressures from his Joint Chiefs to invade Laos openly with up to 60,000 soldiers, empowered, if necessary, to use tactical nuclear weapons. (Nixon also conferred with Kennedy and again urged, at the least, "a commitment of American air power.")[6] Unwilling with his limited reserves to initiate major operations simultaneously in both Laos and Cuba, Kennedy settled for a political solution in Laos, beginning with a cease-fire that went into effect on May 3, 1961. On May 4–5, 1961, Rusk and Kennedy announced the first of a series of measures to strengthen the U.S. military commitment in South Vietnam. The timing suggests that the advocates of a showdown with China in one country had been placated by the quid pro quo of a buildup in another. In like manner the final conclusion of the 1962 Geneva agreements on

Laos came only after the United States had satisfied Asian and domestic hawks by its first commitment of U.S. combat troops to the area, in Thailand.

In 1968, finally, we now know that the "deescalation" announced by President Johnson in March and October, in the form of a cessation of the bombing of North Vietnam, was misleading. In fact the same planes were simply diverted from North Vietnam to Laos: the overall level of bombing, far from decreasing, continued to increase.

Unhappily one has to conclude that up to 1970 there was simply no precedent for a genuine U.S. deescalation in Southeast Asia, though there were illusory appearances of it. The Cambodian and Laotian adventures under Nixon were only more proof, for anyone who still needed it, that the U.S. crisis in Southeast Asia was only the outward manifestation of a continuing crisis of government at home in America.

This book attempted to outline the hidden history of these U.S. escalations in Southeast Asia by focusing on key crises that helped to bring escalation about. Though each chapter was a separate essay, I believed that an understanding of each episode would contribute to the understanding of all the rest, particularly as they helped break down the false picture of these events that was carefully impressed on America.

The initial false picture is of a peace-loving America reluctantly drawn into Asia through a series of "responses" to various acts of aggression by socialist countries, such as a "massive" North Vietnamese invasion of Laos in 1959, an impending invasion of Thailand in 1962, an unprovoked attack on two U.S. destroyers in 1964, and an imminent invasion of South Vietnam from Cambodia in 1970.[7] These episodes will not be properly understood until they have been seen in their context as part of a process or syndrome, the repeated use of intelligence agencies and their allies to prepare the conditions for escalation. This covert preparation, through provocation, connivance, and deceit, is the process which, at the risk of oversimplifying, I called "the war conspiracy."

A second false picture of these same U.S. escalations was found even among elements of the U.S. peace movement. According to this version, U.S. involvement arose accidentally through a series of "mistakes." The distorted claims of aggression to which the U.S. "responded" arose through mistakes of perception on our part, to be attributed to American naïveté or anticommunist paranoia, to failures of communications or of command-and-control procedures, or to the clumsiness of mammoth bureaucracies and the difficulties of handling the vast amounts of information they deal with every day. Every one of these incidents was now attributed to a breakdown of this intelligence, and by an interesting corollary the same incidents could become grounds for increasing the U.S. intelligence establishment so that such "mistakes" would not occur in future.

But, as we shall see, it was precisely the activities of U.S. intelligence personnel (including those with responsibilities for covert or "special" operations) that repeatedly gave rise to these false perceptions in Washington. It would appear that the very apparatus that should have relayed objective intelligence instead manufactured false pretexts for unilateral U.S. aggression. In every one of the critical escalations mentioned (as well as in other episodes for which we have little or no space) U.S. intelligence personnel were chiefly responsible for escalating our involvement.

To correct this picture of accidental or mistaken involvement I spoke of a "war conspiracy," by which I meant the sustained resort to collusion and conspiracy, unauthorized provocations, and fraud by U.S. personnel, particularly intelligence personnel, in order to sustain or increase our military commitment in Asia. I meant no more than this. I was aware that the total picture is more complex than any single phrase or narrative could suggest, and that other factors, not so covert, also contributed to our Asian involvement. War conspiracy itself is as much a symptom as a cause of the war mentality it furthers, for where the management and censorship of news are commonplace, the manipulation and outright invention of it are invited. The war conspiracy is to be seen as a general syndrome, not as the work of a single private cabal; nor is it necessary to think that war was always the intention of these collusions, as well as their result.

On the contrary, both the personnel and the concerns of the war conspiracy changed widely over twenty years. Until the late 1960s this change was continuously in the direction of militarization. In the 1950s our concealed involvement was mostly restricted to a few enterprising individuals like General Chennault and his "private" airline, Civil Air Transport (now known better as Air America), or such flamboyant CIA field operatives as Colonel Lansdale or Robert Campbell James (a cousin of the Socony president, B. B. Jennings). In the 1960s the picture was militarized. CIA field operatives were supplemented or supplanted by the primitive cadres of "special forces," while the labors of military ELINT—electronics intelligence—personnel contributed to our soon being involved in a full-scale U.S. ground and air war. By 1970 the once aggressive CIA seemed to include some of the stronger voices for peace within the administration, while the war camp seemed to be located chiefly within the competing military intelligence services. In other words, the conspiracy must be seen as a continuing process on the model of a long-lived vital organ in which the organizing functions survive the transient cells which make it up. A more down-to-earth analogy would be that of a floating illegal crap game in which the players (and dealers) change, but not the motive of gain.

In a like manner, even though one can talk of U.S. imperialism in Southeast Asia, the specific objectives of this imperialism seem to have varied widely in two decades. In the early 1950s the desire to secure stocks of scarce war materials like tungsten seems to have figured largely in our covert backing of Chinese Nationalist guerrillas in Burma through Chennault's airline. Later the same airline seems to have been used in Laos as part of a new U.S. preoccupation with the technology of a covert or limited war. Doubtless in 1971 U.S. intervention in Asia was backed by prospects of quick-term profits (in the range of 35 percent per annum or even more) from investments in the region, particularly by hopes of new oil discoveries off the shores of Thailand and Cambodia in the South China Sea. After late 1968 offshore drilling activity in Southeast Asia doubled, and there were predictions that the area might soon "emerge as the world's most active exploration and drilling area."[8] In 1970 nearly all of the South China Sea floor north of Java and Sumatra was allocated in concessions to the international oil companies, with the exception of a particularly promising area off the coast of Cambodia and South Vietnam, where offshore drilling had also begun.[9]

Despite the apparent diversity of groups and interests in these successive phases of U.S. involvement, the story in this book reveals a latent continuity underlying them. Take, for example, the private law firm of Thomas G. Corcoran, which organized both Chennault's Flying Tigers and CAT.[10] In the early 1950s Corcoran represented CAT, the insurance interests in Asia of C. V. Starr (a former OSS agent) and United Fruit; and was said by *Fortune* to maintain "the finest intelligence service in Washington":

> Most of [his clients] are companies with international interests and he has a choice clientele in this field. It includes United Fruit Co., American International Underwriters Corp. (part of the C. V. Starr interests in Asia and elsewhere) and General Claire Chennault's Civil Air Transport, Inc. In late 1951 Corcoran, for one example, was working his intelligence service overtime keeping up with American policy on Iran—what the State Department did in this affair would be a guide to what it might or might not do to keep his client, United Fruit, from being thrown out of Guatemala.[11]

After the successful CIA coup against Mossadeq in Iran, Chennault's partner Whiting Willauer went from CAT to be U.S. ambassador in Honduras, where he helped United Fruit officials and the CIA overthrow Arbenz in Guatemala. Miguel Ydigoras Fuentes, an anticommunist who later succeeded the CIA's Castillo Armas as president of Guatemala, tells how a retired executive of United Fruit tried to recruit him for the coup, and how, when in office, a "Washington law firm" told him: "they had financed the 'liberation movement' of Castillo Armas, who had committed himself to certain payments. On his death he still owed them $1,800,000, and as they considered me to be his heir they held me responsible for payment."[12]

In 1960, while Willauer, United Fruit officials, and CAT pilots were participating in the CIA's preparations for the Bay of Pigs, Chennault's airline Civil Air Transport (soon to be better known as Air America) took part in the CIA's overthrow of Souvanna Phouma in Laos, and it served later as part of the infrastructure for the CIA's secret Laotian war. Previously one of the principal U.S. financial interests in Indochina was the Compagnie Franco-Américaine d'Assurances of Saigon owned by Corcoran's client C. V. Starr and Company, whose president by 1960 was Corcoran's law partner William S. Youngman. But after

1950 Corcoran also represented some of the oil companies that since 1963 expressed more and more interest in offshore drilling in the South China Sea. One of these was the Tenneco Corporation, which already held two concessions in the Gulf of Siam between Thailand and Cambodia and acquired further interests in the concession of Frontier Petroleum near Singapore.

Thus, on a functional or operating level, diverse intelligence operations such as in Guatemala and Laos, and diverse overseas economic interests such as in bananas, insurance, and oil, are revealed to be part of one continuous story. At least through 1968 Corcoran's law partners Ernest Cuneo (ex-OSS), Robert Amory (ex-CIA), and James Rowe (one of Lyndon Johnson's earliest advisers along with Corcoran himself) continued to keep closely in touch with Asian developments through both the CIA and the White House. Furthermore, the apparently diverse economic interests who chose to be represented by Corcoran's firm (like United Fruit, CAT, and C. V. Starr) turn out, on closer examination, to be less differentiated than the usual pluralistic models of American society would have us think.

Robert Lehman, for example, was for years a director of both United Fruit and Pan Am Airlines, which after supplying the operating cadres for CAT went on to profit directly as the backup for its Indochina operations. And at least two Pan Am officials associated with Chennault (Gordon Tweedy and John S. Woodbridge) were also intimately involved in C. V. Starr's worldwide insurance operations. The private influence of Corcoran's law firm on U.S. policy appears to be one good reason why in 1957 *Fortune* could report that Robert Lehman's family investment firm of Lehman Brothers (also involved in international oil operations) had experienced by 1957 "the greatest postwar growth of any Wall Street house" and was "one of the biggest profit makers—many believe the biggest."[13]

In other words, powerful economic interests have from the outset been behind the covert instrumentalities such as CAT that contributed to our initial involvement in Southeast Asia. The simple fact of their hidden association with these efforts does not of itself prove to what extent U.S. involvements were motivated by hope of private profit. This is a complex question, and the reader will have to decide for himself (see chapter 11) whether to call CAT (alias Air America) a private "cover" for the implementation of public U.S. policy, or, alternatively, an instrument whereby public resources were committed to the support of private interests. (One cannot talk here narrowly of "private U.S. interests": we shall see that Nationalist Chinese capital, often said to derive from the Soong family, helped to pay for the total Air America operation, just as Nationalist Chinese pilots and personnel helped to man its planes.) The power of intelligence networks is not simply bureaucratic but arises in particular from their close alliance and interaction with private wealth as well as public authority.

The story became more complex in the 1960s, as it became militarized and intensified. After 1959 private economic motives for staying in Indochina were reinforced by bureaucratic motives, the latter sometimes at variance with the former, and U.S. intervention involved far more than the operations of a single agency and paramilitary airline. Air America (which lost its monopoly on covert air operations in 1960) was no longer the central U.S. intelligence enterprise in Southeast Asia combining private wealth with public authority. In the 1960s its wealth and importance were surpassed by those of industries specializing in intelligence technology, such as Itek (the CIA-linked electronics firm) and Ling-Temco-Vought, which supply the supersecret electronic equipment for ELINT operations such as those of *Maddox* and *Pueblo*.[14] Personnel of these intelligence industries were often intimately concerned in preparations for, and occasionally even of the operations of, ELINT missions. There were many other ways in which private companies supplied covers, personnel, or infrastructure for intelligence operations.

Once again, however, this polymorphous and perverse picture of private-public relations is not as pluralistic as at first it might appear. Underlying both the military intelligence operations of the 1960s and the "civilian" intelligence operations of the 1950s, we find the same financial interests. As only one example of this continuing financial base for U.S. involvement, I shall cite the fact that Harper Woodward, who served in the 1950s as a director of CAT, continues to 1970 to serve as a director of Itek. This was not just because Woodward specialized in offering services to the CIA. He was where he was as an "associate" (i.e., employee) of Laurance Rockefeller, a member of a family whose oil and financial interests (chiefly in Standard Oil of New Jersey and Socony Mobil) were worldwide.

It is assuredly no coincidence that Nelson Rockefeller helped sound the alarm about scarce raw materials in 1951,[15] nor that Laurance Rockefeller headed the Rockefeller Brothers Fund Panel Two, which first offered a public blueprint for limited war spending in 1957, nor that the Rockefellers and Socony Mobil hosted Diem and Thai officials in America in the 1950s. (John D. Rockefeller III's Asian Society supplied a forum in 1963 for a Socony Mobil employee who, in the company of several spokesmen with intelligence backgrounds, called publicly for the kind of overt U.S. intervention in Vietnam affairs that began a year later, after the assassinations of Ngo Dinh Diem and John F. Kennedy.)[16] Robert Lehman and the Rockefellers, Wall Street financiers, were personally financially involved in the whole range of economic interests that have been served by the Vietnam War. (James Rockefeller, a cousin, was a fellow director with Lehman of Pan Am.)

In the face of such pervasive economic interest in the background of intelligence operations, particularly those contributing to the Vietnam War, one is tempted to retreat from the "accidental" fallacy about U.S. involvement to the opposite conclusion: acceptance of it as inevitable and unopposable. In the introduction to his valuable essay, Gabriel Kolko asserted, as "a central reality," that "a ruling class makes its policies operate" through a pervasive "business-defined consensus"; and he added that "to understand this essential fact is also to reject conspiratorial theories." [17] From such arguments it is all too easy to conclude that the rest of us do not have the means or institutions to oppose this class.

But it is certain that Kolko underestimated the contradictions underlying U.S. policy in Vietnam since 1944, as for example when he stated that "Despite the almost paranoid belief of the French representative that the O.S.S. was working against France, the O.S.S. only helped consolidate Washington's support for the French. They . . . were unanimous in believing that Ho is . . . a Communist." [18] An Institute of Pacific Relations article by OSS veteran George Sheldon in 1946 spoke favorably of the Viet Minh and critically of French atrocities in the postwar period. It observed that Ho Chi Minh was "formally elected by a vast majority" in the elections of January 1946, and added that "Neutral observers, including Americans, testified that the election was conducted in an efficient and orderly fashion and that the overwhelming popularity of President Ho was undeniable." [19] It is true that such surprising candor from intelligence officers became much rarer after the persecution of the Institute of Pacific Relations for its heresies by the right-wing McCarran Committee in 1952. But that successful campaign by the China lobby, in which Owen Lattimore was defended by top Washington lawyers Thurman Arnold and Abe Fortas, was only one of the many signs in that era of contradictions and struggle *between* powerful American factions.

In like manner, if a single-minded class explanation of U.S. policy were adequate, then there would have been no need for intelligence conspiracies, no Laos invasion fraud in 1959, no second Tonkin Gulf "incident" in 1964. American forces would simply have moved into Laos and Vietnam as nakedly and as arrogantly as the Soviet tanks moved into Czechoslovakia. It may be that we shall see such naked U.S. aggression in the future, but the past suggests that the issue of escalation has up till now divided the U.S. government. The same incidents that showed the grave challenge to our constitutional processes also revealed, by their very resort to connivance and collusion, that these processes are not yet meaningless.

There are legal restrictions on collusive aggressive activity. Sections 956–60 of the U.S. Criminal Code, for example, forbid conspiracies to injure the property of any foreign state, the hiring or retaining of persons within the United States for enlistment in any foreign military service, and the furnishing of money for any military enterprise against the territory of any foreign state. These laws were violated at least six times in the course of our covert intervention in Southeast Asia: with respect to Taiwan (1950 and 1952), Vietnam (1953), and Burma (1951–1953, if not later), Indonesia (1958), and Laos (1959).

In all cases a pretext of legality was supplied by the same fiction: U.S. military officers in foreign service were not employed by the foreign country directly but by a private company with a foreign government contract. This legal cover was first devised by President Roosevelt for Chennault's Flying Tigers in 1941, but he secretly authorized it by an unlisted executive order (April 15, 1941).

It would appear that in late April 1953, when USAF planes and pilots were "loaned" to Chennault's CAT for use by the French in Indochina, this procedure was again authorized "at the highest level."[20] Thus U.S. involvement in the first Indochina war was covert but not conspiratorial: no private individuals had plotted against the authority of the U.S. government.

The legal picture was different in 1950, when Admiral Charles M. Cooke, as head of a private military advisory group for Chiang Kai-shek's government on Taiwan, was employed by a firm known as CIC, or Commerce International (China). Cooke himself later complained that he sought, but failed to obtain, any presidential authorization for his plans ("I never received any action one way or the other on these recommendations; no red light, no green light").[21]

In the case of the Tonkin and *Pueblo* incidents, there were indications in these remarkably similar scenarios that U.S. authorities were presented by intelligence agencies with "unimpeachable" evidence of enemy aggression, in the form of alleged corroborating "intercepts" of enemy orders, which were so distorted as possibly to be fraudulent. Similar misrepresentation of intercepts contributed to the 1970 invasion of Cambodia.

To some it may seem pedantic to dwell on such isolated examples of conspiracy to break the law. The true barbarism of the war is to be found elsewhere, not only in isolable massacres such as at My Lai, but generally in the systematic air war that became central to the so-called Vietnamization program. Can one write a whole book about the Vietnam War that focuses on technical illegalities, while remaining silent about the larger crimes of napalm raids, the wholesale generation of refugees, and possibly even genocide?

Undoubtedly such crimes are in human terms far more serious than those that are the subject of this book. But they were already amply exposed, although their exposure, hitherto, did not seem to have been efficacious. Even the My Lai revelations, chilling though they were, exposed only those who are responsible for carrying out a war, not those who are responsible for starting it. The aim of the present book was exposure on a higher level, that of those who used provocation and escalation as an instrument to sustain an aggressive policy, and resorted to lies and illegalities to achieve those ends.

NOTES

1. In this discussion I likened this process to "a floating illegal crap game," marked by a continuity of motive rather than specific players. Nevertheless, the central roles of CAT/Air America and of Richard Nixon continue to be striking. See chapter 8.

2. *New York Times*, June 6, 1971. According to the story, CIA agents had identified at least twenty-one opium refineries in border area of Laos, Burma, and Thailand that provided constant flow of heroin to American troops in Vietnam; the labs, protected in Laos by of royal Laotian armed forces, had grown until white heroin rated 96 percent pure turned up in Pacific coast cities of United States as well as in Vietnam. Alfred McCoy reveals that the CIA leaked the story after the first bulk shipments of Laotian heroin were

intercepted in Europe and the United States in April 1971 (Alfred McCoy, *The Politics of Heroin: CIA Complicity in the Global Drug Trade* [Brooklyn, N.Y.: Lawrence Hill, 1991], 286, 288).

3. In fact Acheson's response was neither as positive as Pawley had hoped nor as negative as he later complained about to Congress. Acheson "wrote that he did not object to a limited number of private American citizens going to Taiwan, if their services were contracted directly by Chi Govt without responsibility on part of this Govt" (State Department, *Foreign Relations* 9 (1949): 428–31, Acheson to Taipei, November 18, 1949; quoted in Bruce Cumings, *The Origins of the Korean War* (Princeton: Princeton University Press, 1990), 2:510.

4. Peter Dale Scott, *Deep Politics and the Death of JFK* (Berkeley: University of California Press, 1996), 165–69; Cumings, *Origins*, 2:510–12.

5. Chalmers Roberts, "The Day We Didn't Go to War," *Reporter*, September 14, 1954, 35; reprinted in Marvin E. Gettleman, *Vietnam* (New York: Fawcett, 1965), 101.

6. Richard Nixon, "Cuba, Castro, and John F. Kennedy," *Reader's Digest,* November 1964, 291.

7. The *War Conspiracy* chapters on the Tonkin Gulf and *Pueblo* incidents are not reproduced in this volume.

8. *World Oil*, August 15, 1970, 186; cf. *Ocean Industry,* December 1969, 63.

9. *Oil and Gas Journal*, April 28, 1969, 56; map of concessions in *Ocean Industry,* December 1969, 64.

10. It is indicative of Corcoran's deep involvement in covert CIA activities (such as CAT) that throughout the 1950s his Washington law firm of Corcoran and Youngman was not listed in the Martindale-Hubbell law directory). In contrast, Desmond FitzGerald, the CIA officer in Indochina with whom CAT worked, *was* listed in Martindale-Hubbell under the cover of a private practice. Yet we know that in practice FitzGerald "spent many of the ensuing [postwar] years in Vietnam or elsewhere in Asia" (Stewart Alsop, *The Center* [New York: Harper & Row, 1968], 157).

11. "Lawyers and Lobbyists." *Fortune,* February 1952, 142.

12. Miguel Ydigoras Fuentes, *My War with Communism* (Englewood Cliffs, N.J.: Prentice-Hall, 1963), 49–50, 63–64.

13. T. A. Wise, "The Bustling House of Lehman," *Fortune,* December 1957, 157.

14. These chapters not reprinted.

15. Nelson Rockefeller, "Widening Boundaries of National Interest," *Foreign Affairs,* July 1951, 523–38.

16. William Henderson, "Some Reflections on United States Policy in Southeast Asia," in William Henderson, ed., *Southeast Asia: Problems of United States Policy* (Cambridge: MIT Press, 1963), 253–63.

17. Gabriel Kolko, *The Roots of American Foreign Policy* (Boston: Beacon, 1969), xii–xiii.

18. Kolko, *Roots*, 92. In *The Politics of War* (New York: Random House, 1968), Kolko is more cautious: "The [OSS] reports [that Ho was communist] helped to consolidate Washington's support for the French" (p. 610). His later addition of the word "only" seems to be a logical leap without empirical justification.

19. George Sheldon, "Status of the Viet Nam," *Far Eastern Survey*, December 18, 1946, 373–77.

20. Department of State, *Bulletin*, May 18, 1953, 708.

21. U.S. Congress, Senate, Committee on the Judiciary, *Internal Security Report, 1956,* 197.

8

CAT/Air America, 1950–1970

In this chapter I greatly expand on what I wrote in 1969 about how the United States, via its CIA proprietary airline, first began, in Laos, to fight what eventually became a second Indochina war (1959–1975). I have done so for two reasons—one historical, one contemporary.[1]

The historical reason is that, as David Kaiser has written, "the real roots of the Vietnam War lie in the policies the Eisenhower administration adopted toward Southeast Asia after 1954," the chief of which were policies in Laos that, almost unilaterally, "created a serious crisis."[2] *(The incoming Kennedy administration defused this crisis by escalating in Vietnam.)*

In 1969, working from public sources, I attached the blame for a foolishly aggressive and delusional policy in Laos on Air America, backed by CIA and Pentagon hawks, some of whom were hoping against government policy to provoke a war with mainland China.

Now that a declassified version of internal State Department records has been released, we learn how little opposition there was to these policies at the highest level—even from the supposedly irenic Eisenhower, who in 1954 had refrained from supporting with atomic weapons the lost French cause in Indochina.

The following astute conclusion of David Anderson, with respect to Vietnam, remains equally true if for the word "Vietnam" we substitute "Laos":

> *The Eisenhower administration was both the creator and the captive of an illusion in Vietnam. A combination of factors—cold war bipolarism and paranoia, the arrogance of power, cultural and racial chauvinism—blinded U.S. leaders to social, political, historical and military realities in Vietnam. . . . Eisenhower's foreign policy may have been astute in some areas. . . . but in Vietnam . . . the administration oversimplified and overcommitted.*[3]

The root illusion was to think that the brilliant success of the Marshall Plan in restoring the economies of Europe could be replicated in Vietnam and Laos to

119

"build" nations that had not previously existed.[4] *In Laos the illusion of progress in this respect was just as "phony" (to quote Anderson again) as in Vietnam, and for the same reasons: funds earmarked for development were diverted into military priorities, corruption, and perks for the governing class.*[5] *In both countries, furthermore, the chief cause of corruption, and of political squabbling to control it, was the opium traffic.*[6] *In the case of Laos, the corruption and military deformation of a peace-loving Buddhist nation was further enhanced (as in the fall of 1959) by reliance on distorted (or totally false) "intelligence."*

My contemporary reason for focusing on this period is the extent to which we see these illusions resurrected. The Dulles brothers' campaign against neutralism, in which "those who would not stand with the United States were viewed as standing against it,"[7] *strikes a tone of naive arrogance that is again being heard from high places. Those who think that we can achieve a "regime change" in Iraq should be required to study the disastrous and counterproductive results of the militant U.S. efforts in 1959–1960 to achieve "regime change" in Laos, a far smaller and weaker country.*[8]

These similarities should be apparent to any objective observer. Another, less easily recognized, is from the realm of deep politics not usually talked about. The United States, in Afghanistan in 2002, has just replaced the antidrug Taliban regime with a new controversial regime some of whose members have a history as drug traffickers. In Laos, in 1959–1960, the United States did something distressingly similar.

We have reasons also to look at the special interests (notably those allied with Air America, the China lobby, and the KMT) that pushed for the delusional policies of 1959–1960. I shall say more in a moment about these interests: for domestic political reasons, they were well represented in the Eisenhower administration. (It had first been elected by echoing Nixon's McCarthyite attack on the Acheson and the State Department for "losing China.") But we cannot just blame special interests for a paranoia, and a delusion of grandeur, that afflicted the administration as a whole.

It is important to understand why the CIA moved so relentlessly to replace the legal government of Souvanna Phouma in Laos with a group of drug-trafficking generals. In part, as already mentioned, this derived from U.S. dislike of leaders who, like Souvanna Phouma, were neutralist. The U.S. strategy of subversion practiced against Souvanna Phouma in Laos was much like that practiced against Sihanouk in Cambodia, and more conspicuously against Sukarno in Indonesia, where CAT provided "complete logistical and tactical air support for the Indonesian operation."[9]

But there is an instructive difference between what happened in Laos and what happened in Cambodia and Indonesia. Cambodia and particularly Indonesia were countries of interest to U.S. oil companies, and both Sihanouk and Sukarno (unlike Souvanna Phouma) had recognized the government of mainland China. Yet the U.S. effort against Sihanouk was desultory and was essentially called off in July 1960.[10] *Likewise the major campaign in Indonesia was only half-heartedly supported and then swiftly abandoned after a CAT pilot was captured.*

Laos, in contrast, was a small, thinly populated country with few proven resources (other than tin). Yet the "Laotian crisis," a thing of little substance, continued to vex the Eisenhower and Kennedy administrations for years.[11] *How could this be?*

The answer, I think, is twofold. First, Laos bordered with China and North Vietnam. In the early 1950s the U.S. strategy of containment had been directed toward isolating China from the largely urban Chinese populations scattered around the shores of the South China Sea. In the later 1950s ideological talk of a "forward strategy" focused attention increasingly (and some would say absurdly) on the poorly defined and poorly defended Laotian border. Thus a credible version of the domino theory was replaced by an absurdly ideological one, which could never be won inside Laos.

Reports of alleged communist incursions across this border, based on systematic exaggeration of minimal events, were repeatedly used by the U.S. Joint Chiefs to urge the introduction into Laos of U.S. troops armed with tactical atomic weapons. Such a confrontation in Laos served the interests of those who hoped to provoke a U.S. war with the People's Republic of China (PRC).

The second reason, closely related, is that CIA-backed conspiratorial intrigues to gain control of the Laotian government were also de facto struggles to consolidate control of Laotian opium. The defense of a remote region in northeastern Laos led to contracts for a former CAT representative, William Bird, to construct airstrips that were soon used to fly out Hmong opium.[12] *(KMT planes and personnel flew to these airstrips under cover of a "Laotian" airline, Veha Akhat.) In this way the Hmong opium production could be denied to the communist Pathet Lao, even as the latter took over the lowlands of the area from 1959 to 1964.*[13]

This was not a trivial matter. Laotian opium production, concentrated in the northeast, was in the order of fifty to one hundred tons a year and constituted "the country's most valuable export."[14] *In retrospect, it appears that CIA efforts in Laos were focused on denying this opium to the Pathet Lao and possibly on securing it for support of the drug trafficking generals whom it twice, in 1959 and again in 1960, helped install in power.*

The key to this support from 1959 on was the ostensibly Chinese Nationalist civilian airline CAT, which was actually in part a CIA proprietary. In the same year 1959 the CIA firm, CAT Inc. (once owned by Chiang Kai-shek's friend General Claire Chennault) was renamed Air America.

NIXON, THE CHENNAULTS, AIR AMERICA, AND THE CHINA LOBBY

This chapter opens with an understated account (sanitized by the lawyers at Ramparts*) of the conspiratorial and possibly illegal plotting in 1968 by presiden-*

tial candidate Richard Nixon to extend the Vietnam War.[15] Just before the election, with General Chennault's widow, Anna, as an intermediary, Nixon persuaded the head of the Saigon regime to refuse to participate in the Paris peace talks arranged by President Johnson. Nixon's intrigue helped secure his election and also fruitlessly increased the losses of both Vietnamese and American lives.

This chapter explored the background of this conspiratorial link between Nixon and the Chennault circle.[16] It noted that in 1959 and 1960 critical authorizations for CAT in Laos were made when Eisenhower was outside Washington.[17] Later chapters will talk of Nixon's repeated visits to Asia after 1960, on at least one occasion with a representative of oil-drilling interests.[18]

Nixon's extraordinary career is not easily summarized. It is however relevant that it was aided financially by four groups with a common stake in the Far East: organized crime, the China lobby, oilmen, and possibly the CIA.[19] In 1970 I was unaware of Nixon's deep and incriminating financial connections to the mob- and CIA-linked Castle Bank in the Bahamas, a creation of Paul Helliwell, who will emerge in this book as a chief architect of the CIA drug connection in the Far East.[20]

As mentioned in the introduction, I came in time to enlarge my view of the deep political forces pressing for our involvement in Indochina. But as this chapter relates, Chennault, his airline CAT, and his supporting circle of Tom Corcoran, William Pawley, Whiting Willauer, and others, played important roles in projecting a forward U.S. presence into the Third World. This was true both of support for KMT forces and allies (in Taiwan, Burma, Thailand, Korea, Laos, and Vietnam), and also in the covert U.S. interventions against the governments of first Guatemala and then Cuba. I should have commented also on the role of Richard Nixon in these same events, notably with Pawley and Willauer in preparing for the Bay of Pigs.[21]

Nixon was a man of political skills and complexities not reducible to the wishes of those who financed his rise to power. The fact remains that for two decades after World War II, the expansion of U.S. power into the Third World was achieved under presidents who spent much of their time resisting the forces pressing for this expansion. Until 1967 Nixon consistently, whether in office or out, was a leading spokesman for these same forces.

Two murky questions about Nixon's extraordinary career remain unanswered. The first is the extent to which campaign contributions from abroad (including Asia) affected Nixon's policies and career.[22] The second is whether, as recently charged, Nixon's early career, leading up to his use of inside knowledge in the Hiss case, was bolstered by secret and possibly conspiratorial contacts with the Dulles brothers and the fledgling CIA.[23]

In the closing days of the 1968 presidential campaign, the Democrats made an eleventh-hour bid for the presidency through a White House announcement that all bombing in North Vietnam was being stopped and that serious peace negotiations were about to begin. This move was apparently torpedoed within thirty hours by President Thieu of South Vietnam, who publicly rejected the coming negotiations. Three days later, the Democratic candidate lost to Richard Nixon by a narrow margin.

After the election, it was revealed that a major Nixon fund-raiser and supporter had engaged in elaborate machinations in Saigon (including false assurances that Nixon would not enter into such negotiations if elected) to sabotage the Democrats' plan. It was also revealed that, through wire taps, the White House and Humphrey knew of these maneuvers *before* the election and that a heated debate had gone on among Humphrey strategists as to whether the candidate should exploit the discovery in the last moments of the campaign. Humphrey declined to seize the opportunity, he said, because he was sure that Nixon was unaware of and did not approve of the activities of his supporter in Saigon.[24]

The supporter in question was Madame Anna Chan Chennault, the widow of General Claire Chennault (d. 1958) and now an intimate friend of his lawyer Tommy Corcoran. Her covert intervention into the highest affairs of state was by no means an unprecedented act for her and her associates. General Chennault had fought in China with Chiang Kai-shek; after the war he formed a private airline company called Civil Air Transport.

Both husband and wife had, through their involvement with the China lobby and the CIA's complex of private corporations, played a profound role throughout the U.S. involvement in Southeast Asia. General Chennault's airline was, for example, employed by the U.S. government in 1954 to fly in support for the French at Dienbienphu. It was also a key factor in the new fighting which began in Laos in 1959 and 1960. Moreover, it appears that President Eisenhower did not really know when his office and authority were being committed in this Laotian conflict.

In its evasion of international controls over military commitments in Laos and elsewhere, the CIA long relied on the services of its proprietary, General Chennault's "private" airline Civil Air Transport (or, as it was renamed, Air America, Inc.).

HOW AIR AMERICA WAGES WAR

Air America's fleets of transport planes were easily seen in the airports of Laos, South Vietnam, Thailand, and Taiwan. The company was based in Taiwan, where a subsidiary firm, Air Asia, with some eight thousand employees, ran what was for a while one of the world's largest aircraft maintenance and repair facilities. While not all of its operations were paramilitary or even covert, in Vietnam and even more in Laos Air American was the chief airline serving the CIA in its clandestine war activities.

In the 1960s the largest of these operations was the supply of the fortified hilltop positions of the 45,000 Hmong tribesmen fighting against the Pathet Lao behind their lines in northeast Laos. (The Hmong were hill tribesmen on both sides of the Laos-Vietnam border with little sympathy for their Lao rulers.) Most of these Hmong outposts had airstrips that would accommodate special short takeoff and landing aircraft, but because of the danger of enemy fire the American and Nationalist Chinese crews usually relied on parachute drops of guns, mortars, ammunition, rice, even live chickens and pigs. Air America's planes also served to transport the Hmong's main cash crop, opium.

The Hmong units, originally organized and trained by the French, provided a good indigenous army for the Americans in Laos. Together with their CIA and U.S. Special Forces "advisers," the Hmong were used to harass Pathet Lao and North Vietnamese supply lines. In the later 1960s they engaged in conventional battles in which they were transported by Air America's planes and helicopters.[25] The Hmong also defended, until its capture in 1968, the key U.S. radar installation at Pathi near the North Vietnamese border; the station had been used in the bombing of North Vietnam.

Farther south in Laos, Air America flew out of the CIA operations headquarters at Pakse, from which it has supplied an isolated U.S. Army camp at Attopeu in the southeast, as well as the U.S. and South Vietnamese Special Forces operations in the same region. Originally the chief purpose of these activities was to observe and harass the Ho Chi Minh trail, but ultimately the fighting in the Laotian panhandle, as elsewhere in the country, expanded into a general air and ground war. Air America planes were reported to be flying arms, supplies, and reinforcements in this larger campaign as well.[26]

Ostensibly, Air America's planes were only in the business of charter airlift. Before 1968, when the U.S. Air Force transferred its operations from North Vietnam to Laos, air combat operations were largely reserved for "Laotian" planes; but it has been suggested that at least some of these operated out of Thailand with American, Thai, or Nationalist Chinese pilots hired through Air America. In addition, many of Air America's pilots and ground crews were trained for intelligence or "special" missions: a reporter in 1964 was amused to encounter American ground crews whose accents and culture were unmistakably Ivy League.[27] And for years Air America's pilots flew in a combat support role. As early as April 1961, when U.S. "advisers" are first known to have guided the Laotian army in combat, Air America's pilots flew the troops into battle in transports and helicopters supplied by the U.S. Marines.[28]

The 1962 Geneva agreements on Laos prohibited both "foreign paramilitary formations" and "foreign civilians connected with the supply, maintenance, storing and utilization of war materials." Air America's involvement in military and paramilitary operations (under cover of a contract with the U.S. economic aid mission) would thus appear to have been clearly illegal. In calling Air America a paramilitary auxiliary arm, however, it should be stressed that its primary function was logistical: not so much to make war, as to make war possible.

THE EARLY HISTORY OF AIR AMERICA

To understand the complex operations of Air America, one must go back to 1941 and the establishment of the Flying Tigers or American Volunteer Group (AVG), General Claire Chennault's private air force in support of Chiang Kai-shek against the Japanese. At that time President Roosevelt wished to aid Chiang and he also wanted American reserve pilots from the three services to gain combat experience; but America was not yet at war and the U.S. Code forbade the service of active or reserve personnel in foreign wars. The solution was a legal fiction, worked out by Chennault's "Washington squadron," which included Roosevelt's "brain truster" lawyer, Thomas Corcoran, and the young columnist Joseph Alsop. Chennault would visit bases to recruit pilots for the Central Aircraft Manufacturing Company, Federal, Inc. (CAMCO), a corporation wholly owned by William Pawley, a former salesman for the old aircraft producer Curtiss-Wright, Inc., and head of Pan Am's subsidiary in China. According to their contracts, the pilots were merely to engage in "the manufacture, operation, and repair of airplanes" in China, but Chennault explained to them orally that they were going off to fly and fight a war.

In theory, the whole contract was to be paid for by the Chinese government; in practice the funds were supplied by the U.S. government through lend-lease. The operation was highly profitable to both of Pawley's former employers. Curtiss-Wright was able to unload a hundred P-40 pursuit planes, which even the hard-pressed British had just rejected as "obsolescent." Pawley nearly wrecked the whole deal by insisting on a 10 percent agent's commission, or $450,000, on the Curtiss sale. Treasury Secretary Morgenthau protested but was persuaded by the Chinese to approve a payment of $250,000.[29] For its part, Pan Am's Chinese subsidiary was later able to use many of Chennault's pilots in the lucrative charter airlift operations over the "hump" to Chungking.

It was agreed that Pawley's new CAMCO corporation could not take American pilots into the private war business without presidential authorization, and there was some delay in getting this approval. But on April 15, 1941, Roosevelt signed an executive order authorizing the enlistment of U.S. reserve officers and men in the AVG-Flying Tigers. Thus CAMCO became a precedent for the establishment of a private war corporation by government decision. It does not appear, however, that the CIA was always so fastidious about obtaining presidential approval in the postwar period.

After the war Chennault saw that a fortune could be made by obtaining contracts for the airlift of American relief supplies in China. Through Corcoran's connections—and despite much opposition—the relief agency UNRRA supplied Chennault not only with the contracts but also with the planes at bargain prices as well as with a loan to pay for them. One of Corcoran's connections, Whiting Willauer, promptly became Chennault's number two man. With the generous financing of the American taxpayers, Chennault and Willauer needed only a million dollars to set up the new airline. Recurring rumors suggested that CAT was originally bankrolled by Madame Chiang and/or her brother, T. V. Soong, then Chiang's ambassador to the United States, whose personal holdings in the United States—after administering Chinese lend-lease—were reported to have reached $47 million by 1944.[30]

World War II was over, but the Chinese revolution was not. CAT, established for relief flights, was soon flying military airlifts to besieged Nationalist cities, often using the old Flying Tigers as pilots. Chennault himself spent a great deal of time in Washington with Corcoran, Senator William Knowland, and other members of the Soong-financed China lobby; he campaigned in vain for a $700 million aid program to Chiang, half of which would have been earmarked for military airlift.

After the establishment of the Chinese People's Republic in October 1949, Truman and the State Department moved to abandon the Chiang clique and to dissociate themselves from the defense of Taiwan. By contrast, CAT chose to expand its parabusiness operations, appealing for more pilots "of proved loyalty."[31]

To help secure Taiwan from invasion, Chennault and his partners put up personal notes of $4.75 million to buy out China's civil air fleet, then grounded in Hong Kong. The avowed purpose of this "legal kidnapping" was less to acquire the planes than to deny them to the new government pending litigation. It is unclear who backed Chennault financially in this critical maneuver (Soong denied that it was he).[32] But it is known that shortly before the Korean War CAT was refinanced as a Delaware-based corporation [i.e., a CIA proprietary]. By the winter of 1950–1951 CAT was playing a key role in the airlift of supplies to Korea, and Chennault (according to his wife's memoirs) was into "a heavy intelligence assignment for the U.S. government."[33]

CHENNAULT'S AMBITION OF ROLLING BACK COMMUNISM

Chennault's vision for his airline was summed up in 1959, the year of CAT's entry into Laos, by his close friend and biographer, Robert Lee Scott: "Wherever CAT flies it proclaims to the world that somehow the men of Mao will be defeated and driven off the mainland, and all China will return to being free."[34]

As late as March 1952, according to Stewart Alsop, the Truman administration had failed to approve the "forward" policy against China then being proposed by John Foster Dulles.[35] Yet in a CIA operation in 1951, CAT planes were ferrying arms and possibly troops from Taiwan to some 12,000 of Chiang's soldiers who had fled into Burma. In his book Roger Hilsman tells us that the troops, having been equipped by air, undertook a large-scale raid into China's Yunnan province, but the raid was a "colossal failure."[36] Later, in the "crisis" year 1959, some three thousand of the troops moved from Burma to Laos and continued to be resupplied. On another CIA operation in 1952, a CAT plane dropped CIA agents John Downey and Richard Fecteau with a supply of arms for Nationalist guerrillas on the mainland.

In 1954 Chennault conducted a vigorous political campaign in support of a grandiose but detailed proposal whereby his old friends Chiang and Syngman Rhee would be unleashed together against the Chinese mainland with the support of a 470-man "International Volunteer Group" modeled after his old Flying Tigers. "Once Chiang unfurls his banner on the mainland," promised Chennault, "Mao will be blighted by spontaneous peasant uprisings and sabotage."[37]

Chennault actually had a list of pilots and had located training sites for the group in Central America, where his former partner Whiting Willauer, now U.S. ambassador to Honduras, was playing a key role in the CIA-organized deposition of Guatemalan president Arbenz. (Willauer and Pawley were also involved with Nixon in the planning of the Bay of Pigs operation under the Eisenhower administration.) Chennault's plan was sponsored by Admiral Radford, chairman of the Joint Chiefs of Staff, and seems to have had some CIA support. It was defeated, however, by opposition in the State Department, Pentagon, and Nationalist Chinese air force.[38]

CAT, however, had by no means been idle. It flew twenty-four of the twenty-nine C-119s dropping supplies for the French at Dienbienphu. The planes were on "loan" from the U.S. Air Force, and some of the "civilians" flying them were in fact U.S. military pilots. According to Bernard Fall, who flew in these planes, the pilots were "quietly attached to CAT to familiarize themselves with the area in case [as Dulles and Nixon hoped] of American air intervention on behalf of the French."[39]

CAT's C-119s were serviced in Vietnam by two hundred mechanics of the USAF 81st Air Service Unit. Five of these men were declared missing on June 18, 1954. Thus the CAT operation brought about the first official U.S. casualties in the Vietnam War. Senator John Stennis, fearful of a greater U.S. involvement, claimed the Defense Department had violated a "solemn promise" to have the unit removed by June 12.[40]

From the passing of the 1954 Geneva agreements until Chennault's death four years later, CAT seems to have played more of a waiting than an active paramilitary role in Indochina: its planes and pilots being occupied with CIA-supported insurgencies in Indonesia, Burma, and Tibet. At the same time it continued to train large number of Chinese mechanics at its huge Taiwan facility. As a right-wing eulogist observed in 1955, they were thus ready for service "if the Communists thrust at Formosa or Thailand or Southern Indochina. . . . CAT has become a symbol of hope to all Free Asia. Tomorrow the Far Eastern skies may redden with a new war and its loaded cargo carrier may roll down the runways once more."[41]

ALSOP'S "INVASION": AIR AMERICA
ENTERS INTO LAOS

The Quemoy crises of 1954 and 1958 were generated in large part by a buildup of Chiang's troops on the offshore islands, from which battalion-strength commando raids had been launched. While this buildup was encouraged by local military "advisers" and CIA personnel, it was officially disapproved by Washington. The crises generated new pressures in the Pentagon for bombing the mainland, but with their passage the likelihood of a U.S.-backed offensive seemed to recede decisively. American intelligence officials later confirmed that the Soviet Union had disappointed China during the 1958 crisis by promising only defensive support. Some U.S. officials concluded that the United States could therefore risk confrontation with impunity below China's southern border, since any response by China would only intensify the Sino-Soviet split. The fallacy of this reasoning soon became apparent.

After Quemoy, Laos appeared to present the greatest likelihood of war in the Far East, though hardly because of any inherent aggressiveness in the Laotian people themselves. In 1958, the nonaligned government that had been established in Laos under Prince Souvanna Phouma appeared to be close to a neutralist reconciliation with the procommunist Pathet Lao. Fearing that this would lead to the absorption of Laos into the Communist bloc, the United States decided to intervene, and Souvanna Phouma was forced out of office on July 23, 1958, after a timely withholding of U.S. aid.[42] Egged on by its American advisers, the succeeding government of Phoui Sananikone declared itself no longer bound by the provisions of the 1954 Geneva agreements, recognized the KMT Nationalist Chinese government on Taiwan, and moved swiftly toward a covert buildup of U.S. military aid, including nonuniformed advisers.

Even so, the CIA and the military were not satisfied with the new government, which the State Department had approved. Allen Dulles was determined on what in 2002 has become familiar as "regime change," telling the National Security Council on December 23, 1958, that "drastic changes in the [Laotian] government will be required if the Pathet Lao element is to be restrained."[43]

The CIA backed a right-wing power base under Colonel (later General) Phoumi Nosavan, called the Committee for the Defense of National Interests (CDNI); and for the next few years made Phoumi a key figure in its subsequent scenarios.[44] The Pentagon meanwhile backed a plan for "a marked increase" in the number of American military personnel, even though this would entail scrapping the limits established by the 1954 Geneva Accords.[45]

Washington officials were now set on a course, authorized by the National Security Council but often opposed to that of the U.S. ambassador in Vientiane, that led to the further destabilization of Laos and hastened the growth of the Pathet Lao.[46] The CIA's plotting on behalf of General Phoumi has therefore frequently been derided as self-defeating. This assumes, however, that the CIA's interest was confined to the rather amorphous internal politics of Laos; in fact the CIA was pursuing a "forward strategy" for the entire region, while many of its highest officers were hoping for a wider war with mainland China.

In December 1958 both North Vietnam and Yunnan province in southern China began to complain of overflights by American or "Laotian" planes. These charges, Arthur J. Dommen intimates, may refer in fact to "flights of American reconnaissance aircraft"; this is corroborated by the revelation in the *Pentagon Papers* that Civil Air Transport [along with the CIA and KMT] was active in supporting the Tibetan operations of this period.[47] Soon afterward, Peking began to complain of U.S.-supplied Nationalist Chinese Special Forces camps in Yunnan province.

By March 1959, according to Bernard Fall, "some of the Nationalist Chinese guerrillas operating in the Shan states of neighboring Burma had crossed over into Laotian territory and were being supplied by an airlift of 'unknown planes.'"[48] Laos was already beginning to be a cockpit for international confrontation.

Matters escalated in May, when the CDNI-dominated Phoui government moved (against U.S. embassy advice) to force the two Pathet Lao military battalions to accept integration into the Royal Laotian Army. One accepted, but the other was composed largely of tribal Black T'ais, Hmongs and Khas, minorities with long-standing reasons to dislike the Lao government.[49] The latter simply withdrew into its home base of Xieng Khouang province in northeastern Laos.[50]

This was the beginning of expanded Pathet Lao influence in the lowlands of the prime opium-growing area of Laos, which eventually led to the construction of mountain airstrips for Air America and the Hmongs in the same region.[51] (On March 31, 1959, CAT, Inc., the CIA proprietary, had changed its name to Air America, Inc.) It also led to outbreaks of sporadic fighting which General Phoumi quickly labeled a North Vietnamese "invasion."

The first allegations of cross-border fighting began on July 30 at a small border post "mainly concerned with the activities of Méo [Hmong] opium smugglers." Bernard Fall later wrote that the attack had killed one person, the post commander, who was shot from under his house by fellow T'ai tribesmen.[52] Yet on July 30, the day of the incident, Allen Dulles told the National Security Council that "local communist forces aided by *volunteers across the border* had taken control of part of the province of Sam Neua."[53]

On August 23 the *New York Times* reported the arrival of two CAT transports in the Laotian capital, Vientiane. More transports arrived soon thereafter.[54] On August 30 a "crisis" occurred that was to be used retroactively as a pretext for a permanent paramilitary airlift operation.

All through August, reports from three of Phoumi's generals created a minor war hysteria in the U.S. press, which depicted an invasion of Laos by five or more North Vietnamese battalions. At one point, when August rains washed out a bridge, the *New York Times* reported (from "Western military sources") "Laos

Insurgents Take Army Post Close to Capital," and speculated that they were trying to cut off Vientiane from the south. As for the "crisis" of August 30, the
Washington Post wrote that thirty-five hundred Communist rebels, "including
regular Viet-minh troops, have captured eighty villages in a new attack in northern
Laos."[55] Much later, it was learned that in fact not eighty but three villages had
been evacuated, after two of them had been briefly blanketed by 81-millimeter
mortar fire at dawn on August 30. No infantry attack had been observed: the
defending garrisons, as so often happened in Laos, had simply fled.[56]

After it was all over, the Laotian government claimed only that it had lost
ninety-two men during the period of the "invasion" crisis from July 16 to October 7, 1959; more than half of these deaths ("estimated at fifty killed") took place
on August 30. A UN investigating team, after personal interviews, reduced the
latter estimate from fifty to five. No North Vietnamese invaders were ever discovered. Though the Laotians claimed at one point to have seven North Vietnamese
prisoners, it was later admitted that these were deserters who had crossed over
from North Vietnam in order to surrender.

Joseph Alsop, however, who had arrived in Laos just in time to report the
events of August 30, wrote immediately of a "massive new attack on Laos" by
"at least three and perhaps five new battalions of enemy troops from North Vietnam."[57] In the next few days he would write of "aggression, as naked, as flagrant
as a Soviet-East German attack on West Germany," noting that "the age-old
process of Chinese expansion has begun again with a new explosive force."
Unlike most reporters, Alsop could claim to have firsthand reports: on September
1 at the town of Sam Neua, he had seen survivors arrive on foot (one of whom
had a "severe leg wound") from the mortared outposts. Bernard Fall, who was
also in Laos and knew the area well, later called all of this "just so much nonsense," specifying that "a villager with a severe leg wound does not cover 45
miles in two days of march in the Laotian jungle."[58] Alsop, by Fall's account,
had been a willing witness to a charade staged for his benefit by two of Phoumi's
generals.[59]

As on many occasions between 1949 and 1964, Alsop's reports were to play
an important role in shaping the Asian developments he described. The London
Times drew attention to the stir his story created in Washington. Senator Dodd
and others clamored vainly that in the light of the "invasion" Khrushchev's
impending visit to America should be put off. Though this did not happen, there
were other lasting consequences of the "great Laos fraud" of August 1959.[60]

First, on August 26, the State Department announced that additional U.S. aid
and personnel would be sent to Laos: thus the military support program was
stepped up beyond the levels agreed to at Geneva in 1954 at a time when a congressional exposure of its scandal and futility had threatened to terminate it altogether. Second, reportedly under a presidential order dated September 4,
CINCPAC Commander Harry D. Felt moved U.S. ground, sea, and air forces into
a more forward posture for possible action in Laos. (A Signal Corps unit is sup-

posed to have been put in Laos at this time, the first U.S. field unit in Southeast Asia).[61] Third, the planes of CAT (i.e., Air America) were moved into Laos to handle the stepped-up aid, and additional transports (over the approved 1954 levels) were given to the Laotian government. At the same time a Chennault-type "volunteer air force" of U.S. active and reserve officers ("American Fliers for Laos") was said by the *Times* to be negotiating a contract for an operation "like that of the Flying Tigers."[62]

The timing of these germinal decisions is intriguing. On the day of the aid announcement, August 26, Eisenhower had left for Europe at 3:20 in the morning to visit western leaders before receiving Khrushchev in Washington. At a press conference on the eve of his departure, he professed ignorance about the details of the Laotian aid request, which had just been received that morning. He did, however, specify that the State Department had not yet declared the existence of an "invasion" (something it would do during his absence).[63] The date of the "presidential order" on Laos, September 4, was the day allotted in Eisenhower's itinerary for a golf holiday at the secluded Culzean Castle in Scotland.[64] According to his memoirs, which corroborate earlier press reports, "our stolen holiday was interrupted *the following morning* [i.e., September 5] by bad news from Laos." Eisenhower added, "My action *on return to the United States* was to approve increased aid to the pro-United States government" (emphasis added). He is silent about the troop movements he actually authorized while still in Scotland.[65]

Knowing this, one would like to learn why a U.S. response to an artificially inflated "emergency" on August 30 was delayed until Eisenhower's virtual isolation five days later, even though it could not await his return to Washington three days after that. Once again it is the knowledgeable Joseph Alsop who supplies the corroborating details: "Communications are non-existent in little Laos. Hence word of the new 'invasion' took more than 48 hours to reach the commander of the Laotian Army, General Ouane Rathikone. There was, of course, a further delay before the grave news reached Washington. Time also was needed to assess its significance."[66]

Bernard Fall rejects this explanation: "The Laotian Army command . . . *did* know what went on in the border posts since it had radio communications with them."[67] More significantly, the U.S. Army attaché in Laos, himself in Sam Neua, had cabled Army Intelligence reports that (in a State Department summary) "denote a degree of undeniable DRV [North Vietnamese] supported intervention" that could justify intervention by foreign troops.[68] Washington columnist Marquis Childs reported soon after the "invasion" that "a powerful drive is on within the upper bureaucracy of Defense and Intelligence to persuade President Eisenhower that he must send American troops into Laos. . . . They will consist of two Marine regiments of the Third Marine Division now stationed on Okinawa and components of the 1st Marine Air Wing, also on Okinawa [having been moved up in the course of the crisis]. Notice would be served on the Communists—Red China and North Vietnam—that if they did not withdraw in one week, they would be attacked. According to one source, they would use the tactical atomic weapons with which they are in part at least already equipped."[69] The push for additional SEATO and U.S. troops in Laos is now clear from released documents.[70]

Senator Mansfield asked in the Senate on September 7 whether the president and Secretary of State Herter still made foreign policy, or whether the various executive agencies, like Defense and CIA, had taken over. We should learn more about the arrival of CAT's planes in Vientiane on August 22, before the August 30 crisis and the U.S. government's belated authorization.[71]

AIR AMERICA HELPS OVERTHROW
A GOVERNMENT

Although the CIA's General Phoumi was largely responsible for the intrigues of the August "invasion," the State Department's Phoui Sananikone was still in office. On December 30, according to Schlesinger, the CIA "moved in" and toppled Phoui.[72] Phoui's ouster was achieved by an army coup headed by Phoumi Nosavan and the CIA-backed CDNI. After the coup Phoumi Nosavan emerged as the strong man in the new government.

In backing the coup against the opposition of U.S. Ambassador Horace Smith, the CIA had essentially ensured the transfer of power to men like Phoumi who (unlike their opponents) were, or would soon become, involved in the drug traffic.[73] Within the year the CIA would install this coalition of drug traffickers for a second time.

A few months later, in April 1960, the CIA helped to rig an election for the CDNI and Phoumi. Dommen reports that "CIA agents participated in the election rigging, with or without the authority of the American ambassador. A Foreign Service officer . . . had seen CIA agents distribute bagfuls of money to village headmen."[74] But this maneuver was so flagrant that it discredited the government and (according to Denis Warner) "precipitated" a coup in August, restoring the old neutralist premier, Souvanna Phouma.[75]

Over the next few weeks, Souvanna Phouma's new government succeeded in winning the approval of the king, American ambassador Winthrop Brown, and the new right-wing, but pliant, national assembly. In due course his proneutralist government was officially recognized by the United States. Nevertheless General Phoumi, after consulting with his cousin Marshal Sarit in Thailand, decided to move against Souvanna, proclaiming a rival "revolutionary committee" in southern Laos. Phoumi's first announcement of his opposition took the form of leaflets dropped from a C-47 over the Laotian capital.

In the next three months, according to Schlesinger, "A united embassy, including CIA [i.e., CIA station chief Gordon L. Jorgensen] followed Brown in recommending that Washington accept Souvanna's coalition. . . . As for the Defense Department, it was all for Phoumi. Possibly with encouragement from Defense and CIA men in the field, Phoumi . . . proclaimed a new government and denounced Souvanna. The Phoumi regime became the recipient of American military aid, while the Souvanna government in Vientiane continued to receive economic aid. Ambassador Brown still worked to bring them together, but the military support convinced Phoumi that, if he only held out, Washington would put him in power."[76] In fact Phoumi had high-level CIA and Pentagon encouragement to oust Souvanna's supporters in Vientiane. The proof of this was that while Sarit's forces in Thailand blockaded Vientiane, Air America was stepping up its military airlift to Phoumi's base at Savannakhet.

"It was plain," writes Dommen, "that General Phoumi was rapidly building up his materiel and manpower for a march on Vientiane. From mid-September, Savannakhet was the scene of an increased number of landings and take-offs by unmarked C-46 and C-47 transports, manned by American crews. These planes belonged to Air America, Inc., a civilian charter company with U.S. Air Force organizational support and under contract to the U.S. Government."[77]

In October, Hilsman reports, Ambassador Brown was telling Souvanna that the United States "had Phoumi's promise not to use the aid against . . . the neutralist forces" in Vientiane. Yet even as he did so, two men "flew to Savannakhet and gave Phoumi the green light to retake Vientiane."[78] The two men were not some CIA spooks "in the field," but John N. Irwin II, assistant secretary of defense for international security affairs, and Vice Admiral Herbert D. Riley, chief of staff of the U.S. Pacific Command.[79] A declassified State Department cable confirms that Irwin and Riley met Phoumi in Ubon, Thailand: "the thrust of their discussion was that the United States was prepared to support, at least secretly, a march on Vientiane and recapture of the government by Phoumi."[80]

Meanwhile the opium-growing Hmong tribesmen under Vang Pao, encouraged by the CIA, defected from Souvanna in October. At this point Air America began supplying them with materiel and U.S. Special Forces cadres from Savannakhet.

DID THE CIA WANT WAR WITH CHINA?

Why did top U.S. officials deliberately foment a conflict between noncommunist forces in Laos, a conflict that led to rapid increases in the territory held by the Pathet Lao? According to *Time* magazine (March 17, 1961), "The aim, explained the CIA, who called Phoumi 'our boy,' was to 'polarize' the communist and anticommunist factions in Laos." If so, the aim was achieved: the country became a battlefield where U.S. bombings, with between four hundred and five hundred sorties a day in 1970, generated 600,000 refugees. "Polarization," as sanctioned by the Thai blockade of Vientiane and a U.S. refusal of supplies, forced Souvanna Phouma to request an airlift of rice and oil (and later guns) from the Soviet

Union, and in the end to invite in North Vietnamese and Chinese "technicians." The first Soviet transport planes arrived in Vientiane on December 4, 1960, and the Russians were careful to send civilian pilots. As Dommen notes, they were "following the precedent set by the United States."[81]

In late December an American transport was actually fired on by a Soviet Ilyushin-14, and a major international conflict seemed possible. Of course there were some in CIA and Defense who thought that a showdown with "communism" in Asia was inevitable, and better sooner than later. Many more, including most of the Joint Chiefs, believed that America's first priority in Laos was international, to maintain a militant "forward strategy" against an imagined Chinese expansionism. Thus the actual thrust of American policy, if not its avowed intention, was toward the Chennault vision of "rollback" in Asia.

The last weeks of 1960 saw ominous indications that anticommunist forces were only too willing to internationalize the conflict, especially with the first reports in the *Times* and *Le Monde* that General Phoumi's forces were being bolstered by Thai combat troops in Laotian uniforms and by Thai helicopters.[82] The expulsion of Souvanna from Vientiane in mid-December ended nothing; for the next eighteen months Laos would have two "governments," each recognized and supplied by a major power.

For a second time, as a year earlier, the CIA had turned to a coalition of drug traffickers to oust a clean civilian government. This time the drug connections were stronger than before; for the CIA, using Air America, had cemented an alliance between Phoumi in the south and the opium-growing Hmong troops of Vang Pao.[83] (Though the United States had many harsh words for the leaders they ousted, chiefly Souvanna Phouma and Kong Le, these men were never to my knowledge accused of drug trafficking.)[84]

Did Eisenhower authorize this course toward both drugs and escalation? Years later, in 1966, an article in the *New York Times* claimed that the president "had specifically approved" the CIA's backing of Phoumi against Ambassador Brown's advice.[85]

The documentary record now available confirms Ike's approval, but very ambiguously. On September 15 "the President agreed that the U.S. should support Phoumi," and also that it "might be possible to provide Phoumi with some additional C-47s." But at this time the State Department was still hoping to draw Phoumi into a wider anticommunist coalition, as opposed to the Joint Chiefs, who wished to see Phoumi create his own government.[86]

It was the Joint Chiefs who first, on October 3, officially authorized Air America flights to Phoumi.[87] Note that (as mentioned above) Air America had already been supplying Phoumi in Savannakhet since mid-September. The first Air America flight reached Vang Pao on October 5, securing that his allegiance would now be with Phoumi.[88] Not until October 11 was Eisenhower notified that supplies "will [*sic*] be flown in to the non-Communist [Hmong] area in the north."[89] (There is no indication that Ike, or anyone else in Washington, ever heard that these were flights to opium growers.)

After Souvanna Phouma and Phoumi had both made it clear that they would have nothing to do with each other, Eisenhower, on November 21, officially authorized planes and funds to Phoumi's rebel cause. Hearing from Secretary of State Herter that it was time "to take the wraps off Phoumi," the president agreed "to provide Phoumi with CAT planes."[90] The president at the time was staying at his home on the Augusta National golf course.

Eisenhower's own memoirs, in an extraordinary passage, ignore all these developments. He states quite clearly that it was after December 13 (after the crisis posed by the new Soviet airlift) that he approved the use of "United States aircraft" to "transport supplies into the area."

> As Phoumi proceeded to retake Vientiane, General Goodpaster reported the events to me [on December 14]. . . . He then posed several questions: "First, should we seek to have Thai aircraft transport supplies into the area? Second, if the Thais can't do the job, should we use United States aircraft?" . . . I approved the use of Thai transport aircraft and United States aircraft as well![91]

The official record of this phone call confirms Eisenhower's concern about the Soviet aircraft supplying Souvanna Phouma, and the need to "act vigorously, now that we have the cover of legality, in that we are responding to the request of a legally constituted government."[92]

Eisenhower's emphasis on the legal case suggests that he might not have been quite as uninformed as is implied by these last pages of his memoirs. Did he really not know, or not remember, that Thai helicopters were already being used in a combat support role, or that Air America had been flying missions for Laos for over a year, and to rebels for three months?

Air America was central to the Laotian events of 1960, but also secret. A story reporting the crash of an Air America plane in November on the Plain of Jars was not carried in any American newspaper, though it was printed abroad in the *Bangkok Post* of November 28, 1960. (The plane's American pilot was wounded seriously; the KMT Chinese copilot, son of Nationalist Chinese ambassador to Washington Hollington Tong, was killed.)

Meanwhile, six days before Eisenhower authorized the flights, U.S. officials announced that they had "interrupted military air shipments" to Phoumi.[93] Did Eisenhower think he was asked to authorize what was in fact a *resumption* of the airlift to Phoumi, while under the impression that he was *initiating* it? Five hours after the phone call with the president, State cabled that now "no restrictions should be imposed on the utilization of CAT civil aircraft."[94] This meant a return to the Phoumi airlift suspended on December 7.

What is clear is that Air America was "legalized" just in time for the incoming Kennedy administration. For the purposes of this legalization the Soviet airlift—

which CIA and Pentagon machinations had done so much to induce—was not a disaster but a godsend: the airlift could now be justified to the president (as it was to the people) by the formula that (in Sulzberger's words) "we are starting to match" the Soviet airlift.[95]

As in September 1959, so once again Eisenhower's ex post facto authorization of Air America in December 1960 was made when he was in preplanned seclusion. General Phoumi's troops, after pausing for many weeks in their drive up the Mekong River, bestirred themselves in December and finally entered Vientiane at the equivalent of 5:00 A.M. eastern standard time, December 16. Meanwhile Eisenhower's authorization of a U.S. airlift was made to General Goodpaster on December 14.[96] At the time the president was in Walter Reed Army Hospital, not the White House; Eisenhower had entered hospital as planned for his annual physical examination on the evening of December 13 and left it at 10:20 A.M. on December 15. Once again, by coincidence or not, a crucial and belated presidential decision about Air America was implemented, as an "emergency," at a time of Eisenhower's scheduled isolation.[97]

A final indication of constitutional chicanery about the authorization of Air America's airlift is the energy expended by right-wing CIA elements in rewriting Laotian history for the December 1960 period. We can see this in the CIA-inspired attack by Charles Murphy on the role of Eisenhower and Kennedy in the Bay of Pigs fiasco, an attack for which the CIA had the gall to seek an official State Department clearance:

> Phoumi eventually took the capital, Vientiane, early in December, *but at this point the Russians intervened openly*. . . . In concert with a large-scale push by well-trained troops from North Vietnam, they introduced a substantial airlift into northern Laos (an operation that is still continuing). The collapse of the Royal Laotian Army then became inevitable unless the U.S. came in *with at least equal weight* on Phoumi's side. One obvious measure was to put the airlift out of business. The job could have been done by "volunteer" pilots and the challenge would at least have established, at not too high an initial risk for the U.S., how far the Russians were prepared to go. Another measure would have been to bring SEATO forces into the battle, as the SEATO treaty provided. In the end, Eisenhower decided to sheer away from both measures. . . . Even the *modest additional support* that the Defense Department tried to extend to Phoumi's battalions in the field during the last weeks of the Eisenhower Administration was diluted by reason of the conflict between Defense and State.[98]

Phoumi did not secure Vientiane until December 16; the Soviet airlift had begun on December 4. By thus reversing the order of events, the article implies that the United States was sending aid to a legal government, the Soviet Union to rebels; but the genesis of the conflict was in fact the other way round. One should not be surprised to learn that, once again, this rewritten version of history was first published in the column of Joseph Alsop.[99]

The Murphy article, though misleading in its historical facts, correctly shows the magnitude of the choice Eisenhower faced that December. The Laotian crisis of the election year 1960, like the Tonkin Gulf crisis of the election year 1964 and the *Pueblo* crisis of the election year 1968, placed the president under great pressure to put more U.S. troops into Asia. In all three cases, the military wanted a vastly escalated response to a crisis for which they, along with our intelligence community, were largely responsible. The Soviet airlift was apparently presented to Eisenhower as being so reprehensible that the "volunteers" should shoot the planes down; yet it was Air America that set a precedent for this, apparently without presidential authorization.

All of these actions were in fact leading our country into war in Southeast Asia. And it is hard to believe that Air America's directors were unconscious of this. Retired Admiral Felix B. Stump, until 1958 U.S. commander in chief, Pacific, and Air America's board chairman after 1959, told a Los Angeles audience in April 1960, "World War III has already started, and we are deeply involved in it." Later he declared it was "high time" the nation won over communism in the Far East, and he called for the use of tactical nuclear weapons if necessary. Containment was not enough: we must "move beyond this limited objective."[100]

The admiral was not speaking in a vacuum. Now in one country, now in another, the tempo of U.S. operations in Southeast Asia did indeed increase steadily over the next few years. After a disastrous experiment in the latest counterinsurgency techniques in Laos, for example (with Air America planes and pilots transporting the Laotian army), the Kennedy administration agreed in May 1961 to a Laotian cease-fire and negotiations. One day later, Rusk announced the first of a series of steps to increase the involvement of U.S. forces, including Air America, in Vietnam. A year later the United States signed the July 1962 Geneva Agreements to neutralize Laos. Unfortunately, as in 1954 and 1961, the price for U.S. agreement to this apparent deescalation was a further buildup of U.S. (and Air America) deployments in Vietnam and also Thailand.

Despite the 1962 Geneva agreements, Air America did not dismantle its private war enterprise in Laos. Although the agreements providently called for the withdrawal of "foreign civilians connected with the supply, maintenance, storing, and utilization of war materials," Air America continued to fly into northeastern Laos, and it appeared that some of the uniformed U.S. military "advisers" simply reverted to their pre-Kennedy civilian disguise. The first military incident in the resumption of fighting was the shooting down of an Air America plane in November 1962, three days after the Pathet Lao had warned that they would do so.

What made the Pentagon, CIA, and Air America hang on in Laos with such tenacity? Hilsman tells us that, at least as late as 1962, there were those in the Pentagon and CIA "who believed that a direct confrontation with Communist China was inevitable."[101] In his judgment, the basic assumption underlying the CIA's programs in Laos, and particularly the airlift to the Hmong, "seemed to be that Laos was sooner or later to become a major battleground in a military sense between the East and West."[102]

NOTES

1. In addition to the new material about Chennault, CAT, and Air America in chapter 3, the reader can also consult Martha Byrd, *Chennault: Giving Wings to the Tiger* (Tuscaloosa, Ala.: University of Alabama Press, 1987); Christopher Robbins, *Air America* (New York: Avon, 1985); and William M. Leary, *Perilous Missions: Civil Air Transport and CIA Covert Operations in Asia* (University, Ala.: University of Alabama Press, 1984).

2. David Kaiser, *American Tragedy: Kennedy, Johnson, and the Origins of the Vietnam War* (Cambridge: Harvard University Press, Belknap Press, 2000), 11–12.

3. David L. Anderson, *Trapped by Success* (New York: Columbia University Press, 1991), 207–8. I shall argue later that the State Department endorsed these follies because of a political trade-off in which Far Eastern Affairs was entrusted to a veteran of the China lobby, Walter S. Robertson.

4. The idea of "nation building" is an example of shallow thinking concealed by a shallow metaphor. Nations are not normally "built," they grow; and though it is deceptively easy to supply them with outside sustenance, you cannot easily "build" them a digestive system to absorb it.

5. Anderson, *Trapped by Success*, 156. In both Vietnam and Laos the artificial exchange rates of the Commercial Import Program could be easily manipulated to generate profits for those in power.

6. Alfred W. McCoy, *The Politics of Heroin* (Brooklyn, N.Y.: Lawrence Hill, 1991), esp. 211 (Vietnam), 288, 299–305, 331–34 (Laos).

7. Audrey R. Kahin and George McT. Kahin, *Subversion as Foreign Policy* (New York: New Press, 1995), 9.

8. The most conspicuous examples of U.S. "regime changes" in the 1950s were Iran and Guatemala. Who today would not wish to see the return of the moderate democracies that the CIA overturned in 1953 and 1954?

9. Lansdale memo of July 1961(?); *Pentagon Papers* (New York: Bantam, 1971), 137 (CAT); Kahin and Kahin, *Subversion*, 12–13, 179–84. There was also support for the 1958 U.S. intervention in Indonesia from KMT forces in Taiwan and their allies in South Korea (Kahin and Kahin, *Subversion*, 185–88).

10. *Foreign Relations of the United States (FRUS) 1958–1960,* vol. 16, no. 65, p. 218; Kaiser, *American Tragedy*, 21.

11. In the State Department *FRUS* volumes for the Kennedy era, Cambodia and Indonesia are tucked into the volume on Southeast Asia; Laos merits an entire volume to itself.

12. We shall see in chapter 11 that the KMT and APACL collaborated more closely with Laotian military drug traffickers after a CIA-installed Laotian government recognized the KMT government in 1958.

13. The CIA's direct involvement with the opium trade was progressive. Air America started flying the Hmong opium after Ouane Rathikone forced small Corsican airlines out in 1965. But the CIA's airstrips were used by the Corsicans after Kong Le in December

1960 seized the Plain of Jars, which for more than sixty years "had been the hub of the opium trade in northeastern Laos" (McCoy, *Politics*, 316–18).

14. Arthur J. Dommen, *Conflict in Laos: The Politics of Neutralization* (New York: Praeger, 1964), 17. Nevertheless, opium is not mentioned in the published *FRUS* records of the 1959–1960 Laotian crisis, nor in David Kaiser's otherwise excellent history, which is based on them.

15. In the opinion of future U.S. Ambassador Richard Holbrooke, who researched the incident as a coauthor of Clark Clifford's memoirs, "What the Nixon people did [was] perhaps even a violation of the law. They massively, directly and covertly, interfered in a major diplomatic negotiation . . . probably one of the most important negotiations in American diplomatic history" (BBC interview, 2000; quoted in Anthony Summers (with Robbyn Swan), *The Arrogance of Power* [New York: Viking, 2000], 306).

16. I say "circle" because the 1968 intrigue was initiated in 1967 via the intervention of Robert Hill, a Republican foreign policy specialist and former member of the Corcoran-Willauer circle of support for General Chennault and his airline, CAT (Summers, *Arrogance*, 299).

17. In 1971 I wondered if Nixon might have been responsible in Eisenhower's absence. Records released since then show no sign of this; they also suggest that Nixon, while he was vice president, was a team player.

18. In 1964 with Henry Kearns, a representative of Japanese oil interests. Nixon visited the offices in Taiwan of the Asian People's Anti-Communist League.

19. Summers, *Arrogance*, 47–48, 53–57, 62–63, 85, 133–34, 180–81, 194–95, passim. Summers does not mention that Senator Owen Brewster, who was once investigated for passing illicit funds into Nixon's election campaign, was at the heart of the China lobby (Summers, *Arrogance*, 85, 186; Roger Morris, *Richard Milhous Nixon* [New York: Henry Holt, 1990], 576). For the importance of the China lobby in Nixon's early career, understated by Summers, see Stephen E. Ambrose, *Nixon: The Education of a Politician 1913–1962* (New York: Simon & Schuster, 1987), 213–15.

20. Summers, *Arrogance*, 239–45, 253–57, 510 n., 513 n. We shall see that Helliwell was counsel to Lansky's bank in Miami; Summers (pp. 55, 57) claims that Lansky ordered Los Angeles gangster Mickey Cohen to put funds into Nixon's first congressional campaign. Summers also links Nixon's personal fortune in the Bahamas to the Crosby family, which also had a Lansky connection (p. 241). One family member, Francis Peter Crosby, was associated in mob securities fraud with S. G. Fassoulis (see chapter 3). Of course other politicians—notably John F. Kennedy—had their own darker connections. The difference is in the extent to which these connections *invented* Richard Nixon.

21. Summers (*Arrogance*, 185) summons many witnesses in support of the judgment (attributed by Howard Hunt to Nixon's aide Robert Cushman) that Nixon was the "chief architect" of the Bay of Pigs project. Summers argues further (180–81) that Nixon secured CIA support for the project, which had initially been overruled, after receiving a message which originated with Meyer Lansky. When I wrote this chapter in 1969–1970, I had not yet come across the now familiar links between the KMT, CAT, and its successor Air America, and the dramatic postwar expansion of the Asian drug traffic. Also involved was the Asian People's Anti-Communist League, which Nixon visited in Taiwan in 1964. For all this, see chapter 11.

22. Funds are said to have entered Nixon's campaigns from the China lobby, the shah

of Iran, the Greek colonels who seized power in 1967, and possibly the South Vietnamese government in 1968 and 1972 (Summers, *Arrogance*, 85, 164, 286, 519 n.). Earlier, according to former CIA officer Gordon Mason, the CIA destroyed evidence in its possession that Nixon had received a $100,000 bribe from the former Romanian fascist Nicolae Malaxa, by then an asset of the CIA's Frank Wisner (Summers, *Arrogance*, 133–34). Nixon's first campaign for the House in 1946 received funds from both oilmen and Mickey Cohen and other mob figures (via Murray Chotiner), allegedly on orders from Frank Costello and Meyer Lansky (Summers, *Arrogance*, 54–57).

23. Nixon met Allen Dulles back in 1947 in connection with the Hiss case (Ambrose, *Nixon*, 178; Summers, *Arrogance*, 63). John Loftus, a former Justice Department prosecutor who worked on cases of CIA-protected Nazi war criminals, has claimed that Nixon came across these same cases. Allen Dulles then financed Nixon's first campaign to keep him quiet (Summers, *Arrogance*, 62–63; citing John Loftus and Mark Aarons, *The Secret War against the Jews* [New York: St. Martin's, 1994], 221, 557).

24. It is now fully documented that Nixon did know. See Summers, *Arrogance*, 297–308.

25. *New York Times*, October 26, 1969, 24.

26. *New York Times*, September 10, 1969, 10.

27. *New York Times*, August 27, 1964, 6.

28. *Washington Post*, April 6, 1961, A9; *New York Times*, March 25, 1961, 2. In 1969 Americans still piloted helicopters for the Laotian army (*New York Times*, September 24, 1969, 1).

29. Anna Chan Chennault, *Chennault and the Flying Tigers* (New York: Eriksson, 1963), 76–83; Russell Whelan, *The Flying Tigers* (New York: Viking, 1942), 31–32; Claire Lee Chennault, *Way of a Fighter* (New York: Putnam's, 1949), 100–101, cf. 131–33. Corcoran's private law firm dates from this maneuver, when Roosevelt released him from the White House to become counsel for the Flying Tigers' supply corporation, China Defense Supplies, and thus T. V. Soong's contact with the White House (Barbara Tuchman, *Stilwell and the American Experience in China, 1911–45* [New York: Macmillan, 1971], 220).

30. *San Francisco Chronicle*, April 2, 1970, 31; W. T. Wertenbaker, "The China Lobby," *Reporter,* April 15, 1952, 9–10.

31. We now know that "in the summer of 1948 [Frank] Wisner's Office of Policy Coordination [later merged into CIA] 'took increasing control of the airline, which it looked upon as having perfect cover'; CIA funds flowed to it by the summer of 1949, if not earlier, through a dummy corporation [Airdale Corp.] set up by Tommy 'The Cork' Corcoran, T.V. Soong's agent in Washington" (Bruce Cumings, *The Origins of the Korean War* [Princeton: Princeton University Press, 1990], 2:133; quoting Christopher Robbins, *Air America* [New York: Putnam's, 1979], 48–49, 56–57, 70). In September 1949 Frank Wisner began negotiations with State for OPC to buy out the airline. When George Kennan of the State Department "sent Wisner a memo on 4 October that neither approved nor disapproved of Wisner's plans . . . Wisner had all that he needed. OPC was ready to go to war against the Communists in China, and CAT would be part of the action" (Byrd, *Chennault*, 333).

32. Although both Soong and the U.S. government involved themselves actively on Chennault's behalf in this case, the funds consisted of promissory notes from a second

corporation, CATI, unconnected to the CIA/OPC buyout of CAT. The CATI debt was finally resolved in 1954 with a smaller and complex payment, at the same time that CAT was granted the right to operate as Taiwan's civilian airline. See Byrd, *Chennault*, 338, 346–48.

33. Anna Chan Chennault, *A Thousand Springs* (New York: Eriksson, 1962), 248; cf. Chennault, *Chennault and the Flying Tigers*, 275. According to Leary, the CIA gave Chennault the "empty title" of chairman of the new CAT board and called him back to Washington from time to time for consultation because the USG mistrusted Chennault's closeness to America's alienated ex-ally Chiang Kai-shek (Leary, *Perilous Missions*, 137).

34. Robert Lee Scott Jr., *Flying Tiger: Chennault of China* (Garden City, N.Y.: Doubleday, 1959), 282.

35. Stewart Alsop, *Saturday Evening Post*, December 13, 1958, 86.

36. Roger Hilsman, *To Move a Nation* (Garden City, N.Y.: Doubleday, 1967), 300. See chapter 11.

37. Claire Lee Chennault, "Voice of the Tiger" (as reported by Tom McClary), *Flying*, October 1954, 64–68. See also *Look*, September 7, 1954, 80–83; *Flying*, May 1955, 69; *Newsweek*, April 26, 1954, 41.

38. *Pentagon Papers*, 137; Chennault, *Thousand Springs*, 263–64. Chennault and his postwar proposals were viewed with suspicion in Washington, even by the CIA, because of Chennault's proximity to Chiang Kai-shek, Madame Chiang, and T. V. Soong (Leary, *Perilous Missions*, 113, 137).

39. Bernard Fall, *Hell in a Very Small Place* (Philadelphia: Lippincott, 1967), 24.

40. *New York Times*, June 19, 1954, 3.

41. Corey Ford, *Saturday Evening Post*, February 12, 1955, 102. For CAT in other countries, see *Pentagon Papers*, 137.

42. It appears that the State Department objective was not to eliminate Souvanna Phouma but to force him to accept a large representation in his cabinet from the CIA's favorites, what Allen Dulles called "a new and dynamic group, the Committee for the Defense of National Interests" (CDNI). The CDNI, however, refused to serve under Souvanna Phouma, and Ambassador Smith was instructed not to oppose them forcefully on this. Whether or not CIA backed the CDNI in their refusal (as CIA did later in 1960) is not known for 1958. See *FRUS 1958–1960*, vol. 16, nos. 190–91, pp. 471–73.

43. *FRUS 1958–1960*, vol. 16, no. 202, p. 491.

44. Phoumi appears to have been guided initially by Henry Hecksher, the CIA station chief in Laos until 1959, his successor Gordon Jorgensen, and also Robert Jantzen, the CIA station chief in Thailand. In December 1959 Phoumi complained that Ambassador Smith had been responsible for Hecksher leaving Laos earlier than had been expected, and then predicted, correctly, that Smith would soon himself be recalled See *FRUS 1958–1960*, vol. 16, no. 319, p. 723 (Hecksher, not named), no. 421, p. 887 n. (Jantzen).

45. *FRUS 1958–1960*, vol. 16, no. 203, p. 491. I have to acknowledge here that my narration of events is undoubtedly influenced by my four years at this time in the Foreign Service of the Canadian government, which was charged with overseeing the application of the Geneva Accords. Thus I wish to take issue with Kaiser's account of this period, which mentions the Pentagon's plan "for expanding [its] mission" but is silent about the violation of the Geneva Accords, which was the plan's most controversial feature (Kaiser, *American Tragedy*, 23). I also take issue with the following sentence from the same para-

graph: "In January 1959 . . . in an ominous development, Prime Minister Phoui Sananikone spoke to the National Assembly about military incidents along the North Vietnamese
border, and secured special powers to meet this threat." A RAND Corporation report on
Laos concluded that in 1959 it was not the procommunist Pathet Lao but the right-wing
Sananikone government that "precipitated the final crisis which led to war in Laos"
(A. M. Halpern and H. B. Friedman, *Communist Strategy in Laos*, Rand, RM-2561, 51;
cited and amplified in Bernard Fall, *Anatomy of a Crisis: The Laotian Crisis of 1960–
1961*, ed. with an epilogue by Roger M. Smith [Garden City, N.Y.: Doubleday, 1969],
108). Fall in his account notes that Hanoi had complained of Laotian incursions before
Phoui's complaint, and that the main North Vietnamese response was the demand for the
return of the International Control Commission (consisting of India, Canada, and Poland);
the ICC return was strongly opposed by the United States. As a result of the plenary powers vote in response to the "threat," the older ministers of the cabinet were eliminated and
replaced by the younger army colonels of the CIA-backed CDNI. "Sananikone was now
a complete prisoner of the 'Young Turks'" (Fall, *Anatomy*, 96).

46. The opposition by midlevel State Department officials to the CIA and Pentagon
was ineffective because the Republicans and Dulles had placed Far Eastern Affairs in the
hands of Walter Robertson, "a close associate of China lobbyists such as Congressman
Walter Judd" (Anderson, *Trapped by Success*, 180). Robertson's successor, J. Graham
Parsons, had the same mentality.

47. Dommen, *Conflict in Laos*, 115. General Lansdale wrote in a 1961(?) memo on
Laos that CAT had supplied "more than 200 overflights of Mainland China and Tibet, and
extensive air support in Laos during the current crisis" (*Pentagon Papers*, 137). Cf. John
Kenneth Knaus, *Orphans of the Cold War: America and the Tibetan Struggle for Survival*
(New York: Public Affairs, 1999). I have not yet seen James Morrison and Kenneth J.
Conboy, *The CIA's Secret War in Tibet* (Lawrence: University Press of Kansas, 2002).

48. Fall, *Anatomy*, 99. Cf. *FRUS 1958–1960*, 16, no. 226, p. 537. The KMT and
APACL were involved in this support; see chapter 11.

49. Dommen, *Conflict in Laos*, 118; Fall, *Anatomy*, 104.

50. Fall, *Anatomy*, 103–4.

51. I was told in 1971 that this construction began in 1960; McCoy, from firsthand
sources, reports that it began in 1961 (McCoy, *Politics*, 312).

52. Fall, *Anatomy*, 20–21. The post's commander was Deo Van Khoun, a lieutenant in
the Royal Laotian Army and a member of the powerful T'ai family used earlier (before
their expulsion from North Vietnam) by the French, "as their intermediaries with the
Hmong opium growers" (Fall, *Anatomy*, 19; McCoy, *Politics*, 141). It is quite probable
that the August 1959 troubles in the opium-growing provinces of Sam Neua and Phong
Saly were in fact a struggle to control the year's opium harvest. Hugh Toye observes that
the communist Viet Minh had been using opium "to pay for their intelligence services
and propaganda," and the trouble in 1959 began "when much of the opium is still in the
villages." Hugh Toye, *Laos* (London: Oxford University Press, 1968), 130.

53. *FRUS 1958–1960*, vol. 16, no. 232, p. 546; emphasis added. Fall describes the
attackers only as T'ai tribesmen with many relatives in the Sop-Nao area (*Anatomy*, 21).

54. State Department records include a memo of August 19 stating that a proposal to
"help strengthen the Lao Army" was "under urgent study" (*FRUS 1958–1960*, 16, no.
243, p. 562); but there is no evidence of any authorization until that of September 5 (see
below).

55. On September 4 a high-level emergency meeting in Washington was told that "the Lao said at the time that there were five enemy battalions involved, but our army attaché thought there were but three, which would mean some 1500 men. As of September 3 there were two columns moving on Sam Neua" (*FRUS 1958–1960,* vol. 16, no. 257, p. 596).

56. Discussion in Fall, *Anatomy,* 130–38; Dommen, *Conflict in Laos,* 123.

57. Alsop clearly had been briefed by the U.S. Army attaché (see note 55).

58. Bernard Fall, *Street without Joy* (Harrisburg, Pa.: Stackpole, 1964), 334–35; cf. *Anatomy,* 136.

59. Denis Warner, another anticommunist journalist, heard some of the same witnesses and reported that the local general "accepted as fact what the most junior western staff officer would have rejected as fiction" (*The Last Confucian* [New York: Macmillan, 1963], 210). This seems to be a barb directed at Alsop, a former U.S. staff officer in Chungking under Chennault.

60. Another was the preservation of the boondoggle U.S. Laotian aid program, threatened with termination in 1959 after a devastating congressional exposé. Willis Bird, accused of bribery, headed the Bangkok office of Sea Supply, Inc., the CIA proprietary that supplied the KMT opium troops of General Li Mi (see chapter 11). Senator Mansfield issued a public complaint in 1960 that there was little to show for the $300 million in U.S. aid and expenditures for Laos except "chaos, discontent and armies on the loose" (*New York Times,* December 29, 1960).

61. *Bangkok Post,* September 12, 1959. Another consequence was that the groundwork had been laid for Air America's logistic support of the opium-growing Hmong. It is perhaps relevant that the fraudulent reports of a North Vietnamese invasion "were made available to press and [military] attachés together" by General Ouane Rathikone, later the man in charge of the Laos opium monopoly (*FRUS 1958–1960,* vol. 16, no. 252, p. 583).

62. *New York Times,* September 25, 1959, 4; September 27, 1959, 16. The "American Fliers for Laos" would have violated the provisions of the Neutrality Act quite as clearly as had the Flying Tigers: was there then an intention to seek authorization from Eisenhower to parallel that granted by Roosevelt? One who might have known was Joseph Alsop. Like some of the China hands in the CIA and the Pentagon, he had worked for Chennault in China during World War II. Apart from a CIA-inspired article in *Fortune* in 1961 (see note 98 below) I have found no subsequent reference to this "volunteers" project.

63. The State Department's announcement of August 26 caused some congressmen to complain that they had heard nothing about increased assistance in a secret briefing two days before (*New York Times,* August 31, 1959, 10). The *FRUS* documents reveal that the aid increase had been approved on August 24, and that the statement released on August 26 was actually prepared for the president's press conference of August 25; he did not use it (*FRUS 1968–1960,* vol. 16, no. 247, pp. 571–72). It would seem Eisenhower did not yet share his officials' eagerness to act in Laos.

64. The *FRUS* volume reveals that the president approved certain military actions on September 5 (see below). These included a decision to "bring transport aircraft to outloading airfields ready for embarkation of U.S. troops" (*FRUS 1958–1960,* vol. 16, no. 258, p. 600). There was no explicit order for the movement of Air America aircraft.

65. Dwight D. Eisenhower, *Waging Peace: 1956–1961* (Garden City, N.Y.: Doubleday, 1965), 431. These memoirs complicate the picture by the erroneous statement that Eisen-

hower flew to Scotland on the morning of September 3 rather than September 4. The Laotian "crisis" had calmed by the time of the president's return; his only approval action was from Scotland on September 5.

66. Joseph Alsop, *Washington Post*, October 4, 1959, A25.

67. Fall, *Street without Joy*, 334; cf. *Anatomy*, 136.

68. *FRUS 1958–1960*, vol. 16, no. 252, p. 583 n.; cf. p. 584 n. Fall concedes that there were attacks ("the first real attacks of the war"). The attacks consisted of a brief mortar barrage that "had not been followed by an infantry attack; or, if it had been followed by an infantry attack, the garrison was no longer there to witness it because it had begun its retreat much earlier" (Fall, *Anatomy*, 134–35).

69. *Washington Post*, September 11, 1959, A14.

70. *FRUS 1958–1960*, vol. 16, nos. 252, 254, 258, 262 n., passim. Eisenhower, while still in Scotland, was advised on September 6 that a marine task force HQ had been activated in Japan for the Okinawa units named by Childs (*FRUS* no. 260, p. 602, SecState cable to president, September 6, 1959).

71. Deputy CIA Director Charles Cabell emphasized the importance of the Laotian incident in a speech to the National Guard Association on October 6, 1959: "Dismissal of the seriousness of the situation is exactly what the Communists hope to achieve. The fact is, that the loss of even five or six soldiers in a far northern outpost of Laos is important." His speech was later distributed by the Council Against Communist Aggression to rebut skeptical stories downplaying the incident in the *Wall Street Journal* and *Washington Star* (Hoover Institution, Stanley Hornbeck Papers, Box 131). The CACC, later renamed the Council for the Defense of Freedom, joined with the ASC in 1980 to create the Committee for a Free Afghanistan.

72. Arthur J. Schlesinger Jr., *A Thousand Days* (Boston: Houghton Mifflin, 1965), 326. Cf. Kaiser, *American Tragedy*, 25: "One can hardly avoid the conclusion that the CIA had transformed Laotian politics and brought about a military coup."

73. Principals in the 1959 coup were Phoumi Nosavan, Ouane Rathikone, and Prince Sopsaisana (*FRUS* vol. 16, no. 319, p.723). All of these men became known as drug traffickers. Sopsaisana blamed the heroin seized from him in 1971 on Khampan Panya, another CDNI coup leader (McCoy, *Politics*, 300–3, 331–34, 283–84, 379–80).]

74. Dommen, *Laos*, 133.

75. Denis Warner, *Reporting Southeast Asia* (Sydney: Angus and Robertson, 1966), 167.

76. Schlesinger, *Thousand Days*, 326–37. In fact Jorgensen was so close to Phoumi that Kennedy, when he wished to terminate aid to Phoumi in 1962, first had Jorgensen removed.

77. Dommen, *Laos*, 154. Schlesinger, so scathing about "CIA spooks" in Laos, is discreetly silent on the subject of Air America. Even Hilsman, while attacking the "tragedy" of interagency rivalry and the CIA's "attempt to 'play God' in Lao political life," says merely that "air transports of a civilian American airline began a steady shuttle to Phoumi's base in Savannakhet" (*To Move a Nation*, 124).

78. Keyes Beech, "How Uncle Sam Fumbled in Laos," *Saturday Evening Post*, April 22, 1961, 89.

79. Dommen does not mention this important meeting.

80. *FRUS 1958–1960*, vol. 16, no. 431, p. 914; citing Vientiane cable 686 of October 18, 1960.

81. Dommen, *Laos*, 164.

82. *New York Times*, December 21, 1960, 30; *Le Monde*, December 6, 1960, 4.

83. McCoy, *Politics*, 310–11. Other drug traffickers in the second coup included General Kouprasith Abhay and Colonel Oudone Sananikone (cf. McCoy, *Politics*, 331).

84. When Kong Le captured the Plain of Jars in December 1960, the result was to force drug-trafficking Corsican airlines out (McCoy, *Politics*, 316–17). Both Fall (*Anatomy*, 93–94) and Dommen (*Laos*, 111) contrast the reform intentions of the CDNI when created with the "disgraceful trafficking" of old families like the Sananikones around Phoui. Ambassador Smith in December was far less sanguine, charging that some key members of the CDNI were "patently pursuing and have pursued personal not Laos interests and certainly not those of the US" (*FRUS 1958–1960*, vol. 16, no. 312, p. 714; quoted in Kaiser, *American Tragedy*, 24–25). McCoy writes that in 1961, when Phoumi first turned to the opium traffic to fund his army, he already had "controlled the traffic for several years and collected a payoff from both Corsican and Chinese smugglers" (McCoy, *Politics*, 300).

85. *New York Times*, April 28, 1966, 28.

86. *FRUS 1958–1960*, vol. 16, no. 397–98, pp. 846–50.

87. *FRUS 1958–1960*, vol. 16, no. 415, p. 876; Kaiser, *American Tragedy*, 27.

88. McCoy, *Politics*, 311.

89. *FRUS 1958–1960*, vol. 16, no. 424, p. 893.

90. *FRUS 1958–1960*, vol. 16, no. 463, p. 973.

91. Eisenhower, *Waging Peace*, 608–9. Cf. *FRUS 1958–1960*, vol. 16, no. 487, pp. 1008–9; memo of telephone conversation with the president.

92. *FRUS 1958–1960*, vol. 16, no. 487, p. 1009.

93. *New York Times*, December 8, 1960, 7; cf. *FRUS 1958–1960*, vol. 16, no. 480, p. 999. "At the same time, they added, the United States has accelerated delivery to South Vietnam of military equipment needed to fight Communist guerrillas [and] also has recast military training of the Vietnamese Army to emphasize anti-guerrilla operations." The story shows how (as on many later occasions) deescalation in Laos was balanced by escalation in Vietnam; and also how critical military decisions attributed to the Kennedy administration in 1961 had in fact been made by the Pentagon during the lame duck Eisenhower administration.

94. *FRUS 1958–1960*, vol. 16, no. 486, p. 1006.

95. *New York Times*, December 21, 1960, 30. This is the earliest allusion I have been able to find in any American paper to Air America's stepped-up activities after August 1960. State Department records also begin to talk of Air America for the first time on December 23, 1960. As late as December 14, cables use the more ambiguous term "CAT," even though CAT Inc. had officially been renamed Air America back on March 31.

96. Eisenhower, *Waging Peace*, 609.

97. At this point in 1971 I wondered whether the vice president of the United States, Richard Nixon, played any part in these two dubious decisions. We now know that the official records show no trace of Nixon's involvement, and no real need for it. (Nixon may have had a back channel. Summers [*Arrogance*, 184] writes that the CIA "had come to treat the vice president as its 'friend at court' and made certain he received a regular flow of intelligence." A back channel allegedly existed for Vice President Johnson on Vietnam [Newman, *JFK in Vietnam* (New York: Warner, 1992), 225–29], and one clearly existed

for Vice President Bush on Iran-Contra [Theodore Draper, *A Very Thin Line* (New York: Hill & Wang, 1991), 574–76].)

Ike was clearly reluctant to risk war with the other Great Powers, but he was otherwise pliant and not well informed about the details of Laotian politics. A key reason for this was the appalling disinformation he was receiving from intelligence sources. In December 1959 the president was notified in a written memo of the imminent CIA-backed coup by Phoui Sananikone and then was assured that "throughout this matter the U.S. has been making every effort to stand aside" (*FRUS 1958–1960,* vol. 16, no. 316, p. 720). In fact it was only U.S. Ambassador Smith who on December 22 had been told to "step aside" (*FRUS 1958–1960,* vol. 16, no. 309, p. 708). This was because Smith had been trying to prevent the coup that the CIA was promoting.

98. Charles J. V. Murphy, "Cuba: The Record Set Straight," *Fortune,* September 1961, 94, emphasis added; article discussed in Paul W. Blackstock, *The Strategy of Subversion* (Chicago: Quadrangle, 1964), 250.

99. *Washington Post,* January 6, 1961, A19: "The success of Phoumi and Boun Oum produced a result which Washington had not foreseen. The Soviets and North Vietnamese quite flagrantly intervened in Laos, to restore their pawns [i.e., Souvanna Phouma!] to power."

100. Fred J. Cook, *The Warfare State* (New York: Macmillan, 1962), 265; *Los Angeles Times,* April 6, 1960, sec. 3, 2. While still CINCPAC in 1957, Stump was clearly inclined toward military intervention in Indonesia, until Eisenhower intervened to have him brought into line with Washington's views. See Kahin and Kahin, *Subversion,* 86, 262.

101. Hilsman, *To Move,* 311.

102. Hilsman, *To Move,* 115.

9

Laos, 1959–1970

This chapter was originally published in the New York Review of Books *as a critical response to Nixon's statement of March 6, 1970, in support of his escalations in Laos.*[1] *As I researched it, I was struck by the recurrence of intrigues in Laos to increase Air America's presence, intrigues in which one saw the role of not just the CIA but also the KMT in Taiwan, the KMT troops in Laos, and their right-wing Laotian allies. I linked these intrigues (as I still would today) to the fading efforts of Chiang Kai-shek and his American supporters, such as General Claire Chennault, to reestablish the KMT in mainland China.*

What I was still unaware of in 1970 was the extent to which principal players in these intrigues, including the airline itself, were also prominent in the local drug traffic. General Ouane Rathikone of the Royal Laotian Army, who helped perpetrate the "North Vietnamese invasion" hoax of August 1959, had not yet shown to Alfred McCoy the ledgers that he kept as manager of the Laotian opium monopoly (even after the monopoly was declared illegal in 1961).[2] *Nor had McCoy yet exposed the Pepsi-Cola bottling plant near the Mekong River that served as Ouane's front for the import of acetic anhydride, the chief precursor chemical involved in making heroin.*[3]

McCoy's study makes it clear that the principal generals in Laotian politics— Phoumi Nosavan, his cousin Sarit Thanarat in Thailand, and his eventual rival and replacement Ouane Rathikone—were all involved in the drug traffic. McCoy even argues that a major cause of the April 19, 1964, coup discussed in this chapter, which ended the Laotian coalition government and toppled Phoumi from power, was "Phoumi's parsimonious management of his monopolies" (including opium dens in the Vientiane area); this "produced serious tensions in the right-wing camp."[4] *The chief CIA asset in the Nam Tha area, where Phoumi's retreat in 1962 nearly wrecked the 1962 Geneva peace negotiations, was "probably the most important opium merchant in Nam Tha province."*[5]

In the light of McCoy's revelations, every history of Laotian politics in this

147

period (including my own) seems superficial, when the importance of drugs to both Laotian politics and the Laotian economy is left unmentioned. However, my chapter does focus on the key elements in the drug story (CIA, Air America, the KMT and its allies), which I bring together in chapter 11.

As I mention in the introduction, I know of no more recent history of Laos or Indochina that has given equal attention to all these factors. This is unfortunate, given the growing consensus that it is in Laos that we must seek the evolution of the forces leading to U.S. involvement in the Vietnam War.

The inadequacies in my own account pale in comparison to the unreal intelligence dispatches coming out of Laos in this period, some of which are still cited deadpan in otherwise excellent academic histories of Vietnam.

The key to President Nixon's program of overt troop withdrawal in Vietnam was covert escalation in Laos. His Key Biscayne statement on Laos of March 6, 1970, itself drew attention to the connection between the two conflicts, which was soon underlined by Vice President Agnew. In reality the so-called Vietnamization in 1969 of the ground war in South Vietnam was balanced by a sharp escalation of the U.S. air war in Laos, where it could not be observed by Western newsmen. This escalation was then rationalized (though not admitted) by the president's statement on Laos, which put forth a grossly misleading history of North Vietnamese "persistent subversion" and "invasion."

This story was put together long before the Nixon administration. Many of its allegations were supplied years earlier by U.S. intelligence sources, who had a stake in misrepresenting the Laotian war that they had themselves largely helped to create. It is important to see that it was not North Vietnam but the United States, and more particularly its apparatus of civil and military intelligence agencies, that was consistently guilty of the *initial* subversion of whatever order had been established in Laos through international agreements. Thus the Nixon statement should be examined in the light of indubitable CIA and U.S. Air Force activities that it wholly left out.

Although the war in Laos dated back to 1959, the Nixon statement was totally silent about the 1959–1961 period. This is understandable, since virtually every independent observer had condemned the subversive activities in Laos of the CIA and other U.S. agencies during the period when Nixon was vice president. A RAND Corporation report on Laos concluded, for example, that in 1959 it was not the procommunist Pathet Lao but the right-wing Sananikone government (which had been installed by U.S. intrigue and was counseled by U.S. advisers) that "precipitated the final crisis which led to war in Laos."[6]

This "final crisis" followed a probe by a government patrol into the small but sensitive disputed area of Huong Lap on the North Vietnamese border, which had been governed as part of Vietnam in the days of the French. When the patrol was, predictably, fired on, the government charged the North Vietnamese with frontier incursions and claimed that this was related to a planned insurrection by the

Pathet Lao. It then obtained a vote of emergency powers from the assembly and soon ordered the two remaining battalions of the Pathet Lao to be integrated forthwith into the national army.

The Pathet Lao had previously (in November 1957) agreed to this integration, as part of a political settlement in which they received two Cabinet posts and were permitted to participate in elections for specially created seats in the national assembly. In this election the Pathet Lao and their allies (the party of left-leaning neutralist Quinim Pholsena) obtained 32 percent of the votes and thirteen of the twenty-one contested seats, showing that they had grown considerably in popularity in the four years since the 1954 Geneva agreements. (Prince Souphanouvong, the Pathet Lao leader and half-brother of the then premier Prince Souvanna Phouma, received more votes than any other candidate.)

Arthur Schlesinger Jr. recorded the response of the U.S. to the election:

> Washington decided to install a reliably pro-Western regime. CIA spooks put in their appearance, set up a Committee for the Defense of National Interest (CDNI), and brought back from France as its chief an energetic, ambitious and devious officer named Phoumi Nosavan. Prince Souvanna, who had shown himself an honest and respected if impulsive leader, was forced out of office [by a withholding of U.S. aid and CIA encouragement of a parliamentary crisis, allegedly through the use of bribes] . . . a veteran politician named Phoui Sananikone took his place.[7]

The Pathet Lao were then excluded from the new cabinet approved on August 18, 1958.

In May 1959 one Pathet Lao battalion refused, understandably, to be assimilated under the new right-wing government, and it decamped to a valley on the North Vietnamese border. The Sananikone government then declared that the Pathet Lao had committed an act of open rebellion and that only a military solution appeared possible. It thus by its own actions deflected the Pathet Lao from the role of political opposition into a military insurgency for which it was poorly prepared, so that it was forced increasingly to depend on North Vietnamese support.

In August 1959 the government received a large increase in U.S. military support by claiming, falsely, that it had been "invaded" by a North Vietnamese force of as many as eleven battalions. (In February the government had given itself the right to receive this support by declaring unilaterally, with U.S. approval, that it would no longer be bound by the limitations on foreign military aid that it had accepted at Geneva in 1954.) Bernard Fall and the British historian Hugh Toye linked the phony invasion scare to a U.S. congressional exposé at this time of major scandals in the Laos aid program, and to the very real risk that U.S. military aid would be curtailed.[8]

It is frequently claimed that the Pathet Lao was never more than a front for North Vietnamese ambitions in Laos, but this is contradicted by the election

results of 1958 (the last honest elections in Laos). Though before 1954 Souphanouvong and his cadres had fought with the Vietminh against the French, the
indubitable growth in popularity of the Pathet Lao between 1954 and 1958, by
which time it had established a countrywide network of cells at the village level,
must be attributed to its own talent for organization, particularly in exploiting the
resentment of the many hill tribes against the dominant Lao population in the
lowlands and cities.

Let us examine the Nixon statement.

[1] *By 1961 North Vietnamese involvement became marked, the communist forces
made great advances, and a serious situation confronted the Kennedy administration.*

Comment: The crisis facing President Kennedy in early 1961 was the armed
conflict following the successful displacement from the capital city of Vientiane
of Souvanna Phouma's neutralist government (which we officially recognized)
by the CIA-supported right-wing insurrectionary forces of General Phoumi
Nosavan. His rebellion against Souvanna had from the outset received logistical
support from the CIA's proprietary airline, Air America. With its help, Phoumi's
Royal Laotian Army drove the neutralist troops of General Kong Le, Souvanna's
military chief, to the north and into a temporary alliance with the procommunist
Pathet Lao. After Kong Le captured the Plain of Jars from Phoumi's troops, the
Pathet Lao moved south to join him. Souvanna Phouma and Kong Le, genuine
neutralists who feared North Vietnamese influence, nevertheless had been forced
to seek communist support in order to survive Phoumi's attack. Thus CIA-spon-
sored subversion was itself directly responsible for the communists' "great
advances."[9]

It is true that in late 1960 Souvanna Phouma's government, faced with U.S.
encouragement of a rebellion against it, did in response invite in Russian, North
Vietnamese, and Chinese "advisers," thus creating the first known North Vietnamese military presence in Laos since the 1954 Geneva agreements. However,
A. J. Dommen dates the presence of North Vietnamese combat troops (along "the
Laos-Vietnam border") from July-August 1962 and contrasts them with "the
technical experts and cadres that North Vietnam had maintained in Laos since
the end of 1960."[10] Bernard Fall estimated that "the fighting in Laos in 1960–
1962 involved relatively small forces from the [North Vietnamese] 335th and
316th divisions, many of whose men were of the same Thai *montagnard* stock as
the tribesmen on the Laotian side."[11] The British observer Hugh Toye writes that
"on balance, participation by Vietminh infantry, as opposed to cadres and support detachments, in the skirmishes of 1961–2 is unlikely." But by early 1961 the
United States had brought in AT-6s armed with bombs and rockets, U.S. pilots to
fly them, and Special Forces "White Star" teams to encourage guerrilla activity
by Hmong tribesmen behind the Pathet Lao lines. Furthermore, Air America was
using American helicopters and American pilots to move Phoumi's troops into

battle. At this time the Joint Chiefs of Staff pressed for a military showdown over Laos, including the possible use of tactical nuclear weapons, while Richard Nixon himself, in a meeting with Kennedy, urged "a commitment of American air power."[12]

[2] *[In 1962] During the course of those long negotiations [at Geneva for a Laotian settlement] fighting continued and the communists made further advances.*

Comment: This is misleading, since both the delays and the renewal of fighting in 1962 were again clearly attributable to Phoumi Nosavan, not to the communists. For months President Kennedy and his special envoy, Averell Harriman, had been attempting to restore Laotian neutrality and bring about the withdrawal of foreign military elements, by working to establish a tripartite coalition government (Phoumist, neutralist, and Pathet Lao). Phoumi continued to resist Harriman's efforts to involve him in such a coalition for months after Kennedy attempted to coerce him by cutting off his subsidy of $3 million a month. In contravention of the May 1961 cease-fire, and against U.S. official advice, Phoumi also built up a garrison at Nam Tha (only fifteen miles from the Chinese border) to a strength of five thousand and began to probe into enemy territory.

When the Pathet Lao, after giving repeated warnings, fired on Nam Tha in May, Phoumi's troops withdrew precipitously into Thailand. Thus the "further advances" of the Pathet Lao were achieved "after a flurry of firefights but no Pathet Lao attack."[13] The Thai government now requested SEATO aid, and the United States responded by sending troops in accordance with the Thanat-Rusk memorandum, signed just two months before, which provided for unilateral U.S. assistance to Thailand. By all accounts "the Royal Lao Army ran from Nam Tha as soon as the first shells started to fall," claiming falsely (as they had done and continued to do in other crises) that they had been attacked by North Vietnamese and Chinese troops.[14]

This deliberate flight was what President Nixon called "a potential threat to Thailand." Phoumi's purposes at Nam Tha were by most accounts not military but political, to thwart the Geneva negotiations and further involve the United States. According to the London *Times*, the CIA had again encouraged Phoumi to resist the establishment of a neutral government in Laos, made up out of its own funds the subsidy that Kennedy had withheld, and urged Phoumi to build up the Nam Tha garrison in spite of contrary U.S. official advice.[15] A State Department spokesman denied the story, and others suggest that the subsidy may have been paid by Phoumi's kinsman, Sarit Thanarat of Thailand, or by Ngo Dinh Diem.

McCoy offers a credible explanation of Phoumi's new source of income after Kennedy cut off his $3 million a month subsidy:

Phoumi turned to the opium traffic as an alternative source of income for his army and government. Although he had controlled the traffic for several years . . . he was not actively involved. . . . The obvious solution to Phoumi's fiscal crisis was for his government to become directly involved in the import and export of Burmese opium. This decision ultimately led to the growth of northwest Laos as one of the largest heroin-producing centers in the world.

Phoumi delegated responsibility for the Burmese opium connection to Ouane Rathikone, who "was appointed chairman of the semiofficial Laotian Opium Administration in early 1962."[16] Meanwhile the CIA assigned one of its officers, William Young, to defend Nam Tha after Phoumi's withdrawal. Young worked with local tribal leaders like Chao Mai, a Yao who had inherited control over the Yao opium trade from his father.[17]

There were disturbing similarities between Phoumi's Nam Tha buildup and the CIA-KMT "Quemoy ploy" of 1958, when without doubt the CIA encouraged Chiang to build up offensive forces on the offshore island, again in spite of official U.S. advice. One such common feature was the activity of Chinese Nationalist Kuomintang troops, apparently armed and supplied by the CIA and Air America, in the Nam Tha area.[18]

[3] *In approving the 1962 [Geneva agreements] the Kennedy Administration in effect accepted the basic formulation which had been advanced by North Vietnam and the Soviet Union for a Laotian political settlement. . . . The 666 Americans who had been assisting the Royal Lao Government withdrew under ICC supervision. In contrast, the North Vietnamese passed only a token forty men through ICC checkpoints and left over 6,000 troops in the country.*

Comment: As part of the 1962 Geneva agreements, the government of Laos declared that it would "not allow any foreign interference in the internal affairs of the Kingdom of Laos," while the other signing governments agreed to the prohibition of all foreign troops and "paramilitary formations" in Laos, including "advisers" (except for "a precisely limited number of French military instructors"). President Nixon's picture of North Vietnamese violations is created by referring to intelligence reports of six thousand North Vietnamese troops in Laos, which (as we have seen) objective scholars such as Toye do not accept.

It appears that at about this time North Vietnamese border patrol battalions began to move into positions on the Laotian side of the frontier passes. But Dommen and Toye suggest that this action was primarily defensive, in reaction to the five thousand U.S. troops that had been flown into Thailand. Meanwhile, Kennedy's acceptance of the 1962 agreements was violated by the United States in Laos in at least two respects.

First, Roger Hilsman, then State Department intelligence chief, records that the president and National Security Council agreed with Harriman's contention that "the United States should comply with both the letter and the spirit of the agreements in every detail . . . and thereafter there should be no . . . 'black' [covert] reconnaissance flights to confirm whether the North Vietnamese had actually withdrawn."[19]

Yet within one or two weeks after the agreements were signed, such reconnaissance was carried out at low levels over Pathet Lao camps by USAF intelligence using RF-101 Voodoo jets. According to Dommen this was part of "regular aerial surveillance of northern Laos in connection with contingency planning related to the deployment of American troops in Thailand."[20] One RF-101 was hit over the Plain of Jars on August 13, 1964, but made it back to its base in Bangkok. The reconnaissance flights continued until May 1964, when they were belatedly authorized by the new administrations that had come to power in both the United States and Laos.

These overflights seem from the outset to have been concerned less with the Ho Chi Minh trail in southern Laos than with the Plain of Jars some two hundred miles to the northwest. This was the area in which the CIA and Air America had since 1960–1961 armed, trained, and supplied Hmong guerrillas.

Second, inasmuch as the Pathet Lao objected vigorously to the support by the CIA and Special Forces of the Hmong guerrilla tribesmen inside the Pathet Lao area of northeast Laos, the agreements called for the withdrawal of "foreign military advisers, experts, instructors . . . and foreign civilians connected with the supply . . . of war materials."[21] Yet Air America continued its airlift into northeast Laos, if only because (as Roger Hilsman observes) "arming the tribesmen engendered an obligation not only to feed them . . . but also to protect them from vengeance."[22] The Pathet Lao and some neutralists objected violently to Air America's airlift in support of their recent enemies; they objected even more violently to Air America's overt airlift of October 1962 to Kong Le.

The first military incident in the breakdown of the 1962 agreements was the shooting down on November 27, 1962, of an Air America C-123 plane over the Plain of Jars. The plane, it soon developed, had not been shot down by the Pathet Lao, but by a new left-leaning neutralist faction under Colonel Deuane, which now opposed Kong Le and his increasing dependency on the Americans.[23]

As far as Air America's airlift was concerned, Nixon's assertion that "our assistance has always been at the request of the legitimate government of Prime Minister Souvanna Phouma" was false. The government (which was a tripartite coalition) had not been consulted; Souvanna himself, as Dommen writes, "had neither endorsed the Air America airlift (the contract was a carryover from [Phoumi's right-wing] government, and had merely been initialed for the coalition by Keo Vithakone, Secretary of State for Social Welfare, a Phoumist) nor prohibited it."[24] Nor apparently was Souvanna consulted about reconnaissance overflights until May 1964.

These U.S. violations of the 1962 agreements were not in response to North Vietnamese activity; they dated back to the signing of the agreements themselves, one month before the date set for the withdrawal of foreign troops. (In this respect Nixon's claim that "our assistance . . . is directly related to North Vietnamese violations of the agreements" suggested a time sequence of causality which was the reverse of the truth.) In effect, in August 1962 our military and civilian intelligence services invited the other side to violate the newly signed agreements by proving conspicuously to them (though not of course to the U.S. public) that the agreements would be violated on our side.

In addition, the "withdrawal" of U.S. military advisers was illusory. For "several years" several hundred members of the "civilian" USAID mission (working out of the mission's "rural development annex") had been former Special Forces and U.S. Army servicemen responsible to the CIA station chief and working in northeast Laos with the CIA-supported Hmong guerrillas of General Vang Pao. Vang Pao's Armée Clandestine was not even answerable to the Royal Lao government or army, being entirely financed and supported by the CIA.

Dommen's carefully qualified description of U.S. compliance with the 1962 agreements ("Not a single American military man was left in Laos in uniform") says nothing to refute the Pathet Lao charge confirmed by American reporters in Laos: that the Hmong's Special Forces "advisers" simply remained, or soon returned, to work for the CIA in the guise of civilian AID officials.[25]

One country embarrassed by these provocations was the Soviet Union. In 1962, as in 1954, Moscow had helped to persuade its Asian allies to accept a negotiated settlement that the Americans would not honor. The Soviet Union soon moved to extricate itself from its Laotian involvement, since its support of Souvanna now caused it to lose favor not only in Peking but also in Hanoi.

[4] *The political arrangements for a three-way government survived only until April 1963, when the Pathet Lao communist leaders departed from the capital and left their cabinet posts vacant. Fighting soon resumed.*

Comment: The Pathet Lao leaders did not resign their cabinet posts in the coalition government; two of their four ministers withdrew from Vientiane, giving the very good reason that, on April 1 and April 12, two of their allies in Colonel Deuane's left-neutralist faction (one of them Quinim Pholsena, the Laotian foreign minister) had been assassinated. The Pathet Lao attributed these murders to a CIA assassination team recruited by the Laotian military police chief Siho. It is known not only that the CIA was using such teams in Vietnam but that in 1963 it was responsible for collaborating with Siho in training his cadres. But the murders can also be attributed to the growing factionalism between Kong Le and Deuane in the neutralist forces. (One of Deuane's men on February 12 killed Kong Le's deputy commander, a few weeks after the murder of a left-oriented Chinese merchant.)

It seems clear that the resumed fighting on the Plain of Jars in April 1963 was chiefly, if not entirely, between the two neutralist factions, rather than with the Pathet Lao. Moreover, Kong Le's faction, with the support of his old enemy Phoumi, was able to capture certain key outposts, such as Tha Thom, controlling a road north into the Plain of Jars.²⁶ But the negotiations between Souvanna Phouma and Souphanouvong in April and May 1964 (after the opening of a new French peace initiative) suggest that the 1962 political arrangements did not break down irrevocably for almost two years.

[5] *In mid-May 1964 the Pathet Lao supported by the North Vietnamese attacked Prime Minister Souvanna Phouma's neutralist military forces on the Plain of Jars.*

Comment: Dommen confirms that in May 1964, Kong Le's men were attacked by the left-neutralist followers of Colonel Deuane. The Pathet Lao shelled the positions of Phoumist troops flown in since 1962, while the North Vietnamese may have played a supporting role, as did the United States with Kong Le. The result of Deuane's initial attacks was roughly to restore the status quo ante April 1963: the town of Tha Thom in particular was recaptured by his men. By the end of May, Deuane's men and the Pathet Lao held virtually all the territory occupied by the neutralists and the Pathet Lao in June 1962, but no more.²⁷ It is essential to understand these specific events, inasmuch as they were used as a pretext for launching the U.S. bombing of Laos in May, a new policy that soon was extended to both North and South Vietnam.

What Nixon omitted to say was that the fighting in May was, once again, preceded not by a left-wing but by a right-wing initiative. On April 19 a right-wing faction headed by Police Chief Siho staged a coup against Souvanna Phouma—a coup that caused the final collapse of the tripartite coalition government, a restructuring of the cabinet to shift it to the right, the disappearance of an independent neutralist faction, and the eventual decline and fall of the former right-wing leader Phoumi Nosavan.²⁸ Thus it was not true, as Nixon's statement claimed, that "the present government of Laos . . . has been the one originally proposed by the communists": the 1962 political settlement broke down altogether when the cabinet was reconstituted without Pathet Lao permission or participation. It was thus not unreasonable for the Pathet Lao to ask (as it did in early 1970) for a conference of all parties to establish a new coalition government (*New York Times*, March 10, 1970).

The day before Chief Siho's coup, on April 18, Souvanna and Phoumi had met with Pathet Lao leader Prince Souphanouvong on the Plain of Jars, reportedly to work out details of a new agreement to neutralize the royal capital of Luang Prabang and reunite the coalition government there.

Though the details are unclear, it seems that the coup was at least in part designed to prevent the restoration of the neutralist coalition. No one has denied Denis Warner's report that Siho "used the acquiescence of Souvanna Phouma and Phoumi Nosavan in the neutralization of the royal capital of Luang Prabang as the excuse" for the coup.²⁹ Ambassador Unger and William Bundy of the State Department personally persuaded Siho to release Souvanna and restore him as prime minister; but the reconstitution of the Laotian army under a new general staff consisting of nine rightist generals and only one neutralist indicated the real shift of power to the right.[30] The new command then ordered the neutralist troops on the Plain of Jars to be integrated with the right under its authority.

This order was too much for many of Kong Le's men on the Plain of Jars and, instead of complying, six battalions of troops defected, some of them to Deuane's left-neutralist faction. Warner confirms that "the resulting mass defections . . . led [in May] to the rout of Kong Le's troops and the fall of the Plain of Jars."[31] Again, as at Nam Tha in 1962, many troops withdrew, amid charges of a North Vietnamese and Chinese Communist invasion, without ever having been directly attacked.[32]

These right-wing maneuvers in Laos, whether or not they were directly encouraged by American advisers on the scene, cannot but have been indirectly encouraged by the highly publicized debate in Washington over Vietnam. It was known that in early 1964 many generals were calling for U.S. air strikes against so-called communist bases in the north, including the bombing of the Ho Chi Minh trail in Laos. The result of Siho's April coup, if not the intention, was to make way for the initiation of this bombing policy.

One striking feature about the April 19 coup is that it was announced in Bangkok one day before it occurred (*Bangkok Post*, April 18, 1964), and over Taiwan Radio the day before that.

[6] *In May 1964, as North Vietnamese presence increased, the United States, at royal Lao government request, began flying certain interdictory missions against invaders who were violating Lao neutrality.*

Comment: By this important admission it is now for the first time conceded that the United States assumed a combat role in Laos in May 1964, at a time when the North Vietnamese army was still engaged in a support role comparable to that of Air America. (North Vietnam was not formally accused by the United States of violating the Geneva agreements until June 29, 1964.) The air attacks were first carried out by U.S. "civilian" pilots from Air America in T-28 fighter-bombers based in Thailand but carrying Laotian markings. On June 11, 1964, one of these T-28s attacked the Chinese cultural and economic mission at the Pathet Lao capital on the Plain of Jars, killing at least one Chinese. The United States at that time denied responsibility, though the State Department revealed that Thai pilots also flew the T-28s and had been involved.[33]

On May 21, 1964, the United States admitted for the first time that "unarmed United States jets" were flying reconnaissance missions over Laos. Dean Rusk later explained that this was in response to Souvanna Phouma's general request for assistance, but Souvanna Phouma refused to comment on the matter of reconnaissance flights for the next three weeks. In fact these flights had been conducted regularly since at least as early as August 1962. What was new was that in mid-May President Johnson ordered the planes to switch from high-altitude to provoc-

ative low-altitude reconnaissance. At the insistence of the chief of naval operations, he also authorized accompanying escorts of armed jet fighters. These were
ordered not to bomb or strafe Laotian installations until and unless U.S. planes
were damaged.[34] When a navy RF-8 was shot down on June 6, President Johnson
ordered retaliatory strikes.

At this point Souvanna Phouma finally commented publicly on the reconnaissance flights: he reportedly asked that they cease altogether forthwith. (The *New
York Times* on June 10 published a report that he had not agreed to the use of
armed escorts.) On June 12 Souvanna announced that the reconnaissance flights
would continue; this suggested to some observers that since the April 19 coup
and the collapse of the neutralists Souvanna was no longer his own master.[35] His
reluctant ex post facto acquiescence in the use of jet fighter escorts for reconnaissance was the closest approximation in the public record to what Nixon called a
"Royal Lao Government request" for interdictory missions one month earlier.

It has never been explained why the U.S. reconnaissance pilots were ordered
to conduct their flights over Laos at low altitudes and slow speeds, when (as they
informed their superiors) with their modern equipment they could obtain photographs of equal quality if they were permitted to fly higher.[36] The orders seem to
reflect the determination of certain air force and navy officials either to coerce
the other side by a U.S. air presence or, alternatively, to obtain a suitable provocation, as was finally supplied by the Tonkin Gulf incidents, for the bombing of
North Vietnam.

The withdrawals from the Plain of Jars in 1964 produced what Phoumi had
failed to obtain by his withdrawal from Nam Tha in 1962—a direct armed U.S.
intervention in Laos and the frustration of a new initiative (this time by the
French) to restore peace in that country. The similarities between the two withdrawals—the gratuitous right-wing provocations, the flight before being attacked,
and the incredible stories of Chinese Communist invasion—have been attributed
by some to Laotian lack of discipline.

Toye, however, will not accept this explanation for 1962,[37] and there are disturbing indications that in 1964 Laotian and U.S. hawks were still intriguing
together to bring about a further Americanization of the war. Perhaps the chief
indication was the dispatch in May of U.S. Navy aircraft carriers into the Tonkin
Gulf area for the purpose of conducting "reconnaissance" flights and air strikes
against Laos (even the new armed flights could easily have been initiated, as in
the past, by the USAF in Thailand).

By the time the U.S. jet air strikes got under way in June, the rainy season in
Laos had begun, the panic was over, and there was no prospect of ground military
activity in Laos for the next several months. Yet many observers (including Mel-
vin Laird, who had his own Pentagon channels) predicted accurately that the aircraft carriers moved in against Laos might soon be used against North Vietnam.
As *Aviation Week* reported on June 22, 1964, President Johnson appeared to be
awaiting reactions to the Laotian air strikes ("the first U.S. offensive military

action since Korea") before taking "the next big step on the escalation scale."
On June 3, 1964, a *New York Times* correspondent reported "a sense of crisis
and foreboding" in Southeast Asia, attributed "more to the statements of U.S.
Government officials than to any immediate emergency in Laos, South Vietnam
or Cambodia."

[7] *Since this administration has been in office, North Vietnamese pressure has continued. Last spring, the North Vietnamese mounted a campaign which threatened the
royal capital and moved beyond the areas previously occupied by communists. A
counter-attack by the Lao government forces, intended to relieve this military pressure and cut off supply lines, caught the enemy by surprise and succeeded beyond
expectations in pushing them off the . . . Plain of Jars.*

Comment: This statement left out the biggest development under the Nixon
administration. Shortly after November 1968 (when it halted the bombing of
North Vietnam) the United States began to apply to combat zones in Laos the
tactic of massive bombardment hitherto reserved for Vietnam and the region of
the Ho Chi Minh trail in the Laotian panhandle. According to Senator Cranston,
air strikes against Laos increased from 4,500 sorties a month (before the November 1968 halt to the bombing of North Vietnam) to between 12,500 and 15,000
sorties a month in 1970. (Other sources suggest a much more dramatic
increase.)[38]

This new policy led to the total annihilation of many Laotian towns (at first
briefly, but falsely, attributed to a North Vietnamese "scorched earth" policy). It
was also accompanied by the evacuation and resettlement (apparently sometimes
by coercion) of between 500,000 and 600,000 Laotians, or about a quarter of the
total population. (See the *Nation*, January 26, 1970; *New York Times*, March 12,
1970, 3.)

With this new tactic, General Vang Pao's CIA-advised Hmong guerrillas were
ordered to withdraw rather than suffer serious casualties in attempting to hold
forward positions: their function was rather to engage the enemy and thus expose
them to heavy losses through air strikes. These were the tactics once alleged by
U.S. generals to be succeeding in South Vietnam: attrition of the enemy by massive bombardment, rather than serious attempts to hold territory. The new tactics
(like the original covert U.S. military involvements eight years earlier) were inaugurated during the "lame duck" period of a changeover in administrations. In
December 1968 the Pathet Lao protested to the International Control Commission that U.S. planes were dropping four or five times as many bombs in Laos as
they had done two months earlier.[39]

In accordance with their orders to engage the enemy while avoiding heavy casualties, Vang Pao's guerrillas twice in 1969 made spectacular advances into the
enemy Plain of Jars area (on one occasion to about thirty miles from the North
Vietnamese border) and then withdrew from key outposts like Xieng Khouang

and Ban Ban without waiting for the enemy to attack in strength. Just as with General Phoumi in 1962, these withdrawals from isolated advance positions in the face of enemy probes were widely publicized and used as arguments for U.S. escalation. The Kennedy administration did not take this bait; the Nixon administration (with its 1970 B-52 strikes) did.

In the wake of the reported bombing increase, there was also a reported rise in Pathet Lao and North Vietnamese ground activity. Apparently none of this activity violated the 1961–1962 cease-fire line as seriously as Vang Pao's unprecedented forays of April-May and August-September into the Xieng Khouang-Ban Ban area. Most of the Pathet Lao activity in the northeast was directed against Hmong outposts within their base area, notably the forward communications post of Na Khang, which was used for the all-weather bombing of North Vietnam, and the U.S.-Thai base at Muong Soui, which was used to support the Hmong outposts. On August 25, 1969, the *New York Times* said that "if Vang Vieng falls . . . the Laotian government will have been pushed behind the cease-fire line of 1961." But even Vang Vieng was still on the Pathet Lao side of the line.

There were disturbing indications that in 1969 (as in 1962 and 1964) right-wing provocations and escalations were deliberately intended to frustrate Souvanna Phouma's continuing efforts to restore peace and a neutralist coalition government. In May 1969, Souvanna Phouma saw the North Vietnamese ambassador to Laos (at the latter's invitation) for the first time in over four years. On May 15 he announced he was hopeful that the Laotian problem could be solved even before the end of the Vietnam War. It was later revealed that he had offered a formula for the termination of U.S. bombing comparable to that used in Vietnam: a gradual reduction in the bombing in return for a gradual withdrawal of North Vietnamese troops. Souvanna said that he would accept the continued use of the Ho Chi Minh trail by the North Vietnamese troops "with the condition that those troops withdrew" elsewhere.[40] (I was told that in September, four months after this proposal by Souvanna, the North Vietnamese withdrew altogether from the Plain of Jars.)

Four days later, on May 19, the *New York Times* reported that with the advent of the rainy season, Laos was "suddenly quiet." Pathet Lao pressure had tapered off: "Where there is any action government forces appear to be taking the initiative." Only one day later "fierce fighting" was reported from the Plain of Jars: Vang Pao's CIA-supported guerrillas had clashed with the enemy thirteen miles from Xieng Khouang. On May 27 Vang Pao was reported to have withdrawn from Xieng Khouang (which he had held for one month) "following orders . . . not to risk heavy casualties." The next day his troops seized Ban Ban, about thirty miles from North Vietnam, "as Laotian and American bombers continued devastating attacks on North Vietnamese soldiers and supply lines all over northeastern Laos."[41]

This chronology recalled the depressing sequence of occasions in the Vietnam War when a new diplomatic initiative was followed by a new escalation or an intensification of the bombing, instead of a hoped-for reduction.[42] This pattern of a "politics of escalation" appeared to repeat itself in February 1970. In early February

> Souvanna Phouma startled the diplomatic community by publicly offering to go to Hanoi to negotiate an end to the conflict . . . Souvanna was ready, so he said, to agree to the neutralization of the Plain of Jars . . . and . . . promised that his government would "close its eyes" to what goes along the Ho Chi Minh Trail.[43]

On February 17 the Associated Press reported "some of the heaviest air raids ever flown in Southeast Asia" and, on February 19, the first "massive air strikes by U.S. B-52 bombers in the Plain of Jars region." On February 22 the Associated Press fed the American public the typical kind of panic story that had been emanating from northeast Laos ever since the phony "offensive" of August 1959. Vang Pao's guerrillas, it said, had been "swept from the Plain of Jars by an overwhelming North Vietnamese blow . . . with a third of its force dead or missing. . . . The government garrison of 1,500 men based at Xieng Khouang was hit by 6,000 North Vietnamese supported by tanks."

On the next day came the typical corrective story: the attack had been made by four hundred troops, not six thousand; the defenders (who had falsely inflated their strength "for payday purposes") had withdrawn with "very little close-in action." It would appear that once again wildly exaggerated tales from remote areas had resulted in the frustration of a peace initiative, by what was (as Senator Mansfield warned) a significant escalation of the bombing.[44]

[8] *We are trying above all to save American and Allied lives in South Vietnam which are threatened by the continual infiltration of North Vietnamese troops and supplies along the Ho Chi Minh trail. . . . Today there are 67,000 North Vietnamese troops in [Laos]. There are no American troops there. Hanoi is not threatened by Laos; it runs risks only when it moves its forces across borders.*

Comment: The CIA's persistent support, guidance, and encouragement of Hmong guerrilla activities in northeast Laos cannot be rationalized by references to the Ho Chi Minh trail. As anyone can see by looking at a map, the Ho Chi Minh trail runs south from the Mu Gia pass in the southern portion of the Laotian panhandle, two hundred miles to the southeast of the Plain of Jars. These Hmong tribesmen were first trained by the French for paramilitary activities inside what is now North Vietnam, where some of them continued to operate for years after the 1954 Geneva agreements, almost to the time when their French officers were replaced by CIA "Special Forces."[45] Veterans of the Special Forces, now "civilians" working for the CIA, are still working with the Hmong behind enemy lines; Air America and, more recently, Continental Air Services have never ceased airlifting and supplying them.

Hanoi is indeed directly threatened by these CIA activities just across the Laotian border. Heavily fortified Hmong outposts at Pa Thi and Na Khang were developed as forward communications centers for the all-weather pinpoint bombing of North Vietnam.[46] On November 12, 1968, the *Far Eastern Economic Review* reported "evidence that American aircraft, including jets, were flying from a secret base in northern Laos . . . about fifty miles from the North Vietnam border."

It is difficult to explain the tenacity of the CIA's ground operations behind enemy lines in northeast Laos or the conversion of the Plain of Jars into an evacuated "free strike" zone for F-4s, F-105s, and B-52s, except as part of a "forward strategy," to remind North Vietnam of the threat that the United States might resume bombing it. The Nixon statement indeed suggested that the United States hoped to use its escalation in Laos as a means of imposing its peace formula on Vietnam. ("What we do in Laos has thus as its aim to bring about the conditions for progress toward peace in the entire Indochinese Peninsula.")

The 1970 intelligence estimates of 67,000 North Vietnamese in Laos had themselves sharply "escalated" from the figure of 50,000 that was used by the Pentagon up until one month earlier.[47] This was reminiscent of the similar "escalation" of infiltration estimates for South Vietnam in January 1965. The claims then put forward as to the presence of regular North Vietnamese army units in South Vietnam, including at least a battalion if not a division, were tacitly refuted only six months later by no less an authority than McNamara.[48] Six months later it was of course too late. The regular bombing of North and South Vietnam had been initiated; the full "Americanization" of the Vietnam War had been achieved.

The Nixon statement on Laos was an alarming document, not because of what it misrepresented but because of what it might portend. In its skillful retelling of events known only to a few, it resembled the State Department's white paper of February 1965 on Vietnam. The white paper, which also relied heavily on intelligence "estimates," was not really an effort to understand the true developments of the past. It was instead the ominous harbinger for a new strategy of victory through American air power, a document aimed not at serious students of Southeast Asia (who swiftly saw through it) but at the "silent majority" of that era.

The publication of the *Pentagon Papers* confirmed the double roles of the intelligence documents that were finally published as the State Department's white papers of 1961 and 1965 on Vietnam. In both cases the documents first strengthened a particular case for escalation being debated within the bureaucracy, and later were published as part of a carefully concatenated escalation scenario.[49] Not only public opinion but the bureaucratic decision-making process itself was distorted by the dubiously inflated claims of external North Vietnamese intervention contained in both documents. The 1965 white paper in particular doubled the U.S. intelligence estimates of infiltration from North Vietnam which had been publicly released only six months before, on July 29, 1964; these

increased infiltration estimates actually followed the emergence of secret bureaucratic planning to carry the war north, rather than giving rise to it.[50]

The escalated infiltration statistics in the Key Biscayne statement appear to
have played the same controversial double role:

> Hanoi's most recent military build-up in Laos has been particularly escalatory. They
> have poured over 13,000 additional troops into Laos during the past few months,
> raising their total in Laos to over 67,000. Thirty North Vietnamese battalions from
> regular division units participated in the current campaign in the Plain of Jars with
> tanks, armored cars, and long-range artillery.

But thirty North Vietnamese battalions (about 9,000 men) are unlikely to have
participated in a campaign that (as we have seen) involved only 400 combat
troops, who were mostly indigenous Pathet Lao. This figure of 400, a typical
number for a Pathet Lao operation, was later confirmed by U.S. embassy sources
in Vientiane. French and Laotian officials in Vientiane put the total North Vietnamese presence at 30,000–35,000 in mid-1970, of which at least 60 percent
were involved in maintaining the Ho Chi Minh and Sihanouk trails and 5–10
percent remained in the rear. Inasmuch as at least half of the remainder (75 percent, according to the British military attaché) were engaged in support functions,
this would only leave about five thousand or so North Vietnamese troops available for actual combat.[51]

In other words, the North Vietnamese combat presence in Laos was at most
roughly equal to the 4,800 or so Thai irregular troops that Senator Fulbright estimated to be fighting in Laos under CIA auspices. It was vastly outnumbered by
the CIA's whole mercenary force of 30,000 in Laos, said by a Senate Foreign
Relations Committee staff report to provide the "cutting edge" of the Vientiane
armed forces.[52] In this context the Key Biscayne statistics, compiled at the time
of the Pathet Lao's important five-point peace proposals in early 1970, would
appear to be special pleading for the continuation of America's largest covert war
effort, from the very intelligence sources responsible for the prosecution of that
war. In Laos, as soon after in Cambodia, the manipulation of intelligence was the
key to the manipulation of policy.

NOTES

1. Peter Dale Scott, "Laos: The Story Nixon Won't Tell," *New York Review of Books,*
April 9, 1970, 35–45.

2. Alfred W. McCoy, *The Politics of Heroin* (Brooklyn, N.Y.: Lawrence Hill, 1991),
xiv–xv. I doubt that among Chiang's supporters there was any clear demarcation between
the unlikely long-term goal of a return to the mainland and the short-term goal of the drug
traffic that both organized and financed KMT links to the Chinese populations and triads
of Southeast Asia.

3. McCoy, *Politics*, xv. I was never able to establish whether this plant, as well as a similar plant in South Vietnam, was established after Richard Nixon's 1964 visit to Asia, and specifically his visit to the drug-connected Asian People's Anti-Communist League (see chapter 11). Ironically it was under Nixon that the United States initiated relations with the Chinese People's Republic (with Kissinger's secret visit of early July 1971) and simultaneously announced that it would crack down on Laotian, Thai, and South Vietnamese leaders involved in the drug traffic (*New York Times*, July 8, 1971). The key month was June 1971, two months after the chief Laotian APACL delegate, Prince Sopsaisana, was caught in Paris with sixty kilos of high-grade heroin worth $13.5 million on the streets of New York (McCoy, *Politics*, 286).

4. McCoy, *Politics*, 302–3. Phoumi, who had helped instigate the coup but ended up severely weakened by it, had just met in March with Vietnamese General Nguyen Khanh, who was hoping to see the U.S. war effort expand to include North Vietnam and even China. The CIA reported that the coup "was modeled on General Khanh's Saigon coup" of January 1964 (David Kaiser, *American Tragedy: Kennedy, Johnson, and the Origins of the Vietnam War* [Cambridge: Harvard University Press, Belknap Press, 2000], 317). General Siho, publicly identified as the coup's author, was Phoumi's right-hand man and was allegedly corrupt himself (McCoy, *Politics*, 563).

5. McCoy, *Politics*, 337.

6. A. M. Halpern and H. B. Friedman, *Communist Strategy in Laos*, RAND, RM-2561, 51; cited and amplified in Bernard Fall, *Anatomy of a Crisis* (Garden City, N.Y.: Doubleday, 1969), 108.

7. Arthur Schlesinger Jr., *A Thousand Days* (Boston: Houghton Mifflin, 1965), 325–26.

8. Hugh Toye, *Laos: Buffer State or Battleground* (Oxford: Oxford University Press, 1968), 113–31; U.S. Congress, House, Committee on Government Operations, *United States Aid Operations in Laos: Seventh Report*, 86th Cong., 1st sess., June 15, 1969.

9. Text of the president's statement as printed in the *San Francisco Chronicle*, March 6, 1970, 9. The late Bernard Fall observed that the CIA policy of deliberate "polarization" in Laos in this period "had thrown into communism's arms a great many people who essentially were not communists (just as in 1946 many Vietnamese who at first merely wanted the French to get out as colonial masters in Vietnam were finally pushed into Ho Chi Minh's Vietminh) but who, by deliberate action on our side, were left with no alternative" (Fall, *Anatomy of a Crisis*, 199; cf. 189).

According to Arthur Schlesinger Jr. (*A Thousand Days*, 328): "The Eisenhower Administration, by rejecting the neutralist alternative, had driven the neutralists into reluctant alliance with the communists and provoked (and in many eyes legitimized) open Soviet aid to the Pathet Lao. All this was done without serious consultation with the incoming administration which would shortly inherit the problem." For further details, see Toye, *Laos*, 145–65.

10. Arthur J. Dommen, *Conflict in Laos: The Politics of Neutralization* (New York: Praeger, 1964), 238. Even though he conceded that North Vietnam in 1962 was "very probably" moved by fear of the five thousand U.S. troops airlifted into Thailand, Dommen was no apologist for the North Vietnamese presence in Laos. On the contrary, his book (prepared with assistance from the Council on Foreign Relations staff) urged "the sudden encirclement of one of the Vietnamese border patrol battalions . . . and its noiseless liqui-

dation by a determined and highly trained [US] Special Forces unit." This, he argued, "would have a tremendous shock effect in Hanoi" (p. 301).

11. Bernard Fall, *Vietnam Witness, 1953–66* (New York: Praeger, 1966), 249.

12. Toye, *Laos*, 178; Roger Hilsman, *To Move a Nation* (Garden City, N.Y.: Doubleday, 1967), 127; *New York Times*, March 25, 1961, 2; Fall, *Anatomy of a Crisis*, 206; *Fortune*, September 1961, 94; Schlesinger, *Thousand Days*, 336–37.

13. Toye, *Laos*, 182; cf. Hilsman, *To Move a Nation*, 140.

14. Denis Warner, *The Last Confucian* (New York: Macmillan, 1963), 217–18.

15. London *Times*, May 24, 1962; May 31, 1962. A story in the *Saturday Evening Post*, April 7, 1962, 87–88, also identified a "handful" of CIA and MAAG members as working "industriously to undermine our present policy in Laos." Kennedy, when he approved cutting off aid to Phoumi, overruled CIA Director McCone (Kaiser, *American Tragedy*, 127; citing *FRUS 1961–1963*, vol. 24, no. 223, p. 264). See also Kaiser, *American Tragedy*, 134–39.

16. McCoy, *Politics*, 300; cf. 288.

17. McCoy, *Politics*, 335–37.

18. President Kennedy made another effort to have the KMT troops removed from the area in the spring of 1961, but some four thousand were reported to have insisted on remaining in Laos and Thailand (*Washington Post*, March 16, 1970, A10). According to Alfred McCoy, "some 2,000 to 3,000 KMT regulars had been left behind in Laos, and they were hired by the CIA to strengthen the rightist position in the area" (McCoy, *Politics*, 349).

19. Hilsman, *To Move a Nation*, 152–53.

20. Dommen, *Conflict in Laos,* 238; Grant Wolfkill, *Reported to Be Alive* (London: W. H. Allen, 1966), 273–74.

21. *Protocol to the Declaration on the Neutrality of Laos*; Articles 1(a), 2, 4; in Dommen, *Conflict in Laos*, 314–15.

22. Hilsman, *To Move a Nation*, 115; cf. Bernard Fall, *Street without Joy* (Harrisburg, Pa.: Stackpole, 1967), 340; Dommen, *Conflict in Laos*, 233.

23. *New York Times*, December 5, 1962, 3; Dommen, *Conflict in Laos*, 243.

24. Dommen, *Conflict in Laos*, 244.

25. Jack Foisie, *San Francisco Chronicle*, March 10, 1970, 16; Dommen, *Conflict in Laos*, 239, italics added. According to Foisie, "There is the possibility that some [annex] men have gained temporary leave from the Armed Forces and can return to the military after their contract expires." Some of the U.S. "civilian" pilots working in Laos are also reported to have been recruited from the USAF on this basis.

On March 13, 1970, Senator Fulbright reported that Richard Helms, director of Central Intelligence, had "generally confirmed" the accuracy of news dispatches from Laos reporting the CIA activity (*New York Times*, March 14, 1970, 11).

26. As late as May 4, 1964, William Bundy could tell a House Committee that the power change since July 1962 in the Plain of Jars area had "been favorable . . . to the non-communist elements of the Government"; House Committee on Appropriations, *Foreign Operations Appropriations for 1965, Hearings before a Subcommittee*, 88th Cong., 2d sess., 414.

27. Dommen, *Conflict in Laos*, 256: "On May 16, the dissident followers of Colonel Deuane Siphaseuth, with Pathet Lao and North Vietnamese support, compelled Kong Le

to abandon a number of positions on the Plain and to evacuate his Muong Phanh command post. . . . By the end of May, the Pathet Lao and the 'true neutralists' [under Deuane] occupied virtually all the ground that had been held jointly by themselves and Kong Le . . . in June 1962." Cf. Toye, *Laos*, 193.

28. "Although the ostensible motivation for the right-wing coup of April 19, 1964 was to eliminate the neutralist army . . . the generals seem to have devoted most of their energy to breaking up Phoumi's financial empire" (McCoy, *Politics*, 302). The troops in the coup were commanded by General Kouprasith Abhay, who "inherited most of [Phoumi's] real estate holdings, brothels, and opium dens in the Vientiane region" (p. 303). McCoy's informative account of the coup does not mention the role played by KMT officers from Taiwan.

29. Denis Warner, *Reporting Southeast Asia* (Sydney: Angus & Robertson, 1966), 190. Wilfred Burchett (*The Second Indochina War* [New York: International Publishers, 1970], 162–63) says that although the April 18 tripartite meeting was in fact fruitless, fear of its success caused the CIA to proceed with the April 19 coup.

30. *New York Times*, May 14, 1964, 11; May 19, 1964, 5; Fall, *Street without Joy*, 341.

31. Warner, *Reporting Southeast Asia*, 191. The integration order recalled a similar rightist order in 1959 to the Pathet Lao, an order that was instrumental in triggering the Laotian war.

32. *New York Times*, May 16, 1964, 2; May 28, 1964, 10.

33. *Pentagon Papers*, 239; Dommen, *Conflict in Laos*, 259; Toye, *Laos*, 194. The first substantial reports of North Vietnamese infiltration followed the new U.S. bombing policy. Cf. T. D. Allman, *Far Eastern Economic Review*, January 1, 1970, 21: "When the Vientiane government permitted the Americans to start the bombing, the North Vietnamese committed increasing amounts of troops in an effort to discredit that government."

34. *Pentagon Papers*, 239; Dommen, *Conflict in Laos*, 238; Joseph C. Goulden, *Truth Is the First Casualty: The Gulf of Tonkin Affair—Illusion and Reality* (New York: Rand McNally, 1969), 97.

35. Toye, *Laos*, 194; Dommen, *Conflict in Laos*, 258: "Souvanna . . . became daily more of a figurehead in a situation over which he had little control." In response to the news of Souvanna's objections, the United States announced that it was suspending the reconnaissance flights "for at least 48 hours." But at the same time the State Department announced that the flights would continue "subject to consultation." This was by no means the first time that the United States had treated Souvanna in so humiliating a fashion; cf. Fall, *Anatomy of a Crisis*, 193ff., 223.

36. Goulden, *Truth Is the First Casualty*, 97. Grant Wolfkill, then a prisoner of the Pathet Lao, testifies to the lowness of the flights in 1962 (*Reported to Be Alive*, 273–74): "Flying at a thousand feet, it [an unmarked jet F-101] whipped through the valley and swung around leisurely at one end. I could see the pilot's head as the plane turned. . . . Three days later the F-101 returned. . . . Every gun in the camp blazed away at it this time. With arrogant indifference the jet maintained its course." Statement of Secretary Rusk, July 30, 1964, in U.S. Department of State, *American Foreign Policy*, 1964, 943; see also Dommen, *Conflict in Laos*, 258.

37. Toye, *Laos*, 182: "After a flurry of fire fights but no Pathet Lao attack, Nam Tha was abandoned. This time there could be no doubt about it; General Boun Leut is no poltroon; he had obeyed Phoumi's orders."

38. T. D. Allman reported in the *Far Eastern Economic Review,* January 1, 1970, 21, that "the U.S. now flies as many as 20,000 bombing sorties a month in Laos." Richard Dudman (*St. Louis Post-Dispatch,* December 23, 1969) put the level one year earlier at one thousand a month. The higher figure was correct: "By the end of 1969, the number of American bombing missions over Laos had reached a total of 242,000, an average of more than 650 missions a day" (Seymour Hersh, *The Price of Power* [New York: Summit, 1983], 168).

39. *New York Times,* December 31, 1968, 6.

40. *New York Times,* May 15, 1969, 13; May 17, 3; *Far Eastern Economic Review,* June 5, 1969, 569; *San Francisco Chronicle,* March 6, 1970, 26.

41. *New York Times,* May 19, 1969, 6; May 20, 3; May 27, 5; May 28, 9.

42. Franz Schurmann, Peter Dale Scott, and Reginald Zelnik, *The Politics of Escalation in Vietnam* (Boston: Beacon, 1966); David Kraslow and Stuart H. Loory, *The Secret Search for Peace in Vietnam* (New York: Random House, 1968), 3–74; *Ramparts,* March 1968, 56–58; *New York Times,* January 6, 1968, 28.

43. *Newsweek,* February 16, 1970, 37.

44. *San Francisco Chronicle,* February 17, 1970; February 19; February 22; February 23. In August 1969 there was also the mysterious episode of the tribal double agent who, on Vang Pao's instruction, sold a map of the secret Hmong headquarters at Long Cheng to six members of the North Vietnamese embassy. According to T. D. Allman, "The affair . . . appeared to be at least in part a right-wing effort to reduce the Prime Minister's room to maneuver and perhaps even force a break in diplomatic relations between the two countries," *Far Eastern Economic Review,* September 11, 1969, 648.

45. Fall, *Street without Joy,* 341.

46. Robert Shaplen, *Time Out of Hand* (New York: Harper & Row, 1969), 346; *New York Times,* October 26, 1969, 24.

47. Nixon's Key Biscayne estimate of 67,000 troops ("put out . . . without clearing it with any of the experts") infuriated a USIA official, Jerome H. Doolittle, who was a press attaché in Laos. "The night before the statement was issued, Doolittle had told a press briefing in Vientiane that there were 40,000 North Vietnamese troops in the country." Doolittle recalled later that "what they'd done was add up every conceivable estimate" (Hersh, *Price of Power,* 171 n.).

48. Secretary McNamara on June 17, 1965, Department of State *Bulletin,* July 5, 1965, 18; cf. Department of State *Bulletin,* March 22, 1965, 414; May 17, 1965, 750, 753; Theodore Draper, "How Not to Negotiate," *New York Review of Books,* May 4, 1967, 27 n.; Theodore Draper, *Abuse of Power* (New York: Viking, 1967), 76–77; Schurmann, Scott, and Zelnik, *Politics of Escalation,* 47 n.

49. *Pentagon Papers,* 107, 152–53, 338, 422. The 1965 white paper was drafted by Chester Cooper, a former CIA officer attached to the White House staff.

50. *New York Times,* January 27, 1965, 2; cf. *Pentagon Papers.*

51. These statistics are taken from the valuable appendix to Fred Branfman, "Presidential War in Laos, 1964–1970," in Nina Adams and Alfred W. McCoy, eds., *Laos: War and Revolution* (New York: Harper & Row, 1970), 278–80.

52. *San Francisco Chronicle,* August 3, 1971, 1, 18.

10

Cambodia and Oil, 1970

What I have to say about Cambodian politics in this chapter is less up-to-date than what I have to say about oil. Two recent excellent studies, one by Australian David P. Chandler and the other by French Marie Alexandrine Martin, tell us much more about the internal reasons for Cambodia's collapse in the 1970s.[1] But both books either discount or ignore external factors to which I refer, above all the intervention of U.S., Japanese, and Indonesian covert operators.

Neither book addresses the detailed charges of Seymour Hersh in 1983 that "Sihanouk's overthrow [in 1970] had been for years a high priority of the [U.S.] Green Berets reconnaissance units operating inside Cambodia since the late 1960s."[2] Hersh reports in particular that U.S. intelligence officials proposed "to insert a U.S.-trained assassination team disguised as Vietcong insurgents into Phnom Penh to kill Prince Sihanouk as a pretext for revolution."[3] I say more about this in a later addition to the chapter.

With respect to what I say below about Union Oil's (now Unocal's) offshore concessions in Cambodia, Unocal now has at least three petroleum concessions in what is referred to as the Thailand-Cambodia overlapping area in the Gulf of Thailand. All three are held conjointly with the Japanese Mitsui Oil Exploration Company, also referred to in this chapter. The oldest of these, Gas Sale Agreement No. 1, dates back to March 1, 1972, in the brief period while Richard Nixon was still successfully propping up General Lon Nol in Phnom Penh. Another concession, held by Chevron with British Gas Asia, Inc., is dated March 8, 1972.[4]

When in 1995 Cambodia first offered three offshore blocks near Sihanoukville for bidding, Unocal was reported to have been among the seventeen firms expressing interest.[5] Two years later, the offshore border disputes between Thailand, Cambodia, and Vietnam were finally resolved. It was announced then that "after decades of waiting, Unocal Thailand now expects to begin next year an exploration programme over an area . . . awarded to it in 1968 by the Thai Government."[6]

167

I would like to supplement my earlier analysis, published in June 1970 in the *New York Review of Books*, of the secret "crisis" decision to send regular U.S. ground troops into Cambodia. That analysis, which detailed the strategic require-ments of the air war impelling the Joint Chiefs and the National Security Council, was limited in the same way as the *Pentagon Papers*. At the same time, there are clues in the *Pentagon Papers* (e.g., that covert U.S. air operations against North Vietnam immediately *preceded* the Tonkin Gulf incidents)[7] which justify greater emphasis on the role of the covert U.S. air and ground operations in Cambodia, preceding Nixon's decision to invade that country.

One can now see the strategic requirements of the air war in a broader context, political and economic rather than military, both in Cambodia and in America itself. At first glance these other considerations might seem to overshadow the role of intelligence agencies to which I drew passing attention. On the contrary this larger perspective reinforces and even explains the role of covert operations and bureaucratic intrigues, rather than overshadows them. It also raises grave questions about the role of President Nixon and his political backers.

An undoubted crisis had been slowly developing for some years in Cambodia, under the more and more nominal leadership of Sihanouk. In retrospect one can see that Sihanouk's efforts to maintain a neutralist posture were increasingly hopeless and anachronistic, for economic as well as strategic reasons. Lon Nol's coup[8] of March 1970, which paved the way for the American and South Vietnam-ese invasion, was only the ultimate and most visible stage in a rightward shift of power that had begun some three years before. This was due to

> pressures which were in part the result of steadily deteriorating economic conditions. Over the past several years the Cambodian economy has become subject to increas-ing strains. Cambodia has been extraordinarily dependent on manufactured imports, both for day-to-day consumption and . . . for industrial development. The exports exchanged for these goods have been rubber and rice. But the surplus of these com-modities has never been enough to meet the country's foreign exchange needs. Until 1963 these needs had been met largely by U.S. economic and military assistance. When in 1963 Sihanouk terminated the aid agreements with the United States in his efforts to remain free of political pressure from Washington, the flow of dollars stopped, and since 1964 there has been a growing balance of payments deficit.[9]

By the fall of 1967 Sihanouk was forced to seek a rapprochement with the American-dominated World Bank, International Monetary Fund, and Asian Development Bank (all of which linked the prospects of aid to the abandonment by Sihanouk of his faltering experiments in "Buddhist socialism" and national-ized foreign trade). In this context Sihanouk shifted to the right, received Chester Bowles in January 1968, and began increasingly to crack down on Khmer Rouge and NLF troops. In August 1969 Sihanouk formed a new government headed by Lon Nol and Sirik Matak, the men who would soon overthrow him. Meanwhile, in June 1969, Sihanouk resumed diplomatic relations with Washington; the U.S.

embassy, in 1959 caught red-handed in the act of plotting against him, was allowed to reopen. "Economic necessity, not fear of the Vietnamese Communists, seems to have been the prime reason."[10]

In Washington new political and economic pressures lent weight to the strategic arguments of the Joint Chiefs of Staff for widening the war into Cambodia. Defense Secretary Laird, a "hawk" by anyone's standards in 1968, found himself increasingly bypassed and overruled by military demands for escalation in 1969 and 1970. The reason lay in the White House. A president who had been recently elected on a program of peace proved to be highly receptive to military proposals that promised to end the war quickly, more receptive than a defense secretary who saw these proposals as an overcommitment of limited resources that increasingly weakened the U.S. military posture in the world as a whole. Nixon and Kissinger began to deal with the Joint Chiefs over the head of Laird.

By the time of Nixon's election in 1968, moreover, the interests of large American oil companies had been drawn to the possibility of offshore oil discoveries in the neighborhood of Cambodia. The first offshore geological surveys were made in the late 1950s by Chinese mainland geologists, as a result of which a French company drilled the first oil well, unsuccessfully, in 1971.[11] Leases in the adjacent offshore waters of Thailand had been awarded in September 1967 to six oil companies (five of them American); this lent urgency to unresolved offshore border disputes between Thailand and Cambodia that were initially resolved after the Lon Nol regime took over in 1970.[12]

Meanwhile, in the wake of U.S. Navy–sponsored hydrographic and geomagnetic surveys dating back to 1957, the months of November and December 1968 saw a "highly successful" seismic refraction oil exploration survey around the South Vietnamese island of Poulo Panjang, which lies directly south of Cambodia.[13] This survey was only the last and most promising of a preliminary series, conducted under the auspices of the United Nations Economic Commission for Asia and the Far East (ECAFE). State Department denials notwithstanding, official documents reveal that the great bulk of the technical assistance for these surveys came from the U.S. Naval Oceanographic Office (NAVOCEANO).

According to NAVOCEANO's annual report for 1968, "the Navy's coastal survey ships [which included no less than seven chartered from commercial petroleum survey services] were completely employed in charting operations off the east and west coasts of South Vietnam. Furthermore,

The following magnetic studies were carried out during [fiscal year] 1968: A complete low-level aeromagnetic survey of South Vietnam [including all of the land surface and at least part of the offshore waters, "for military and/or scientific purposes"]; a detailed survey of the Formosa Strait off the coast of Taiwan (in fulfillment of a U.S. offer to provide aeromagnetic surveys of the Asian continental shelf area as a contribution to the United Nations Economic Commission for Asia and the Far East.[14]

This language explains the chicanery of the State Department's written assurances to Senator Fulbright that the U.S. government "has not provided South Vietnam any technical assistance relating to offshore oil exploration."[15] Strictly speaking, the assistance was not provided to South Vietnam, but either as "support of the fleet" (in the case of the charting) or "as a contribution to" ECAFE (in the case of the aeromagnetic surveys).

The Poulo Panjang seismic survey was in an area close to Cambodia and affected by the unresolved border dispute between the two countries over offshore islands. It was also very close to an Esso concession northeast of Malaysia in which, according to reported rumors, oil had already been discovered.[16] This may help explain why ECAFE proceeded, before June 1967, to make "a broad regional study of the northeastern portion of the Sunda shelf of Southeastern Asia, including the Gulf of Thailand and the adjoining offshore areas of Cambodia and the Republic of South Vietnam,"[17] even though Cambodia at this time was not a member of ECAFE and may not even have been consulted. In 1969 the same ECAFE committee formulated proposals for further seismic refraction surveys in selected Cambodian offshore waters, as "suggestions" to be forwarded "to the Cambodian authorities for consideration."[18]

Meanwhile, the special aeromagnetic survey planes of the U.S. Navy proposed to carry out aeromagnetic profiles across the Sunda shelf "at opportune times while in transit between major projects in this region," ostensibly as part of the U.S. Navy's Project MAGNET (originally a project "to provide world-wide charts of magnetic declination for safety in navigation at sea").[19] These surveys of Cambodia's offshore areas, apparently never asked for by Sihanouk's government, should be investigated closely by Congress. By the end of 1970, when it appeared to many that the Lon Nol regime could not possibly survive without increased U.S. support, "Union Oil of California . . . had a concession for all onshore Cambodian oil and much of the off-shore, former French, concession as well."[20]

All these diverse economic and political factors, both in Cambodia and in America, will suggest to liberal minds a picture of historical complexity and to Marxist minds a picture of historical inevitability; either of these pictures might seem to rule out the hypothesis that conspiracy played any major role in prompting the U.S. invasion of Cambodia. However, if we now look at covert U.S. military and intelligence operations for the same period, the complex picture becomes a much simpler one in which the long-range operation of economic factors turns out to have been helped along considerably by bureaucratic means.

In particular the Cambodian balance of payments crisis, which forced Sihanouk to install his domestic enemies in power and reopen relations with a hostile U.S. bureaucracy, represented a historical process that had been considerably accelerated by U.S. covert operations. From as early as 1964, but with particular intensity in April-May 1969, U.S. planes from South Vietnam systematically defoliated as much as one-third of the French-owned rubber plantations in Cambodia, the chief source of Cambodia's export revenue. Although the Department of Defense denied at first that the plantations had been deliberately sprayed, a visiting team of American biologists found this denial incredible:

> The fact that rubber plantations (which are readily distinguishable from the air) were so heavily hit (one-third of all this major Cambodian crop) suggests an attempt at punitive action on the part of the United States. That U.S. pilots are, we are told, under standing orders in South Vietnam to avoid the spraying of rubber adds further support to the hypothesis that this particular action was deliberate.[21]

The biologists concluded that the spraying, carried out just before the beginning of the growing season, had caused up to 80 percent damage in some areas; it represented an economic loss in 1969 of approximately $11 million in rubber, plus an additional $1.2 million in other crops. These losses totaled more than half of Cambodia's exports in 1968 ($22.9 million), of which rubber represented 64 percent ($14.6 million).[22] An ensuing economic crisis (including a budgetary deficit of $20 million) induced Sihanouk to talk publicly in July and August 1969 of accepting direct U.S. aid, and even of resigning.[23]

After being questioned by a House foreign affairs subcommittee, Thomas R. Pickering of the State Department finally sent written confirmation "that the greatest part of the damage was caused by a deliberate and direct overflight of the rubber plantations."[24] He claimed, however, that "there were no U.S. missions targeted for the Cambodian areas involved, nor were the investigators able to determine that any U.S. aircraft were directly involved in spraying these areas."

As in the case of covert U.S. operations against Cambodia in 1959 and 1967, the public was allowed to draw the conclusion that some other government, presumably South Vietnam, was responsible. But one cannot accept this excuse for a defoliation program dating back eight years, to the days when the rudimentary South Vietnamese air force was in fact largely flown by U.S. pilots. Another explanation might be that Air America planes and pilots were involved, since Air America officials have admitted to extensive defoliation programs against insurgent areas in Thailand, and U.S. officials have frequently fallen back on the excuse that Air America's planes, based in Taiwan, Thailand, and South Vietnam, are not "U.S. aircraft."[25]

American responsibility for this extensive and repeated use of its defoliants for international aggression cannot be denied. It is particularly instructive to learn from a pre-invasion article in the authoritative *Far Eastern Economic Review* that "last spring (April-May 1969) . . . Henry Kissinger and Nixon ordered bombing strikes against communist bases in Cambodia."[26] In other words, secret strikes for the two months of the covert defoliation program were ordered by the adviser who, as chairman of the National Security Council's Special Action Group, presided over the secret decision to invade Cambodia one year later.

President Nixon's covert operations against Cambodia in the first year of his presidency are part of a series dating back to the era when he was vice president. In 1958 and 1959 the CIA financed, equipped, and advised the brief military uprising of the Khmer Serei, whose part-Vietnamese political leader, Son Ngoc Thanh, had been premier of Cambodia under the Japanese. To show CIA complicity in the uprising, Sihanouk is said to have given as evidence the fact that a political officer from the U.S. embassy, Victor Masao Matsui, was found in the Khmer Serei rebel headquarters. As far as I am aware, it was eleven years before this fact was even alluded to in the "responsible" U.S. press: "South Vietnamese undercover agents who had directed the uprising subsequently explained that Matsui's presence on the scene was only accidental. They disclosed, however, that the CIA had financed the operation."[27] Matsui's presence appears less accidental when we learn that he was with the U.S. Army for twelve years before joining the U.S. embassy in Cambodia as a "political officer." In 1966 he was expelled for a second time from Pakistan for renewed charges of subversion.

Throughout the 1960s the CIA in Saigon continued to use its contacts with Son Ngoc Thanh and the Khmer Serei in at least three ways: for intelligence gathering (in both Cambodia and South Vietnam), for special missions inside Cambodia, and for the recruitment and training of paramilitary forces from the large ethnic Khmer minority of the delta provinces of South Vietnam.[28] Many if not most of the latter were taken in from the armed bandit Khmer Kampuchea Krom (KKK), of whom an unflattering portrait is found in Robin Moore's book *The Green Berets*. Trained by U.S. Special Forces, by the Khmer Serei, and later by Thai officers in Thailand, these troops became part of the CIDG or so-called Mike Force of ethnic minorities, who were controlled (along with U.S. Green Berets and the 34-A ops teams working against North Vietnam) by the Saigon-based Studies and Operations Group (SOG, or MACSOG). SOG in turn reported in theory to Generals Westmoreland and Abrams (COMUSMACV), but it is said to have reported in practice to the CIA, which originally set it up.

The U.S. public was given a hint of the deep splits within both the U.S. military and the intelligence communities in the wake of the two Green Beret murder scandals of 1969; some of the resulting leaks concerned Cambodia. Both of the murdered agents, it developed, had operated in Cambodia; at least one of them (Inchin Hai Lam) had been a member of the Khmer Serei. Shortly before Sihanouk's overthrow, a *New York Times* report revealed that the United States had used the Khmer Serei, an organization "dedicated to the overthrow of the legitimate government of Cambodia, on covert missions into that country in 1967, according to testimony at the trial of a Green Beret captain convicted in 1968 of killing one of the members of the sect."[29]

In 1967 Sihanouk renewed his charges that the CIA was still plotting against him (as it had in 1959), and Khmer Serei harassment, especially along the Thai border, markedly increased.[30] The charges have since been corroborated: "A Green Beret officer says he took part in a secret mission in 1967 designed to aid in the overthrow of Cambodia's Prince Norodom Sihanouk. . . . Capt. John

McCarthy . . . said the clandestine operation in Cambodia was directed from South Vietnam by the Central Intelligence Agency. . . . The mission was known as 'Operation Cherry' . . . and involved McCarthy, working under cover, and members of the Khmer Serai."[31]

According to the same *New York Times* story, "sources said that the several hundred former [Khmer Serei] members in Cambodia had pledged allegiance" to the Sihanouk government. This happened in 1967, when Lon Nol was briefly prime minister, but the indications are that the Khmer Serei retained their identity, their militant opposition to proleft elements in Sihanouk's coalition, and their links with U.S. intelligence circles. Of these last, DIA at least continued to maintain a "safe house" in Phnom Penh, even when diplomatic relations with Cambodia were broken off and U.S. personnel officially withdrawn.[32]

Wilfred Burchett has charged that the more violent events surrounding the overthrow of Sihanouk—the planned raids against the North Vietnamese and PRG embassies on March 11 and the ensuing massacres of ethnic Vietnamese civilians in the Cambodian countryside—were all spearheaded by CIA-trained Khmer Serei cadres.[33] In the weeks and months following the coup of March 18, 1970, it became abundantly clear that the most reliable cadres in the Cambodian army were those recruited and trained by the Khmer Serei and Green Berets in South Vietnam.[34] Although the majority of these entered Cambodia after the coup, their central role lent credence to the Burchett hypothesis. So did the unprecedented and unexplained "demonstrations on March 8th and 9th . . . in the eastern province of Svay Rieng, where villagers [*sic*], with the help of Cambodian troops, seized weapons from Vietnamese guerrillas."[35]

These must have been well-trained villagers to accomplish, without U.S. air support, what the best Cambodian troops were unable to do afterwards. Their prodigious achievement was followed on March 15, three days *before* the coup, by the first publicly announced and conducted joint operation between Cambodia and South Vietnamese troops.[36] Given the usual suspicion and hostility between the two peoples and their armies, it seems likely that special Khmer Serei cadres from South Vietnam were involved.

The special relationship between Lon Nol's army and the Khmer Serei-KKK units at its center implicates the U.S. intelligence community, not only in the coup itself but also in the ensuing "strategy of provocation," in which a series of hopeless attacks on larger and superior enemy forces brought about a debacle followed by official U.S. intervention. This involvement of U.S. intelligence personnel, above all the paramilitary personnel under SOG and the CIA, does not imply that Cambodian history in 1970 followed a master blueprint emanating from CIA headquarters. The intelligence parastructures of other nations were also involved, in addition to those of the United States, Thailand, and South Vietnam.

Sihanouk himself claimed that much of the plotting took place in Japan, between Prince Sirik Matak (a coup leader who was then ambassador to Tokyo), Song Sak (a Khmer Serei leader and alleged CIA agent who fled Phnom Penh in

1964 with $10 million), and CIA personnel.[37] An analysis of the coup in *Le Monde Diplomatique* refers to the contacts of a third coup leader with "Japanese secret societies manipulated by the CIA,"[38] and Son Ngoc Thanh himself owes much of his influence to his three years in Japan during World War II. As noted above, this collaboration in Cambodia between CIA and Japanese elements was followed in March 1972 by the granting of a joint concession in Thai-Cambodian offshore waters to Union Oil of California and the Mitsui Oil Exploration Company.

A country that was more directly involved, as *Newsweek* reported, was General Suharto's Indonesia, although it was later suggested that in Cambodia Indonesia was fronting for Japan:[39]

> A team of Cambodian officers secretly visited Indonesia last November [1969], and again in January, to study in depth how the Indonesian Army managed to overthrow President Sukarno [in 1965]. This, some Indonesians say, gave Djakarta advance knowledge of Cambodian General Lon Nol's coup against Prince Norodom Siha-nouk last March. It also helps explain Indonesia's prompt offer to send arms to Lon Nol.[40]

Psychological warfare "experts" from Indonesia arrived in Phnom Penh within days of the coup. According to Wilfred Burchett, they "advised" in the xenophobic anticommunist campaign against ethnic Vietnamese that is one of the most striking similarities between the Indonesian and Cambodian coups.[41]

These additional external factors suggest a prevailing trend toward right-wing repressive capitalism for which the United States and its agencies are not solely responsible. At the same time, all the known facts about foreign involvement reemphasize the central coordinating role of U.S. intelligence, and in particular of the paramilitary faction in the CIA, that faction known to the public through the operations of Civil Air Transport/Air America. CAT supplied "complete and tactical air support" for the abortive Indonesian military uprising of 1958;[42] Tony Poe, their legendary ground operative who spearheaded guerrilla operations against Tibet and (in Laos) South China from 1958 to 1970, has been identified as working also with the Khmer Serei insurgents in southwestern Cambodia.[43] Air America and its personnel, finally, do contract work in Southeast Asia for the large oil companies,[44] many of which maintain their own "intelligence" networks recruited largely from veterans of the CIA.

In contrast to nineteenth-century flag imperialism, the twentieth-century equivalent is multinational, like the large corporations whose sphere of influence is enlarged and whose syndicates, after the fall of Sihanouk, proceeded to divide up the whole of the southern South China Sea for oil exploration.[45] Indonesian participation in the planning of the Lon Nol coup is in this respect particularly instructive, for it is a striking fact that the successful military coup against Sukarno in 1965, like the unsuccessful military uprising of 1958, was not only linked to the CIA but followed publicly announced moves by Sukarno to nationalize the rich Indonesian oil industry. The power of U.S. and Japanese oil interests with the new Suharto regime is likewise a matter of public record.[46]

The Lon Nol coup of 1970, like the right-wing coups of January 1964 in Saigon and April 1964 in Laos, would have been counterproductive if they had not been swiftly followed by a stepped-up U.S. involvement. In 1964 U.S. clandestine ops also came first, with the initiation of 34-A operations against North Vietnam in February 1964 and T-28 bombing raids, with Thai and Air America pilots, in Laos in April and May.[47] In both cases these provocations, although inadequate by themselves to improve the U.S. military position, aggravated the conflict in a way that brought about the first open commitment of U.S. military forces.[48] In this respect the "coinciding" of the first covert T-28 and 34-A marine attacks against North Vietnam, in a way that helped provoke the Tonkin Gulf incidents, indicates that some U.S. officials wanted escalation.

The *Pentagon Papers* indicated that the hawks had the support of Director McCone[49] but kept other key administration personnel in the dark as to their plans. McNamara in particular claimed to have been ignorant of 34-A operations accompanying the ELINT mission of the USS *Maddox*, even while he released the order for the August 5 bombing of North Vietnam. Later in 1964 a State Department official could only report that the T-28 bombings of August 1–2 "probably" took place, as the North Vietnamese had claimed, and McNamara denied.[50]

In like manner the overt U.S. intervention in Cambodia in 1970, although vital if months of covert U.S. operations were not to collapse, seems only to have been accomplished after intrigue, secrecy, and deception within the massive U.S. bureaucracy. The only significant change in role from 1964 seems to have been that of the CIA director. In 1964 John A. McCone, an in-and-outer, held $1 million worth of stock in Standard Oil of California, one of the two largest U.S. oil firms in Indonesia and Southeast Asia, whose subsidiary Caltex accounted for 70 percent of Sumatran oil production. That he should be revealed as one of Washington's most ardent hawks in 1964 and 1965 does not weaken the case of those who offer an economic explanation for U.S. military policy. Richard Helms, director in 1970, by contrast, was a career intelligence officer with no particular commitment to, or economic stake in, the Far East.

Like other disputed escalations in the Indochina war, the 1970 invasion of Cambodia was preceded by an "intelligence battle" in Washington. A policy debate was disguised as a factual one over the relevance of the deteriorating scene in Cambodia to U.S. prospects in Vietnam. In this debate the issues that emerged were the truth or falsity of two propositions, finally subscribed to by President Nixon in his invasion announcement of April 30: (1) in the so-called Cambodian sanctuaries lay "the key control center" COSVN, "the headquarters for the entire communist military operation in South Vietnam"; (2) the enemy was "concentrating his main forces in these sanctuaries where they are building up to launch massive attacks on our forces [in South Vietnam]."[51]

The military imagination, as revealed to *Newsweek*, seems to have envisioned COSVN (Central Office for South Vietnam) as a setting for the denouement of a James Bond spy thriller: "Near the town of Memot [Mimot] . . . COSVN's reinforced concrete bunkers are believed to spread 15 to 20 feet beneath the jungle's surface and to house some 5,000 men, many of them specialists in communications and ordnance."[52] But other "intelligence analysts" in Saigon said flatly that COSVN "is not a static location" but "a mobile group of individuals . . . who seldom sleep more than one night in the same bed."[53] The latter analysts predicted confidently and correctly that COSVN would not be found.

There was similar skepticism within the bureaucracy about alleged captured documents from "Allied intelligence sources" revealing plans for "a series of attacks in South Vietnam the first week in May," "as violent as those of the 1968 Tet offensive," even though these plans were taken seriously by the National Security Council apparatus.[54] Two staff members of the Fulbright committee, who received a quite different impression from briefings in Washington before April 29 and in Vietnam on May 2–3, alluded to these documents acidulously in their report: "There seem to be captured documents to prove almost any point or to support, retrospectively, almost any conclusion."[55]

Nixon's two propositions were finally discredited by the failure of U.S. forces to find either COSVN or massed troop formations in the Cambodian sanctuaries. But long before April 30 the propositions had been authoritatively and repeatedly refuted in the U.S. press. Robert Shaplen, an informed journalist with "left-CIA" contacts since at least the early 1950s, cited "reliable reports" that the so-called COSVN had been moved out of the sanctuaries area "at the time of the [March 18] coup against Sihanouk." He was corroborating "authoritative reports" in the *New York Times* a month earlier, with a detailed map, showing that COSVN had been moved from near Mimot in Cambodia into virtually inaccessible areas in South Vietnam itself, "in Tayninh between Katum and Somracht" and "in Binhlong between Cheampdau and Khtarek."[56]

Early reports pinpointed General Wheeler and Admiral Moorer as the key hawks in the administration, with plans for a 30,000-man amphibious U.S. invasion,[57] and corroborated columnist Jack Anderson's ex post facto report that the Joint Chiefs endorsed the false picture of COSVN:

> The President is furious with the Joint Chiefs for misleading him about the possibility of destroying the Communist headquarters. They visualized the enemy command center, apparently, as a jungle version of their own elaborate, Pentagon-style headquarters. But other intelligence specialists had warned the headquarters, like a floating crap game, could be folded up quickly and re-established later in some other jungle hideout.[58]

Although this story appears to be itself one more missile in the intelligence battle, it has the ring of truth. In early 1971 there were rumors that the president then relied far less on DIA and more on CIA than he did before Cambodia.

In another leak Jack Anderson traced the false information about COSVN to alleged enemy radio messages intercepted by U.S. Army Intelligence in Vietnam:

> General Creighton Abrams . . . thought he knew where COSVN was located, because the Army had intercepted radio messages from the North Vietnamese command center. Crack troops quickly zeroed in on the location but found no sign of the headquarters. By continuing to monitor enemy radio transmissions, the Army frantically chased but never caught up with COSVN. Army Intelligence finally concluded that the North Vietnamese had set up their mobile radio transmitters a safe distance from the secret headquarters, with runners to carry the messages back and forth.[59]

This new information does not "explain" the error of Army Intelligence and the Joint Chiefs. On the contrary, it increases the probability of an "intelligence conspiracy" to bring about the April 30 invasion of Cambodia by deliberate misrepresentation. What was at issue was not a particular set of geographic coordinates but the army's claim of a fixed concrete installation housing five thousand men. Did the intercepted messages corroborate the existence of such an installation or not? Was the reported volume of communications compatible with the failure of 25,000 U.S. and Vietnamese troops to find a headquarters any where in the Fishhook area, not just at one location? Above all, did the content of the intercepts corroborate the "captured documents" that spoke of a new Tet offensive in early May, or did they refute them? If the former, the intercepts were probably false; if the latter, they were probably concealed from the White House decision makers.

Much was unclear about these intercepts, but one conclusion was clear. If Senator Fulbright's committee was serious about unearthing the origins and course of U.S. intervention in Indochina, it would have to examine the recurring importance of alleged "intercepts" in provoking escalation in response to the Tonkin Gulf incidents in 1964 and incidents in Cambodia in 1970. In particular it would have to examine the recurring pattern of 1964 and 1970, in which covert aggression by Air America and paramilitary forces under SOG and the CIA, which helped provoke a crisis, were followed by intelligence "intercepts" falsely indicating enemy offensive actions, and/or provide grounds for open U.S. military retaliation.

The possibility of an intelligence conspiracy, by no means proved but demanding to be investigated, suggests the context of a U.S. president who for some reason is reluctant to escalate. The complex role played by Nixon in the election year 1970 is suggestively like that played by Johnson in the election year 1964. Both men, early in their administration, had committed themselves to a long-range policy of hanging on in Indochina, even while cultivating a popular public image as peace seekers. Both men had thus given initial encouragement to CINC-PAC and Pentagon fantasies of "victory" in Indochina. As days of electoral reckoning neared, however, both men were increasingly reluctant to approve escalation proposals favored by the Joint Chiefs of Staff. Both Nixon and Johnson reverted to a posture of reluctance and indecision, with overtones of increasing tension between them and their Joint Chiefs, *after* as well as before their swift, spectacular, and highly dubious escalations.

Nixon and Johnson were no doves; what they above all wished to avoid was not escalation but personal responsibility for the decision to escalate. Such indecision invited parapolitics in the form of covert operations and manipulated intelligence that effectively took the decision out of the president's hands. What was subsequently resented, by Nixon in particular, was not so much the presentation of false intelligence but the embarrassment that this falsity was so swiftly and easily penetrated by the public.

Such speculations—they are only that—do not address the question whether either president may have encouraged such an intelligence conspiracy against his own administrative procedures. This question too is worth exploring, for both leaders owed much of their political success to the oil and aerospace interests that have been lobbying for a strong stand in Indochina.

Nixon's personal role in the Cambodian "crisis" is particularly open to question. On April 28, the day of the Fishhook decision and two days before his own congressional leaders would hear of it, Nixon told "several private citizens" from eleven "veterans and patriotic organizations" that the action he was soon to order "was imperative if we were to escape the probability of total and humiliating defeat in Vietnam."[60] One needs to ask why Nixon, the professed strict constructionist of the Constitution, did not consult with his own Congress over an impending invasion but instead shared his secret with a small group of retired military officers and their friends. The answer may well be that some of these officers were linked to the American Security Council, a powerful lobby with strong links to Nixon himself, to the U.S. intelligence community, and to the Los Angeles oil and aerospace interests that contributed so much to elect Nixon in 1968.

It is, I think, no digression to look at these links more closely. Among the members of the ASC's National Strategy Committee were Admiral Felix B. Stump, Air America's board chairman and former CINCPAC, and Henry O'Melveny Duque, Nixon's former law partner who sat on the board of California's Union Bank with two directors each from Union Oil of California (the beneficiaries of the Cambodia coup) and TRW (Thompson-Ramo-Wooldridge, a leading defense aerospace contractor). Also working with the ASC were vice presidents from Atlantic-Richfield, Standard Oil of California, and General Dynamics, and Admiral Robert W. Berry, Pacific coast director for the rarely mentioned but powerful National Security Industrial Association. These interlocks between the

ASC, Nixon, intelligence personnel, and Pacific-oriented oil companies could be expanded to fill pages.[61]

An additional word should be said here about the NSIA, which describes itself as a "non-lobbying organization of more than 400 [defense contractors] conceived by James Forrestal in 1944": "NSIA has won a reputation with both Industry and Government for fair dealing by expressing only those points of view which can provide a stronger national defense program."[62] Since April 1964 a large percentage of NSIA publications have dealt with industrial support for the National Oceanographic Program, a program under which the ships and planes of the U.S. Naval Oceanographic Office have been used for preliminary oil explorations off the shores of Indochina."[63] The same program also supplies a cover for ELINT missions such as that of *Pueblo*.

Nixon's connections with the intelligence and petroleum establishments were more prominent in 1964, when he was one of the earliest and most sustained advocates of "carrying the Vietnam war north." What business interests did Nixon represent during his two visits to the Far East in 1964, one of which lasted twenty-four days? Why was he accompanied by Henry Kearns, a representative of the Japanese Mitsui interests who had contracted in 1963 for a ten-year oil-drilling program in Indonesia?[64] Is it relevant that Nixon's New York law firm represented Mitsui interests in the United States, and that his former law partner Attorney-General John Mitchell was by all accounts the only strong voice inside Nixon's cabinet in support of the 1970 Cambodian invasion?

In raising these questions I do not wish to suggest that Nixon in 1970 was either an omnipotent Machiavellian or a slavish puppet of hidden economic interests. His own inability to envisage the consequences of his escalation, pathetically like that of Johnson in 1964 and 1965, is revealed by his public statement on May 8, 1970: "I would expect that the South Vietnamese would come out approximately at the same time that we do, because when we come out our logistical support and air support will also come out with them."[65] That both of these predictions were soon proved false is no more evidence of outright dishonesty than the Johnson administration's assurances in early 1965 that U.S. and Korean forces were being sent to Vietnam for defensive purposes.

But neither should we simply speak, as some have, of the "illusion of presidential command" over recalcitrant generals. In particular Nixon cannot be exempted from responsibility for systematic programs of covert operations against Cambodia, some of which at least emanated from the White House, like the bombings of April-May 1969, and some of which reached their peak under his administration, like the defoliation program of the same two months.

NOTES

1. David P. Chandler, *The Tragedy of Cambodian History: Politics, War, and Revolution since 1945* (New Haven: Yale University Press, 1991); Marie Alexandrine Martin,

Cambodia: A Shattered Society, trans. Mark W. McLeod (Berkeley: University of California Press, 1994).

2. Seymour Hersh, *The Price of Power: Kissinger in the White House* (New York: Summit, 1983), 176. Hersh also talks of "incontrovertible evidence that Lon Nol was approached by agents of American military intelligence and asked to overthrow the Sihanouk government."

3. Hersh, *Price of Power*, 179.

4. Government of Thailand, "Petroleum Concessionaires in Thailand (as of March 20, 2002)," mfd02.dmr.go.th/resources/petroleum/concession/concessionairs.pdf.

5. *Journal of Commerce*, February 17, 1995.

6. *Bangkok Post*, October 29, 1997.

7. Report to Assistant Secretary of State Bundy, November 7, 1964, in *New York Times*, June 13, 1971, 37; *The Pentagon Papers* (New York: Bantam, 1971), 306.

8. The phrase "Lon Nol's coup," though frequently encountered, is admittedly an oversimplification: many others participated in the overthrow of Sihanouk, which was finally approved by an unanimous vote of the Cambodian legislature. The technical point that such a vote had no constitutional validity is less important than the weakness of the Sangkum in the face of a prior de facto takeover by Lon Nol and his allies. At least two successive coups in Laos were similarly "ratified" by votes of the Laotian legislature in 1960. Both Chandler and Martin agree that the key figure in the coup was not the ambivalent Lon Nol but Sirik Matak (Chandler, *Tragedy,* 198; Martin, *Cambodia,* 122).

9. William Rosoff, "Dissension in the Kingdom," in Jonathan Grant, Laurence Moss, and Jonathan Unger, eds., *Cambodia: The Widening War in Indochina* (New York: Washington Square, 1971), 89.

10. Rosoff, "Dissension," 90.

11. *Journal of Commerce*, February 17, 1995.

12. Malcolm Caldwell, "Oil and the War," *Liberation,* Spring 1971, 59. The American companies now operating in the offshore area are Unocal (formerly Union Oil of California), Chevron, Amoco, and Amerada Hess; ExxonMobil is operating onshore, mfd02.dmr-.go.th/resources/petroleum/concession/concessionairs.pdf. Before 1970 Union Oil of California had already developed an oilfield in the Khorat plateau of Thailand near Laos (*World Oil*, August 15, 1963, 203).

13. United Nations Economic Commission for Asia and the Far East, Committee for Coordination of Joint Prospecting for Mineral Resources in Asian Offshore Areas, *Report of the Sixth Session, May 21–27, 1969* (E/CN.11/L.239), 9, 66–70.

14. U.S. Naval Oceanographic Office, *Annual Report, 1968,* 1, 16; cf. 7, 73, UN Doc. E/CN.11/L.216, 5. The seven charter survey vessels were leased from Alpine Geophysical Associates, Marine Acoustical Services, and Texas Instruments, Inc.

15. Letter of February 10, 1971, from David M. Abshire, assistant secretary of state for congressional relations; quoted in *San Francisco Chronicle*, June 11, 1971, 17.

16. *Wall Street Journal*, September 22, 1970, 34.

17. United Nations Economic Commission for Asia and the Far East, Committee for Coordination of Joint Prospecting, *Report of the Third Session (June 24–July 4, 1967)* (E/CN.11/L.186), 32.

18. UN Doc. E/CN.11/L.239, 9.

19. UN Doc. E/CN.11/L.239, 93; E/CN.11/186, 36; cf. E/CN.11/L.216, 7–8. One sus-

pects that "safety in navigation at sea" was as important in this survey as in the same planes' aeromagnetic survey of the entire land area of South Vietnam.

20. Malcolm Caldwell, *Liberation,* Spring 1971, 59. However in 1971, a recent French report announced that the new Cambodian government would allow no foreign oil companies to drill independently in its offshore waters. All would have to work through a government board in which French oil interests were still prominent (July 2, 1971). This would suggest that covert U.S.-French competition for Cambodia was not resolved in 1971. As noted above, Unocal (formerly Union Oil of California) now has three different concessions in the Thailand-Cambodia overlapping area of the Gulf of Thailand, the oldest of which dates back to March 1, 1972.

21. *Report on Herbicidal Damage by the United States in Southeastern Cambodia,* by A. H. Westing (Windham College), E. W. Pfeiffer (University of Montana), J. Lavorel, and L. Matarasso, reprinted in Thomas Whiteside, *Defoliation* (New York: Ballantine, 1970), 131.

22. United Nations Statistical Office, *World Trade Annual,* 1968 Supplement (New York: Walker, 1969), 5:410. It is alleged that the primary motive of the defoliation was to facilitate hot pursuit of NLF troops in the Vietnam War. This was in conjunction with the secret bombing of Cambodia, which began at the same time. Both Chandler (p. 179) and Martin (p. 133) mention the severity of the financial crisis and the role of the falloff in rubber exports. Chandler also mentions the defoliation, but only in passing.

23. Rosoff, in Grant, *Cambodia,* 90.

24. U.S. Congress, House, Committee on Foreign Affairs, *Chemical-Biological Warfare . . . Hearings,* 91st Cong., 1st sess., 198; cf. Whiteside, *Defoliation,* 130.

25. Pickering's claim of "no U.S. missions" is now completely incredible, since the revelation of the sustained secret bombing campaign that began in early 1969. "Over the next fourteen months, until a month after the coup d'état in Phnom Penh, over 3,500 bombing sorties were carried out along the Cambodian side of the frontier" (Chandler, *Tragedy,* 184).

26. Harold Munthe-Kaas, *Far Eastern Economic Review,* December 25, 1969, 668.

27. Stanley Karnow, *Washington Post,* March 28, 1970, A10. For a typical press censorship of Sihanouk's charge, cf. *Time,* March 16, 1959, 34. William Worthy, "The CIA Plot against Cambodia" (*Le Sangkum,* Phnom Penh, September 1965, 17), speaks of a covert flight to Siem Reap by an Air Vietnam plane on February 7, 1959. It is known that many of Air Vietnam's pilots were in fact Americans flying with Civil Air Transport. Chandler (101–7) confirms both that Matsui was "a CIA agent" and that he was peripherally involved in a South Vietnamese–backed plot against Sihanouk in 1959 with Dap Chhuon, the governor of Siem Reap province. According to Audrey and George Kahin, the Eisenhower-Dulles administration encouraged Thailand and South Vietnam in support of this plot, in which the Khmer Serei were also involved (Audrey R. and George McT. Kahin, *Subversion as Foreign Policy* [New York: New Press, 1995], 12–13).

28. *New York Times,* January 28, 1970, 1; *San Francisco Chronicle,* May 29, 1970, 14.

29. *New York Times,* January 28, 1970, 1. The testimony was offered by Major Patrick J. McKernan, "chief of the Army counterintelligence operations branch" in Saigon.

30. *New York Times,* February 19, 1967, 25; *Le Monde,* May 6, 1967, 1, 3.

31. *San Francisco Chronicle,* May 23, 1971. See also John L. Plaster, *SOG: The Secret Wars of America's Commandos in Vietnam* (New York: Simon & Schuster, 1997), 97–98;

Douglas Valentine, *The Phoenix Program* (New York: Morrow, 1990), 328. Not yet explained is the presence at the Nha Trang base in 1970 of Helliwell's old associate Mitchell WerBell, who six years later would be indicted on drug charges.

32. Andrew Tully, *The Super Spies* (New York: William Morrow, 1969), 201.

33. *Guardian* (New York), April 25, 1970, 1.

34. *New York Times*, May 5, 1970, 16; *San Francisco Chronicle*, May 29, 1970, 14.

35. Robert Shaplen, *New Yorker*, May 9, 1970, 136.

36. *Bangkok World*, March 18, 1970, 1.

37. Press conference of Prince Sihanouk, as reported in Wilfred Burchett, *The Second Indochina War* (New York: International Publishers, 1970), 55–56.

38. Daniel Roy, "Le Coup de Phnompenh," *Le Monde Diplomatique*, April 1970, 12–13; translated in Martin Gettleman et al., eds., *Conflict in Indochina* (New York: Random House, 1970), 350. These charges were amplified by Sihanouk's French adviser Charles Meyer, *Derrière le sourir khmer* (Paris: Plon, 171), 321–24, cf. 181. The allegation that Sim Var was guided by the "occult leadership" of a pro-Japanese secret society, the Black Stars, is denounced by Chandler (p. 32) as an old concoction of French intelligence. But Sim Var did have a connection to Sasakawa Ryoichi, a former suspected war criminal and close associate of the high-level CIA asset Kodama Yoshio. Sasakawa, who was also a friend of Son Ngoc Thanh, invited Sim Var to Japan right after the 1970 coup (*AMPO* [Tokyo], January 1974, 44). Sasakawa and Kodama were prominent members of the Black Dragon Society during World War II and collaborated with the Kempeitai (Japanese Gestapo) on the Asian mainland. Sasakawa helped create the Japan chapter of the Asian People's Anti-Communist League. For more on the Black Dragon Society and Cambodia, see Noam Chomsky and Edward S. Herman, *The Political Economy of Human Rights* (Boston: South End, 1979), 2:194; Jean Claude Pomonti and Serge Thien, *Des courtisans aux partisans* (Paris: Gallimard, 1971).

39. *Far Eastern Economic Review Yearbook*, 1971.

40. *Newsweek*, May 25, 1970, 25.

41. Burchett, *Second Indochina War*, 65; cf. Jonathan Grant, "The Regime of Lon Nol," in Grant, *Cambodia*, 121. Both Chandler (p. 203) and Martin (p. 184) mention the Indonesia-like xenophobic massacres, complete with "strings of corpses floating down the Mekong" (Chandler, *Tragedy,* 203). But neither, astonishingly, mentions the arrival of Indonesian experts amid such terrorizing practices. Meanwhile, according to a former U.S. Navy intelligence specialist, Samuel Thornton, the initial U.S. military plan to overthrow Sihanouk "included a request for authorization to insert a U.S.-trained assassination team disguised as Vietcong insurgents into Phnom Penh to kill Prince Sihanouk as a pretext for revolution" (Hersh, *Price*, p. 179). (Thornton said that the assassination part of the plot was rejected by Lon Nol himself, which is entirely credible given what we now know about Lon Nol's role in 1970.) As Hersh points out, Green Beret assassination teams that operated inside South Vietnam routinely dressed as Vietcong cadre while on missions. Thus the alleged U.S. plan of 1968, which was reportedly approved "shortly after Nixon's inauguration . . . 'at the highest level of government,'" called for an assassination of a moderate at the center by apparent leftists, as a pretext for a right-wing seizure of power. This is the formula underlaying the right-wing Indonesian coup against Sukarno in 1965, and it raises a question: Did the earlier anti-Sukarno operation call for foreign elements to be infiltrated into the Gestapu forces who murdered the pro-Sukarno generals? Coen

Holtzappel ("The 30 September Movement," *Journal of Contemporary Asia* 11, no. 2 [1979]: 222) suspected "the use of outsiders who are given suitable disguises to do a dirty job." See Peter Dale Scott, "The United States and the Overthrow of Sukarno, 1965–1967," *Pacific Affairs*, Summer 1985, 239–64, www.pir.org/scott.html.

42. Lansdale memo of July 1961, in *Pentagon Papers*, 137; cf. David Wise and Thomas B. Ross, *The Invisible Government* (New York: Bantam, 1965), 145–56.

43. *San Francisco Chronicle*, September 4, 1970, 24.

44. *New York Times*, April 5, 1970, 1, 22.

45. However, the CIA role may have been more central than I realized in 1971. Douglas Valentine, whose book is based on over one hundred interviews with veterans of CIA and Special Forces, gives the following succinct account of the Lon Nol coup: "The final phase began on March 12, 1970, while Sihanouk was abroad and his prime minister, Lon Nol, under instructions from the CIA, ordered all North Vietnamese out of Cambodia within seventy-two hours. That same day Deputy Minister Sirik Matak canceled a trade treaty between Cambodia and the Provisional Revolutionary Government [of Vietnam]. Four days later the U.S. merchant ship *Columbia Eagle*, which was ostensibly carrying munitions for U.S. Air Force units in Thailand, was commandeered by two CIA officers, who steered it into the port of Sihanoukville. Armed with guns and ammunition from the *Columbia Eagle*, and backed by the Khmer Kampuchea Krom (Cambodia exiles trained by the CIA in South Vietnam) and the Khmer Serai (Cambodians under Son Ngoc Thanh, trained by the CIA in Thailand), Lon Nol's forces seized control of the government and moved against the Khmer Rouge (Cambodian Communists) and the Vietnamese who supported Prince Sihanouk" (*The Phoenix Program* [New York: William Morrow, 1990], 327). Valentine then implicates the CIA in the subsequent massacre of ethnic Vietnamese in Cambodia (p. 328).

46. *Wall Street Journal*, April 18, 1967, 30; quoted in Michael Tanzer, *The Political Economy of International Oil and the Underdeveloped Countries* (Boston: Beacon, 1969), 363–64.

47. 34-A and Special Force–Air America operations in Vietnam were controlled by the CIA's Studies and Operations Group (SOG), as were the Mike Force ethnic mercenaries later infiltrated into Cambodia. Lieutenant Colonel Conein, who acted as General Khanh's case officer and maintained contact with the 1963 and 1964 coups, is said to have also handled covert operations inside North Vietnam.

48. "At least two academic researchers have reported that the (CIA-backed) Khmer Kampuchea Krom were operating inside Cambodia before the March coup against Sihanouk. Gerald C. Hickey, an anthropologist . . . told the Pentagon that KKK soldiers had been involved in the sacking of the North Vietnamese and PRG embassies in Phnom Penh on March 16 . . . George McT. Kahin (told) the Senate Foreign Relations Committee on March 6, 1975 . . . he had learned that as many as 4,800 KKK soldiers serving with the Green Berets and the South Vietnamese Army had been pulled from their units and flown by American aircraft into Cambodia within a few weeks of the coup" (Hersh, *Price*, 181 n.; cf. Kahin and Kahin, *Subversion*, 13, 246).

49. *Pentagon Papers*, 386, 440.

50. *Pentagon Papers*, 261.

51. President Nixon, speech, April 30, 1970; reprinted in Gettleman, *Conflict in Indochina* (New York: Random House, 1970), 382, 384.

52. *Newsweek*, May 11, 1970, 25.

53. *San Francisco Chronicle*, May 4, 1970, 13.

54. *San Francisco Chronicle*, May 2, 1970, 7; *Wall Street Journal*, April 28, 1970, 1.

55. U.S. Congress, Senate, Committee on Foreign Relations, *Cambodia: May 1970*, Staff Report (Washington, D.C.: GPO, 1970), 5; cf. 6.

56. Robert Shaplen, "Letter from Indochina," *New Yorker*, May 9, 1970, 139; *New York Times*, April 4, 1970, 3; cf. *Washington Post*, April 5, 1970, A6.

57. *Oakland Tribune*, May 2, 1970, 1.

58. *San Francisco Chronicle*, May 14, 1970, 43. Cf. "End Run by Joint Chiefs? Laird Pushes JCS Reorganization," *Christian Science Monitor*, May 14, 1970: "Many civilians in the Defense Department believe that the Joint Chiefs pulled an end run in their efforts to get the attacks against the border areas approved."

59. *San Francisco Chronicle*, March 30, 1971, 33.

60. *San Francisco Examiner*, May 21, 1970, 1.

61. In the ASC library was a bound set of hearings of the House Un-American Activities Committee from 1938 to 1941 "which the flyleaf says is the property of Senator Richard M. Nixon" (*New York Times*, August 17, 1970, 21).

62. Richard D. Terry, *Ocean Engineering* (Washington: National Security Industrial Association, 1966), 1.

63. For titles, see National Union Catalogue, author list, 1963–1967, 39, 50–51.

64. *World Petroleum,* September 1963, 66. Henry Kearns served in 1955 on the Hoover Commission Task Force on Intelligence Activities, under General Mark Clark, a sometime business associate of Nixon's who served in 1971 on the National Strategy Committee of the ASC.

65. *New York Times*, May 9, 1971, 8.

11

Opium, the China Lobby, and the CIA

THE UNDERREPORTED U.S. INVOLVEMENT
WITH DRUG TRAFFICKING

I do not believe that any book has so far advanced my revelations in 1970 about the involvement of Air America (previously named Civil Air Transport, or CAT) and its personnel in the Asian drug traffic.[1] The deep political element here is the presence of organized crime, both Asian and American, in the background at every stage of the story, from the first postwar involvement of the United States with the infrastructure of the Asian drug traffic to the recycling of Asian funds into the American political mainstream, via the China lobby and later the law firm of Corcoran and Rowe.

Where else do we find all these aspects viewed synoptically? The new edition of Alfred McCoy's massive and invaluable study, The Politics of Heroin, *notes the importance of Paul Helliwell in arranging for the U.S. government to subsidize CAT but describes him only as "a lawyer," ignoring the significant relationships he developed with organized crime, including Meyer Lansky's bank.[2] Furthermore, while confirming the movement of opium in CAT planes, McCoy understates the structural role of CAT in building up the postwar opium and heroin traffic. His statement that General Claire Chennault "sold CAT to the CIA in August [i.e., July] 1950" omits the relevant fact that Chinese KMT interests eventually retained a 60 percent ownership of the company owning CAT planes, which could then be used on drug missions.[3] His subject being broadly defined by the interviews he conducted in 1971, he has little or nothing to say about the links in the 1960s between Laos and the KMT on Taiwan.*

Other statements scattered through McCoy's book sometimes suggest that CIA and CAT/Air America were only passively complicitous with the drug traffickers, or that involvement was at the agent level.[4] The truth is that the massive postwar restructuring of the drug trade under KMT auspices was one in which both the

185

CIA and CAT played a key organizing role. I also believe that to understand the full range of McCoy's subject, the politics of heroin, one has to look also at the role played by the drug-financed China lobby in the United States.[5] We still need the kind of in-depth study of opium in postwar Asian politics that has begun to emerge for the prewar period.[6]

Such a study might help us determine why the CIA has repeatedly allied itself with key drug-trafficking elements in Europe, Afghanistan, the Middle East, Latin America, and elsewhere—most recently in Kosovo, Colombia, and Afghanistan. This might contribute to a much needed political response to the complaint a decade ago by a former top DEA investigator that "in my 30-year history in the Drug Enforcement Administration and related agencies, the major targets of my investigations almost invariably turned out to be working for the CIA."[7]

This phenomenon can only be understood by seeing how the interface of crime and policy served both drug traffickers and high-level financial interests and affected developments both in Asia and in the United States. This chapter, though it did not have the benefit of McCoy's two excellent books, has the merit of attempting such an overview.[8]

Professor Samuel Eliot Morison has written how in 1903 Theodore Roosevelt, "in the face of international law and morality," secretly ordered the U.S. Navy to support the "revolutionary" secession of Panama from Colombia. The secession, which led swiftly to the Canal Zone treaty, is described by him as a plan by "Panama businessmen, agents of the French company [which stood to gain $40 million in compensation under the treaty] and United States army officers."[9] He neglects to add that the "agents" of the French Panama Canal Company were the New York investment bankers J. & W. Seligman and their Washington lobbyist Bunau-Varilla, who organized and financed the "revolution" out of a suite in the Waldorf-Astoria. The intervention of the U.S. Navy was not Roosevelt's idea but Bunau-Varilla's, who called on the president and spoke to him about "American lives and interests." Even the flag of the new Panamanian Republic, for which later generations of more idealistic nationalists have demonstrated and died, was designed and hand-stitched by Bunau-Varilla out of Macy's silk, at the summer house of James Seligman in Westchester, New York.[10]

In some ways the Panama exercise in "big stick" partition, with its subsequent thorough but ineffective congressional exposure and its hidden economic interests, including a "French company" financed through Wall Street, is an instructive precedent for the postwar U.S. involvement in Indochina.[11] Legally, however, the picture might appear to be different, for many of Bunau-Varilla's activities in preparing for revolution and war would today be outlawed under section 956–60 of the U.S. Criminal Code. In theory at least, responsibility for this kind of defense of American "interests" is now a monopoly of the CIA, even if the CIA continues to maintain close contact with J. & W. Seligman and similar Wall Street institutions.

These contacts were powerful, and in 1948 it was pressure from Wall Street that succeeded in pushing the infant CIA into its first covert operations. President Truman later declared his unhappiness at this deflection of the CIA from its intelligence function: "I never had any thought . . . when I set up the CIA that it would be injected into peacetime cloak-and-dagger operations."[12] His intentions, however, counted for less than those of Allen Dulles, then a New York corporation lawyer and president of the Council on Foreign Relations. The administration became concerned that the communists might shortly win the Italian elections:

> Forrestal felt that secret counteraction was vital, but his initial assessment was that the Italian operation would have to be private. The wealthy industrialists in Milan were hesitant to provide the money, fearing reprisals if the Communists won, and so the hat was passed at the Brook Club in New York. But Allen Dulles felt the problem could not be handled effectively in private hands. He urged strongly that the government establish a covert organization. Because of the desire to finance the organization with unvouchered funds, the decision was made to create it under the National Security Council.[13]

This fateful essay in nonaccountability is instructive: the defense secretary felt the operation should be private, but a private corporation lawyer determined it should be public. By this arrangement, presumably, the men in the Brook Club even got their money back; since then the funds (unvouchered) have been the public's.

Truman's lack of sympathy for the way the CIA was being "diverted" into covert operations did not result in any measures to curb control of the CIA by Wall Street Republicans. On the contrary, as the CIA began to burgeon under Bedell Smith, *all seven* persons who are known to have served as deputy directors of the CIA under Smith and Truman came from New York legal and financial circles.[14]

These men used their corporate experience and connections to set up a number of dummy private enterprises as "proprietaries" or wholly owned fronts for the CIA, particularly for Far Eastern operations. On the model of William Pawley's CAMCO company, which had fronted for General Chennault and the Flying Tigers in 1941, the capital came from government sources, but profits (if any) are said to have been retained by the proprietary in question.

Thus William Ray Peers, an OSS hand from Burma and China who later was the army chief of staff's special assistant for special warfare activities, headed up Western Enterprises, Inc., in Taiwan, a cover for the launching of Kuomintang commando raids from Quemoy and Matsu.[15] Willis Bird (OSS China) headed a Bangkok "trading company" called Sea Supply, Inc., which supplied arms and other supplies to the KMT troops of General Li Mi in Burma,[16] and later trained the Thai border police under Thai Interior Minister Phao Sriyanon.[17]

By far the largest CIA proprietary in Asia was the Delaware corporation CAT,

Inc., chartered in July 1950 and known since March 31, 1959, as Air America, Inc. General Lansdale's memorandum of July 1961 to Maxwell Taylor on unconventional warfare, published as part of the *Pentagon Papers,* confirmed this commonly known fact:

> CAT. Civil Air Transport (Chinese Nationalist). CAT is a commercial airline engaged in scheduled and nonscheduled air operations throughout the Far East, with headquarters and large maintenance facilities located in Taiwan. CAT, a CIA proprietary, provides air logistical support under commercial cover to most CIA and other U.S. Government agencies' requirements. . . . During the past ten years, it has had some notable achievements, including support of the Chinese Nationalist withdrawal from the mainland, air drop support to the French at Dien Bien Phu, complete logistical and tactical air support for the [1958] Indonesian operation, air lifts of refugees from North Vietnam, more than 200 overflights of Mainland China and Tibet, and extensive support in Laos during the current [1961] crisis.[18]

General Lansdale erred, however, in failing to distinguish between the Taiwan Commercial Airline CAT Co., Ltd., alias Civil Air Transport (CATCL), and the American operating firm CAT, Inc., the CIA proprietary that supplied CATCL with pilots and other personnel. Sixty percent of the capital and control of CATCL was KMT-Chinese Nationalist, represented by officers of the former Kincheng Bank in Shanghai who allegedly fronted for T. V. Soong and/or his sister Madame Chiang Kai-shek.[19]

CATCL had been set up by General Chennault in 1946, after the U.S. State Department cited pressure from T. V. Soong and Madame Chiang as grounds for forcing UNRRA to reverse itself and subsidize the creation of Chennault's airline.[20] Chennault's partner in CAT was Whiting Willauer, a U.S. "economic intelligence" officer who during World War II supplied the Flying Tigers as an officer of China Defense Supplies under T. V. Soong. CAT's treasurer in the 1940s was James J. Brennan, another member of the wartime Chennault-Corcoran-Alsop "Washington squadron," who after the war served as T. V. Soong's personal secretary in China. The lawyer for CAT, as for the Flying Tigers, was Tommy Corcoran, who after the war was rumored to be handling T. V. Soong's multimillion-dollar investments in the United States.[21]

In the late 1940s CAT flew military support missions for the Kuomintang against the communists, while Chennault lobbied openly from a Washington office against the more cautious China policy of the Truman-Acheson State Department. In November 1949 Chennault, after a similar visit by Chiang, flew to Syngman Rhee in Korea, "to give him a plan for the Korean military air force," even though at this time it was still U.S. official policy to deny Rhee planes to discourage him from invading North Korea.[22] In December 1949, *Time* later claimed, Dean Acheson told one of its correspondents that "what we must do now is shake loose from the Chinese Nationalists," while in January 1949 George Kennan predicted that "by next year at this time we will have recognized the Chinese Communists."[23] All such thoughts were frustrated by the sudden out-break of the Korean War on June 25, 1950—an event still imperfectly understood, which may have been anticipated by certain KMT speculators who because of the war "cleared an estimated profit of about $30,000,000" in soybeans.[24] Efforts at rapprochement with Peking were again frustrated by the Quemoy crises of 1954 and 1958.

Shortly after the outbreak of the Korean War, on July 10, 1950, CAT, Inc. (along with its holding company Airdale Corporation) was chartered with OPC funds in Delaware.[25] The American company CAT, Inc., promptly supplied planes, pilots, and U.S. airlift contracts to the Taiwan company CATCL, which in this period was the sole flag air carrier of Chiang's new republic.[26] While Tommy Corcoran continued to represent Soong, Chennault, and CATCL, the aviation law firm of Pogue and Neal handled the incorporation of CAT, Inc., whose later counsel Brackley Shaw was a former army intelligence officer and general counsel for the air force. During this period of formation a vice president of the National City Bank of New York, Walter Reid Wolf, was recruited briefly as a CIA deputy director from 1951 to 1953; soon afterward two of Wolf's fellow directors in the small Empire City Savings Bank (Samuel Sloan Walker and Arthur B. Richard-son) were named to the board of CAT, Inc., and later Air America..

At the same time, Desmond FitzGerald entered the CIA from the Citibank-related law firm of Samuel Sloan Duryee, Walker's cousin and a director with Wolf of Citibank's investment subsidiary (City Bank Farmers Trust). FitzGerald, a former liaison officer with the Chinese New Sixth Army, spent much of the next decade in Asia and had charge of the CIA Laos operatives "in the field" whom President Kennedy found so hard to control. What Hilsman calls the "problem of CIA" arose not because of the remoteness of FitzGerald and CAT from the center of power, but because of their proximity to it. FitzGerald too was a member of New York's four-hundred-member Brook Club, "perhaps club-dom's richest from the point of view of inherited wealth."[27] Other Brook Club members included three directors of CAT, Inc., two directors of Pan Am, and Chiang Kai-shek's promoters Walter S. Robertson, who for six years was Eisen-hower's assistant secretary of state for Far Eastern Affairs, and Joe Alsop.

In this pyramid the CIA's official control over CATCL was remote and unrelia-ble. Its proprietary Airdale Corporation (in 1957 renamed Pacific Corporation) owned 100 percent of CAT, Inc./Air America, Inc. (which hired pilots), and of CAT Inc.'s subsidiary the Asiatic Aeronautical Company, later Air Asia, which owned both aircraft and "one of the world's largest aircraft maintenance and repair facilities . . . at Tainan in southern Taiwan."[28] But Airdale owned only 40 percent of CATCL and thus could hardly be called to account when (as frequently occurred) CAT planes flew in support of operations conforming to Taiwan and KMT foreign policy, but at odds with the official foreign policy of the United States.

Even the CIA's control over Airdale/Pacific Corporation, which was said to clear profits in the order of $10 million a year, is open to question: it is possible that the proprietary relationship is as useful in supplying an "official" cover for private profit as it is in supplying a "private" cover for the CIA.[29] Air America itself had a private stake in Southeast Asia's burgeoning oil economy, for it flew "prospectors looking for copper and geologists searching for oil in Indonesia, and provide[d] pilots for commercial airlines such as Air Vietnam and Thai Airways, and for China Airlines [Taiwan's new Chinese-owned flag airline which in 1968 took over CAT's passenger services]."[30] Much larger has been the economic stake of the financial interests represented on the boards of Pacific Corporation and CAT, Inc., over the years (such as Dillon Read, represented by William A. Read Jr., and the Rockefellers, represented by Laurance Rockefeller's employee Harper Woodward).

Perhaps the most obvious stake has been that of Pan Am (on whose board sit Robert Lehman of Lehman Brothers and James Sterling Rockefeller of the National City Bank). Like the National City Bank itself and the larger Bank of America, which in the early postwar period was still allied with it,[31] so also Pan Am was particularly oriented toward development of a "Pacific rim community," as opposed to an "Atlantic community." It has been shown that Pan Am's staggering profits in the 1960s were built about its early monopoly of commercial air service to Thailand and Indochina. Pan Am's Indochina service was opened with the assistance of the U.S. government "in the national interest" on May 22, 1953, seventeen days after CAT, using planes and pilots "loaned" by the USAF, began its military airlift to Dienbienphu.

The inauguration of CAT's airlift to Laos in September 1959, which continued with little interruption for a decade, was likewise a godsend to Pan Am and the other big U.S. airlines at a time when they were suffering badly. Laos generated a need for additional military airlift which, after considerable lobbying and threats of quitting international service, was awarded by contract to the commercial carriers.[32] Thanks to its Pacific operations, Pan Am saw its charter revenues soar almost 300 percent in four years and showed a profit in 1961 for the first time since 1956, even though its Atlantic service continued to operate at a loss.[33]

One can note with some cynicism that at the heart of the so-called China lobby in Congress in the early 1950s (Claire Boothe Luce, Pat McCarran, and Owen Brewster) was to be found the heart of the Pan Am lobby. Senator Pat McCarran of Nevada, who chaired the congressional inquiry into Owen Lattimore and the Institute of Pacific Relations, had first achieved fame as author of the 1938 Civil Aeronautics Act and later as an oil lobbyist. In his heyday as a China lobbyist, McCarran was also known as "the gambler's senator" and is said to have sat in court at the Riverside Hotel in Reno, making deals for syndicate men with criminal records to obtain casino licenses contrary to the law.[34] Despite such dubious representatives, one cannot call lobbying a conspiracy, any more than one can discern anything illegal in the fact that Air America's top operating personnel were also recruited from Pan Am.[35] When, however, one looks beyond the Washington offices of Air America to the Asian field operations of CAT, with its 60 percent Chinese Nationalist control, the possibility of KMT-criminal connections and activity demands to be explored.

The most questionable of CAT's activities was its sustained supply of arms and other matériel to KMT General Li Mi and his successors in Burma and North Thailand between 1949 and 1961. Li Mi is probably the only major opium dealer in the world to have been honored with the U.S. Legion of Merit and Medal of Freedom; his Ninety-third Division began collecting opium from the Hmong of northern Laos as early as 1946.[36] Faced with a public scandal after Burma complained about these foreign intruders on its soil, the United States hired CAT, Inc., to fly them out in 1954. Nevertheless, the bulk of the troops refused to move and CATCL continued to supply them, possibly using some of the very same planes chartered for the illusory repatriation. According to an informed source, "the CIA saw these troops as a thorn in Mao's side and continued to supply them with arms *and money*," even though they had "decided to settle down and become rich by growing opium."[37]

The decision to finance and supply the remnants of Li Mi's troops had grave consequences for the world opium and heroin traffic, and also for that part of it handled by the so-called National Crime Syndicate in the United States. The new right-wing Thai government of Phibun Songgram, having seized power in an 1948 coup (over the issue of controlling the local Chinese),[38] legalized the sale of opium and established an official Thai government opium monopoly on September 17, 1949. This happened just as the Chinese communists were expelling the last of the KMT-linked warlords who had supplied the Far East and America with opium before World War II. Shortly thereafter, prepared opium in the containers of the Thai government opium monopoly was seized in a raid in Boston, Massachusetts, an event not noted in the U.S. press but duly reported by the U.S. government to the United Nations Commission on Narcotic Drugs.[39] Throughout the 1950s U.S. government representatives continued to notice quietly that Thailand was a source for the opium and heroin imported into the United States, though this relative candor waned in the 1960s with the escalation of the second Indochina war.[40] They also reported the rapid increase in both opium trading and opium growing in northern Thailand, where the KMT troops were established, and noted that most of this opium was exported out of Thailand for illicit traffic abroad.[41]

Up until about 1964, the United States also complained officially and ostentatiously to the UN Narcotics Commission about "Yunnan opium," brand "999" morphine, and heroin from "the Chinese mainland," as part of Peking's "twenty-year plan to finance political activities and spread addiction."[42] In 1958, for example, it reported that 154 pounds of heroin "from mainland China" had been smuggled into the United States and in 1960 that "the principal sources of the diacetylmorphine [heroin] seized in the United States were Hong Kong, Mexico, and communist China."[43] But other delegates and the commission itself would complete this misleading picture: "Yunnan opium" was opium that came from anywhere in the "fertile triangle" (the Burma-Thai-Laos-Yunnan border area). The Hong Kong authorities "were not aware of a traffic in narcotics from the mainland of China through Hong Kong," but "quantities of narcotics reached Hong Kong via Thailand" (E/CN.7/395, 18). The bulk of "Yunnan opium" and the "999" morphine in particular were in fact trafficked under the protection of the KMT troops in Burma and north Thailand supplied by CAT. In 1960 the UN Commission discreetly noted the presence in the Burmese sector of the "fertile triangle" of "remnants of KMT troops who were maintaining themselves largely on the profits of the opium trade. It was reported that they received their supplies periodically by air" (E/CN.7/395, 15).

Why did CAT planes continue until 1961 to support the suppliers of heroin, which was flooding, via Thailand and Hong Kong, into the United States? One reason was indeed military: to use the KMT troops and raids "as a thorn in Mao's side," especially during the CIA/CAT-supported operation in Tibet (adjacent to Yunnan) from 1956 to 1960, for which the CIA agent Tony Poe (later stationed in the Laotian opium center of Ban Houei Sai) trained Tibetan guerrillas in the mountains of Colorado.[44]

A second reason was political: to maintain contact with the elaborate fabric of Chinese secret societies or "Triads" throughout Southeast Asia. The profits and relationships of the opium trade, in other words, would help preserve the prewar KMT ascendancy among the Chinese middle class of these countries, and thus challenge their allegiance to the new Chinese People's Republic. This question of Chinese allegiance was particularly acute in the early 1950s in Malaya, where the farming of the opium franchise among Chinese Triads had been resorted to by the British authorities since at least the 1870s.[45] The organized opium traffic had become a well-established accommodation and control mechanism, and after World War II the opium was supplied by the "fertile triangle."[46]

Although the British by and large resisted Triad-KMT offers to mobilize against the Chinese insurgency in Malaya, they also found it difficult to crack down on the opium and gambling activities of the Wa Kei secret society, "without disrupting the fabric" of the Wa Kei and leaving a vacuum for the communists to fill.[47] Meanwhile the wealthy Chinese owners of tin mines in the more exposed countryside found it expedient to subsidize a Wa Kei-Triad private army "with strong KMT backing" as a mobile armed force against the communist guerrillas. This "Kinta Valley Home Guard" is given credit for restoring security to the Malayan tin industry by 1954.[48]

In Thailand also the farming of the opium franchise was used by the government for over a century as a means of controlling the local Chinese population, and the enormous profits from the opium traffic were a traditional source of corruption inside the Siamese government.[49] In the 1950s the Thai interior minister, General Phao Sriyanon, after an initial phase of anti-Sinitism, "showed every willingness to co-operate with Kuomintang Chinese in the campaign against

Communism."[50] At the same time his police, and in particular his border police, collaborated with Li Mi's KMT troops in Burma by officially "confiscating" their contraband opium in return for a reward to KMT "informers." (As early as 1950 a U.S. government representative noted cynical reports that it was profitable for the opium trader to be seized and to share the reward with police.)[51]

It seems indisputable that some elements in the KMT used opium as a means to organize and finance KMT links with and control over the important Chinese communities of Southeast Asia. This is not surprising: the KMT had relied on the Triads and gangs involved in the opium traffic since as early as 1927, when Chiang Kai-shek, encouraged by foreign bankers, used the Ch'ing Pang "Green Gang" of Tu Yueh-sheng to break the communist insurrection in Shanghai. (Chiang Kai-shek is said by some authorities to have been a Ch'ing Pang member.)[52]

After the remnants of the Shanghai "Green" and "Red Gangs" had relocated in Hong Kong, one finds increasing references in UN Reports to the narcotics traffic of Triad societies in Hong Kong and throughout the world. In 1963, for example, the U.S. representative to the UN Narcotics Commission "observed that the problem of the Triad organizations (Chinese groups involved in the illicit traffic in the Far East and Europe) appeared to be significant in recent trafficking developments." Other delegates, confirming that "many heroin traffickers . . . had Triad backgrounds," noted the activities of Hong Kong Triad representatives in Germany, Spain, and Switzerland.[53]

This worldwide network of Chinese secret societies in the opium traffic extended both before and after World War II to the Hip Sings, one of the Chinese tongs in the United States, and also to the Bing Kong and other American tongs. In the 1930s the national president of the Hip Sings, Yee On Li, was convicted for a Mafia-linked narcotics operation involving the wife of Lucky Luciano's partner, Thomas Pennachio; Yee was also involved with "Hip Sing dope dealers in Chicago, San Francisco, Pittsburgh, New York, Cleveland, Dallas, and other important cities."[54] In January 1959 a new generation of Hip Sing officials, including San Francisco president George W. Yee, were again indicted for narcotics smuggling. A U.S. government report on the indictments noted that the tong's activities possibly paralleled "the operations of the Triad societies in Hong Kong."[55]

It has been claimed that profits from narcotics smuggling in the United States have been channeled into the China lobby, thus helping to keep open the opium supply lines through Laos and Thailand. In 1960 Ross Y. Koen, in his book *The China Lobby in American Politics*, wrote that

> there is . . . considerable evidence that a number of [Nationalist] Chinese officials engaged in the illegal smuggling of narcotics into the United States with the full knowledge and connivance of the Nationalist Chinese Government. The evidence indicates that several prominent Americans have participated in and profited from

these transactions. It indicates further that the narcotics business has been an important factor in the activities and permutations of the China Lobby.[56]

Professor Koen expressed the hope that his charges would lead to a fuller legal investigation; they led, instead, after a denial from Narcotics Commissioner Anslinger, to his book's being recalled by the publisher. But Anslinger's denial, recently published, does not touch on Mr. Koen's charge about the China lobby:

> I can give you an unqualified statement that this is manufactured out of the whole cloth: that there is no scintilla of evidence that any Chinese officials have engaged in illegal smuggling of narcotics into the United States *with the full knowledge and connivance of the Chinese Nationalist Government.*[57]

Without the italicized qualification, Anslinger's refutation would be hard to believe. For Chiang's consul general in San Francisco at the time of the Hip Sing arrests in the late 1930s, Huang Chao-chin himself "narrowly escaped conviction . . . on charges of smuggling narcotics in the US."[58] After 1952 Huang was a member of the KMT Central Committee, and in 1971 he was chairman of the First Commercial Bank of Taiwan.[59]

The KMT's stake in the CAT airlift to its troops in the "fertile triangle" became obvious in 1961, when Fang Chih, a member of the KMT Central Supervisory Committee and secretary-general of the Free China Relief Agency (FCRA), admitted responsibility for an unlisted CAT plane that had just been shot down over Thailand by the Burmese air force.[60] The Asian People's Anti-Communist League (APACL), of which the FCRA at the same address was a member agency, was itself an organization through which the KMT maintained overt contact with right-wing political and financial interests in Europe and America, as well as with overseas Chinese communities. APACL enlarged after 1967 into the World Anti-Communist League (WACL), whose Latin American branch coordinated such right-wing drug-financed plots as the so-called Bolivian cocaine coup of 1980.[61]

The chairman of the APACL's secret liaison group in America (in effect the heart of the American China lobby) was in 1959 Charles Edison, yet another right-wing member of the Brook Club.[62] The APACL also wrote of its collaboration with psychological warfare experts in the Department of Defense and with the John Birch Society. The unpublicized visit to Laos of Fang Chih, in the weeks immediately preceding the phony Laos "invasion" of 1959, suggests that the narcotics traffic, as well as Pathet Lao activity, may have been a reason why CAT's planes inaugurated their flights in that year into the opium-growing Hmong areas of Sam Neua province. This in turn would explain the extraordinary rumors, reported in the *Christian Science Monitor*, that the Laotian Air Force's "opium runs are made with CIA 'protection.'"[63]

Is it too much to suggest that CAT entry into Laos in 1959 had less to do with

North Vietnam and the nonexistent "invasion" of Laos, reported by Brook Club member Joe Alsop, than with opium? The U.S. government itself, commenting on the nearby rebellion of the same year in the Shan states of Burma, called it "an instance of a rebellion precipitated by the opium traffic."[64] The KMT-sponsored Shan rebellion followed a crackdown in the summer of 1959 by the Burmese government, after Pai Che-jen and some two thousand KMT troops had been driven from Sanskyin Mountain in Yunnan into Burma in 1958.[65]

By March 1959, according to Bernard Fall, "some of the Nationalist guerrillas operating in the Shan states of neighboring Burma had crossed into Laotian territory and were being supplied by an airlift of 'unknown planes.'"[66] Their old opium routes were being threatened to the south as well. In July 1959 the Thai government, in response to years of U.S. government pressure, ended its opium monopoly and announced it would clamp down on the narcotics traffic.[67] Shortly after this prohibition heroin, in the place of the bulkier opium, "came to be regarded as the major problem" in Thailand.[68] By September 1959 CAT had commenced charter airlift in Laos at the expense of the American taxpayer.

Meanwhile, in May-June 1959, Fang Chih of APACL visited KMT camps in Laos, Burma, and Thailand, as he did again in 1960. On August 18, 1959, five days before the arrival of the two CAT planes in Vientiane, and twelve days before the alleged "invasion," Ku Cheng-kang, who was president of the FCRA as well as of the Taiwan APACL, received in Taiwan the mysterious but influential Colonel Oudone Sananikone, a member of what was then the ruling Laotian family and nephew of Laotian Premier Phoui Sananikone.[69] On August 26, 1959, in Washington, Oudone's father, Ngon Sananikone, signed the United States-Laos emergency aid agreement that would pay to charter the CAT planes, three days after their arrival. This was only a few hours after Eisenhower had left for Europe on the same day, not having had time to study the aid request, for Ngon had only submitted it on August 25. On August 27 Oudone Sananikone attended the founding in Taiwan of a Sino-Laotian friendship society, whose trustees included Ku Cheng-kang and Fang Chih.[70]

Oudone Sananikone headed a "Laotian" paramilitary airline, Veha Akhat, which in those days serviced the opium-growing areas north of the Plain of Jars with Chinese Nationalist planes and personnel (CAT had not yet begun its operations to the Hmong in this region, which offered such profitable opportunities for smuggling as a sideline for enterprising pilots).[71] Oudone Sananikone also figured prominently in the secret three-way talks between officers of Laos, South Vietnam, and Taiwan that preceded the Vientiane coup and resulting crisis of April 19, 1964, the coup that was reported two days in advance by Taiwan Radio.[72]

Another major figure in the 1959 and 1964 Laotian plots was General Ouane Rathikone, who flew with Joe Alsop to Sam Neua and showed him the staged evidence of the 1959 "invasion." General Ouane is said to have admitted in a 1970s interview that he was "the real boss" of opium operations in Laos.[73]

What is extraordinary, and quite possibly criminal under U.S. law, is not the involvement in narcotics of the KMT nor that of the Taiwan airline CATCL that it controlled, but of Americans exercising the authority of the CIA. The CIA as an agency, it is true, cannot be identified with the narcotics trade any more than can the whole of the Kuomintang. In 1955, for example, when the CIA ran airlift to the opium trade in Thailand, General Lansdale in Vietnam used CIA funds to smash the pro-French Binh Xuyen apparatus that controlled the dope and gambling activities of Saigon and its Chinese suburb, much as the Triads operated in Malaya.[74] In 1971 Air America planes were reported to have taken part in the growing U.S. crackdown on the narcotics traffic, while a former-CIA congressman, Robert Steele of Connecticut, produced a useful report, *The World Heroin Problem,* after a worldwide tour in the company of a former CIA Saigon station chief.[75]

Although General Lansdale was cracking down on narcotics in Vietnam, William H. Bird, the CAT representative in Bangkok, was said to have coordinated CAT airdrops to Li Mi's troops in the "fertile triangle." In 1960, after CAT began flying in Laos through "the great Laos fraud," his private engineering firm Bird and Son began the construction of short airstrips in Hmong territory which were soon used for the collection of Laos opium, some of it destined to be manufactured into heroin in Marseilles, and forwarded to the National Crime Syndicate in the United States.[76] Soon Bird and Son had its own airline of fifty planes flying U.S. contract airlift to the opium growing tribesmen, and rumors soon arose that these planes, like Air America's in the same area, were not infrequently used for smuggling.[77]

William Bird's alleged brother or cousin in Bangkok, China OSS veteran Willis Bird, headed the Bangkok office of a "trading company" called Sea Supply, Inc. As we noted before, Sea Supply first supplied arms to the KMT troops of General Li Mi, and later trained Phao Sriyanon's Thai border police who were also implicated in KMT opium-smuggling activities. Like William, Willis Bird also branched into construction business on his own. In 1959, as vice president of the Universal Construction Company, Bird was said by a congressional committee investigating corruption in Laos to have bribed an International Cooperation Administration (ICA) aid official in Vientiane.[78] In 1962, when President Kennedy was struggling to bring the CIA hawks in Thailand under control, his brother, the attorney general, belatedly returned an indictment against Willis Bird, who never returned to this country to stand trial.[79]

What particularly concerns us is of course not the personal venality of a U.S. construction official or of pilots dabbling in opium on the side, so much as the sustained support by CIA proprietaries of narcotics-smuggling activities that affected the continental United States. It is not at all clear that this policy had sanction at the highest level. As I argued in chapter 4, Eisenhower seems to have had only the vaguest awareness of realities in Laos. By all accounts the Kennedy administration was exerting pressure to remove the "estimated 4,000 Chinese Nationalists" who "were reportedly operating in western Laos in 1961," having been "flown from Taiwan into bases in northern Thailand."[80] Even the Johnson administration announced in February 1964 that it would withdraw Air America (i.e., CATCL) from Laos. This announcement came to naught after the organizer of CAT's American replacement, John Davidson of Seaboard World Services, was "accidentally" killed in a dubious and controversial explosion of a CAT plane.[81]

How could the objectives of U.S. presidents be at odds with those of a CIA proprietary? The obvious stake of KMT interests in CATCL is a partial explanation, to which one can perhaps add the stake of private American interests as well. For it is a striking fact that the law firm of Tommy Corcoran, the Washington lawyer for CATCL and T. V. Soong, has had its own links to the interlocking worlds of the China lobby and of organized crime. His partner W. S. Youngman joined the board of U.S. Life and other domestic insurance companies, controlled by C. V. Starr (OSS China) with the help of Philippine and other Asian capital.[82] Youngman's fellow directors of Starr's companies have included John S. Woodbridge of Pan Am, Francis F. Randolph of J. & W. Seligman, W. Palmer Dixon of Loeb Rhoades, Charles Edison of the postwar China lobby, and Alfred B. Jones of the Nationalist Chinese government's registered agency, the Universal Trading Corporation. The McClellan Committee heard that in 1950 U.S. Life (with Edison a director) and a much smaller company (Union Casualty of New York) were allotted a major Teamsters insurance contract, after a lower bid from a larger and safer company had been rejected. Hoffa was accused by a fellow trustee, testifying under oath before another committee, of intervening on behalf of U.S. Life and Union Casualty, whose agents were Hoffa's close business associates Paul Dorfman and Allen Dorfman.[83]

The National City Bank itself had once leased its racetrack in Havana (and also, through a subsidiary, the Hotel Nacional de Cuba's casino) to Meyer Lansky of the organized crime syndicate.[84] In 1950 Citibank's largest shareholder, Transamerica Corporation, was represented, through James F. Cavagnaro, in the shadowy World Commerce Corporation organized by several OSS veterans. In 1950 the World Commerce Corporation was involved in dubious soybean operations[85] while its subsidiary Commerce International (China) sponsored the unauthorized Pawley-Cooke military assistance mission to Taiwan[86] and the illegal smuggling of airplanes from California to the government of Chiang Kai-shek.[87] Satiris "Sonny" Fassoulis, accused of passing bribes as the vice president of Commerce International, was under indictment ten years later when he surfaced in the syndicate-linked Guterma scandals.[88]

A director of Air America through the years has been Robert Guestier Goelet of the City Investing Co., where his fellow-directors have included Joseph Binns of U.S. Life (Binns was involved in Bahamas and other land speculations with Meyer Lansky's business associate Lou Chesler),[89] and John W. Houser (an intelligence veteran from the Pacific who negotiated the lease of the Havana Hilton hotel casino to Cuban associates of the syndicate).[90]

We find the same network linking CIA proprietaries, war lobbies, and organized crime, when we turn our attention from CAT to the other identified supporter of opium activities, Sea Supply, Inc. Sea Supply was organized in Miami, Florida, where its counsel, Paul L. E. Helliwell, doubled after 1951 as the counsel for C. V. Starr insurance interests, and also as Thai consul in Miami. It would be hard to say whether Helliwell (the former OSS chief of special intelligence in China) was more active in representing U.S. or Thai government interests; in 1955 and 1956, for example, the Thai consulate in Miami (operating out of Helliwell's office as secretary for the American Bankers Insurance Company of Florida) passed over $30,000 to its registered foreign lobbyist in Washington, Tommy Corcoran's law partner James Rowe. Inasmuch as Corcoran and Rowe were two of the closest personal advisers to Lyndon Baines Johnson, then the rapidly rising Senate majority leader, Helliwell's lobbying activities for the opium-dealing government of Phibun and Phao Sriyanon may well have had a more powerful impact on U.S. policy than his legal activities for the CIA.

Miami of course has been frequently identified as "a point where many of the more important United States and Canadian and even the French [narcotics] traffickers congregate."[91] American Bankers Insurance, the company from whose office Helliwell doubled as Thai consul general and counsel for Sea Supply, Inc., appears to have maintained its own marginal links with the institutions servicing the world of organized crime and narcotics.[92] The most striking interlock is that of its director J. L. King, who in 1964 was also a director of the Miami National Bank. The Miami National Bank was identified in 1969 as having served between 1963 and 1967 as a conduit through which "hot" syndicate money was exported by Meyer Lansky's couriers and "laundered" through the interlocking Exchange and Investment Bank in Geneva.[93] (Lou Poller, King's fellow director of the Miami National Bank and a director also of the Swiss Exchange and Investment Bank, was investigated by the McClellan Committee about his use of Teamster capital to acquire the Miami National Bank, and subsequently indicted for perjury.)[94]

It is said that rich Thai and other Asian capitalists, like wealthy syndicate gangsters such as "Trigger Mike" Coppola, have invested heavily in Florida's postwar land boom, through companies such as the General Development Corporation of Meyer Lansky's business associate Lou Chesler.[95] Such business associations might help explain why, for example, Prince Puchartra of Thailand became the only royal representative at the 1966 opening of Caesar's Palace in Las Vegas, a hotel-casino said to be controlled by Jimmy Hoffa.[96] The same associations, if they were exposed, might cast light on the unexplained 1968 business trip to Hong Kong and Southeast Asia of Santos Trafficante, an old Lansky associate named in narcotics investigations.[97] Trafficante had been preceded in 1965 by John Pullman, Meyer Lansky's courier to the Miami National Bank. In April 1965 Pullman visited "the Peninsular Hotel in Hong Kong, where the syndicate had casinos and obtained much of its narcotics."[98]

The apparent involvement of CIA proprietaries with foreign narcotics operations is paralleled by their apparent interlock with the domestic institutions serving organized crime. The thrust of this admittedly sketchy inquiry has been to suggest that, with the maturation of both capitalism and Third World nationalism, and with the outlawing of private war operations like those financed by Seligman in 1903, wealthy U.S. interests (using the secret authorities delegated to the CIA) have resorted systematically to organized outlaws to pursue their operations.

It is true that the embarrassing links between Air America and CATCL diminished after 1965. But the opium-based economy of Laos continued to be protected by a coalition of opium-growing CIA mercenaries, Air America planes, and Thai troops.[99] Nixon's crackdown in 1971 on Turkish opium production handled by Corsicans in France only increased the importance of heroin deriving from (and refined in) the "fertile triangle," which was already estimated to supply possibly 25 percent of American heroin consumption.[100]

Official U.S. doubletalk about the domestic heroin problem (and the reluctance in the 1960s to recognize the "fertile triangle" as a source for it) is only one further symptom that the public sanctions of law and the constitution have yielded ground to private interests and the secret sanctions provided through the CIA. More specifically, the use of illegal narcotics networks to fight communism, resorted to by capitalists in Shanghai in 1927 and in Southeast Asia in the 1950s, seems without our knowledge to have been sanctioned inside the United States.[101]

NOTES

1. See also chapter 3.

2. Alfred McCoy, *The Politics of Heroin* (Brooklyn, N.Y.: Lawrence Hill, 1991), 167–68; cf. this book, 207n93. For Helliwell's criminal connections, see Alan A. Block, *Masters of Paradise* (New Brunswick, N.J.: Transaction, 1991), 165, 168–71, 189–90.

3. McCoy, *Politics of Heroin*, 167 ("sold CAT"). Elsewhere McCoy notes the importance of "unmarked C-46 and C-47 transport aircraft" to the KMT presence in Burma (p. 169). The 60 percent arrangement that I wrote about in 1972 is described in detail in William Leary, *Perilous Missions* (University, Ala.: University of Alabama Press, 1984), 204–8. However, Leary's archival account, based on CAT and Air America documents and files, does not adequately describe the extent of KMT/CAT links to the drug trafficking troops in Burma. For example, in describing the 1953–1954 CAT evacuation of troops from Burma to Taiwan (pp. 195–96), Leary does not mention the reports that return flights brought fresh and younger troops back in. On this point McCoy's account is much better (pp. 174–76).

4. For example, McCoy, *Politics of Heroin*, 19: "The CIA adopted a complicitous posture toward the traffic, allowing the Hmong commander, General Vang Pao to use the CIA's Air America to collect opium from his scattered highland villages." Other examples at pages 129 ("A CIA agent could achieve"), 291 ("The agency . . . did not object"), 307, and so on.

Again, McCoy does not mention Operation Mosquito, the program launched by Casey, Reagan, and French intelligence chief Alexandre de Marenches to demoralize the Soviet Army in Afghanistan with a flood of drugs (see chapter 2 of this volume; Stéphane Allix, *La petite cuillère de Schéhérazade* [Paris: Editions Ramsay, 1998], 95; Alexandre de Marenches, *Dans le secret des princes* [Paris: Stock, 1986]). McCoy relies too heavily on official U.S. sources. Thus he suggests, for example, that drug flows through Iran increased after the fall of the Shah (p. 446). Most credible non-U.S. sources indicate the opposite: "'After the revolution in 1979, Iran, which had cultivated drugs for years, managed to eradicate growing of opium poppies in a year and a half,' says Antonio Mazzitelli, the Teheran representative of the UN Drug Control Programme (UNDCP)." *Le Monde Diplomatique*, March 13, 2002; mondediplo.com/2002/03/13drug?var_s = afghanistan + %2B + heroin; see also M. Emdad-ul Haq, *Drugs in South Asia* (New York: St. Martin's, 2000), 198. Despite these details, McCoy's study remains the best by far that we have.

5. See this book, 193–94.

6. For example, Carl A. Trocki, *Opium, Empire, and the Global Political Economy: A Study of the Asian Opium Trade, 1750–1950* (London: Routledge, 1999); Timothy Brook and Bob Tadashi Wakabayashi, eds., *Opium Regimes: China, Britain, and Japan, 1839–1952* (Berkeley: University of California Press, 2000).

7. Peter Dale Scott and Jonathan Marshall, *Cocaine Politics: Drugs, Armies, and the CIA in Central America* (Berkeley: University of California Press, 1998), xviii–xix.

8. See also Peter Dale Scott, *Deep Politics and the Death of JFK* (Berkeley: University of California Press, 1996), esp. 164–91.

9. Samuel Eliot Morison, *The Oxford History of the American People* (New York: Oxford University Press, 1965), 825–26. Pointing to the subsequent impact on all Latin America, Morison concludes that "the United States is paying dear today for Roosevelt's impetuosity in 1903."

10. Stephen Birmingham, *"Our Crowd": The Great Jewish Families of New York* (New York: Harper & Row, 1967), 236–38; U.S. Congress, Senate, *Documents,* 58th Cong., 2d sess., no. 53; House, *Documents,* 58th Cong., 1st sess., no. 8. The French government was so far from involving itself in this campaign to recuperate the assets of the defunct Paris company that "the French Foreign Minister in Washington wired Bunau-Varilla's brother in Paris, saying that Philippe's [congressional lobbying] activities were embarrassing to France, and suggesting that Philippe had lost his mind" (Birmingham, *"Our Crowd,"* 237).

11. For example, the "nation building" activities in Vietnam of the immigrant European liberal Joseph Buttinger can be compared to those of the French liberal Bunau-Varilla, "who had first caught the attention of the Seligmans through his activities in the Dreyfus case."

12. *Washington Post,* December 22, 1963, A11; quoted in Roger Hilsman, *To Move a Nation* (Garden City, N.Y.: Doubleday, 1967), 63.

13. David Wise and Thomas B. Ross, *The Espionage Establishment* (New York: Random House, 1967), 166.

14. Frank G. Wisner (OSS) came to the government in 1948 from the Wall Street legal firm of Carter, Ledyard, and Milburn, which represented various Rockefeller, Whitney, and Standard Oil interests. As director of the Office of Policy Coordination, which became

the CIA's Plans Division on January 4, 1951, Wisner was in charge of the CIA's covert operations.

William Harding Jackson (Republican), Smith's deputy director in 1950–1951, had been with Carter, Ledyard, and Milburn from 1934 to 1947 and was now an investment partner of John Hay Whitney on the board of Bankers Trust.

Allen Welsh Dulles (OSS, Republican), a wartime director of J. Henry Schroder Banking Corporation and longtime partner of Sullivan and Cromwell (linked with various Rockefeller and Schroeder interests), succeeded Jackson as deputy director in August 1951.

Murray McConnel, president of the Manufacturers Capital Corporation on Wall Street, was the CIA's deputy director for administration in 1950 and 1951.

Walter Reid Wolf (Republican), a vice president of the National City Bank of New York and of its investment affiliate City Bank Farmers Trust, was a CIA deputy director (presumably McConnel's successor) from 1951 to 1953.

Robert Amory Jr. (son of a New York manufacturer who was a codirector of at least three Boston firms with directors of United Fruit) came to the CIA as deputy director for intelligence in 1952 (according to *Who's Who*).

Loftus E. Becker, of the Wall Street law firm Cahill, Gordon, Reindel, and Ohl (representing the investment firms of Dillon Read and Stone and Webster), went on leave to the CIA in April 1951 and was named deputy director "for Intelligence" (according to the Martindale-Hubbard law directory, 1965, 4707) for a year beginning January 21, 1952.

All of these men except Becker were listed in the select *New York Social Register*, and thus they were members of not only New York's financial-legal elite but also its hereditary upper class. The known links between the CIA and Civil Air Transport-Air America date from this period, when New York finance enjoyed a monopoly over the CIA's top civilian appointments.

15. David Wise and Thomas B. Ross, *The Invisible Government* (New York: Bantam, 1965), 115–16; *New Republic*, April 12, 1969, 8.

16. Wise and Ross, *Invisible Government*, 140.

17. *New York Times*, September 20, 1957, 7.

18. *The Pentagon Papers* (New York: Bantam, 1971), 137.

19. Arnold Dibble, "The Nine Lives of CAT II," *Saturday Evening Post*, May 18, 1968, 50; *New York Times*, November 11, 1949, 14; April 5, 1970, 22; *Free China Review*, November 1963, 31. In 1949 the Kincheng Bank ostensibly severed its connections with CAT, in the vain hope of continuing to operate on the mainland. But Wang Wen-san, then manager of the Kincheng Bank, was in 1972 still chairman of CATCL's board, on which the KMT Chinese Nationalists had three of the five seats. Air America pilots long circulated the rumor that "Madame Chiang owns the planes and we lease them from her" (*San Francisco Chronicle*, April 2, 1970, 31). The complex details of the CIA–Wang Wen-san arrangement are given in Leary, *Perilous Missions*, 106–12, 199–208.

20. Charles Wertenbaker, "The China Lobby," *Reporter*, April 15, 1952, 9.

21. John R. Beal, *Marshall in China* (New York: Doubleday, 1970), 85.

22. U.S. Congress, House, Committee on Un-American Activities, *International Communism: Consultation with Major-General Claire Lee Chennault*, 85th Cong., 2d sess., April 23, 1958, 9–10; U.S. Department of State, *U.S. Policy in the Korean Crisis* (Washington, D.C.: GPO, 1950), 21–22.

23. *Time*, October 15, 1951, 23.

24. *New York Times*, July 6, 1951, 9; cf. June 9, 1951, 6; I. F. Stone, *The Hidden History of the Korean War* (New York: Monthly Review Press, 1969), xi. The *New York Times* wrote that "the soybean is expected to come under any Congressional inquiry of the China Lobby," but no such inquiry ever took place. It may be relevant that Joe McCarthy took part in the profitable soybean speculations on the advice of a Pepsi-Cola lobbyist.

25. Leary, *Perilous Missions*, 110–12; Christopher Robbins, *Air America* (New York: Putnam's, 1979), 48–49, 56–57, 70.

26. The bulk of U.S. military airlift inside Korea was flown by CATCL, which soon boasted assets of some $5.5 million and income in the order of from $6 to $12 million a year (*Collier's*, August 11, 1951, 35).

27. Cleveland Amory, *Who Killed Society?* (New York: Pocket Books, 1960), 202.

28. Dibble, "Nine Lives," 50.

29. One indication of this mutual advantage between political and economic concerns is the later convergence in the board of one enterprise (Cuno Engineering) of former CIA director Bedell Smith, of his deputy director Murray McConnel, and of McConnel's successor Walter Reid Wolf, who was involved in setting up CAT, Inc.

30. *New York Times*, April 5, 1970, 1, 22. Air America pilots, like Lockheed's U-2 pilots, are mostly recruited from the USAF, and are said to have the same rights of return into USAF at the end of their "civilian" tour.

31. Transamerica Corporation, the Giannini holding corporation, was in the late 1940s the largest stockholder in both banks, owning about 9 percent of Citibank and 22 percent of the Bank of America.

32. *New York Times*, April 8, 1960, 62; U.S. Congress, House, Committee on Armed Services, Special Subcommittee on National Airlift, *Hearings*, 86th Cong., 2d sess. (Washington, D.C.: GPO, 1960), 4616–50, 4730–34. The president of Pan Am testified that his company would have to release three hundred pilots during the next six months "if traffic—other than normal civil traffic—doesn't become available." It has been noted that the congressional compromise between the Pentagon and the commercial airlines contained "no recommendation about what to do if the combination of more strategic airlift and continuing guarantees to the [airlines] industry produced too much airlift in nonwar situations" (Frederick C. Thayer, *Air Transport Policy and National Security* [Chapel Hill: University of North Carolina Press, 1965], 225). Thanks to the Laotian airlift and war, that problem was not faced.

33. Angus McDonald and Al McCoy, "Pan Am Makes the Going Great," *Scanlon's,* April 1970, 53. In 1961 Pan Am's Atlantic competitor, TWA, lost $38 million. In 1962 Pan Am's total air cargo load rose 500 percent, thanks in part to the airlift in that year of U.S. troops to Thailand.

34. Ed Reid, *The Grim Reapers* (Chicago: Henry Regnery, 1969), 219; Wallace Turner, *Gamblers' Money: The New Force in American Life* (Cambridge, Mass.: Houghton Mifflin, 1965), 10, 274.

35. George A. Doole, chief executive officer of Air America, Amos Hiatt, treasurer, and Hugh Grundy, president of Air Asia, were all recruited from Pan Am and its foreign subsidiaries, just as William Pawley had worked for Pan Am's China subsidy CNAC before setting up the Flying Tigers in 1941. One also notes that the "American Fliers for Laos," who volunteered in response to the 1959 Laos "invasion," were recruited by Clif-

ford L. Speer, a "major in the Air Force Reserve and civilian employee at Fort Huachuca, Arizona" (*New York Times*, September 27, 1959, 16). Pan Am has a contract at Fort Huachuca to conduct highly secret "electronics weapons" research for the USAF.

36. J. T. McAlister, *Vietnam: The Origins of a Revolution* (New York: Knopf, 1969), 228; cited in David Feingold, "Opium and Politics in Laos," in Nina Adams and Al McCoy, eds., *Laos: War and Revolution* (New York: Harper, 1970), 335.

37. George Thayer, *The War Business* (New York: Simon & Schuster, 1969), 158, emphasis added. Even the U.S. government publication *Area Book for Thailand* (Washington, D.C.: GPO, 1968) records of the KMT troops that "their principal income allegedly comes from serving as armed escort for the opium caravans moving southward" [to Bangkok] (p. 454).

38. G. William Skinner, *Chinese Society in Thailand: An Analytical History* (Ithaca, N.Y.: Cornell University Press, 1957), 289.

39. UN Document E/CN.7/213 (communicated by the U.S. representative), November 17, 1950, 9.

40. For example, a statement by Harry J. Anslinger, then U.S. commissioner of narcotics, before the Senate Committee on the Judiciary, *Illicit Narcotics Traffic, Hearings*, 84th Cong., 2d sess. (Washington, D.C.: GPO, 1955), 13; UN Document E/CN.7/394, April 29, 1960, 2.

41. U.S. Congress, Senate, Committee on the Judiciary, *Narcotic Control Act of 1956, Hearing*, 84th Cong., 2d sess., May 4, 1956, 34. Before the tenth session (1955) of the UN Narcotics Commission, the U.S. representative noted that from two hundred to four hundred tons of opium were imported annually south into Thailand across the Burma-Laos border, of which only one hundred tons were consumed in Thailand itself (UN Document E/CN.7/303/Rev. 1, 34).

42. UN Commission on Narcotic Drugs, *Report of the Ninth Session* (1954), E/CN.7/283, 22.

43. UN Commission on Narcotic Drugs, *Report of the Thirteenth Session* (1958), E/CN.7/354, 26, cf. 22; *Report of the Fifteenth Session* (1960), E/CN.7/395, 19, cf. 18. For details of how a KMT-Hip Sing heroin shipment was manipulated by CIA officer George White into a "communist" shipment, see Peter Dale Scott, foreword to Henrik Krüger, *The Great Heroin Coup* (Boston: South End, 1980), 15–16; Peter Dale Scott, *Deep Politics and the Death of JFK* (Berkeley: University of California Press, 1976), 167.

44. *San Francisco Chronicle*, September 4, 1970, 1. *Free China and Asia*, a journal published by the KMT agency responsible for chartering the CAT flights, gave details of Yunnan military operations and wrote of "plans to rise up in coordination with the efforts of the Tibetans against the Communist rule, particularly those in Yunnan and Sikang" (*Free China and Asia*, June 1959, 21; cf. January 1959, 10). The tragic but relevant story of CIA operations in Tibet has now been told by one of the CIA officers responsible: John Kenneth Knaus, *Orphans of the Cold War: America and the Tibetan Struggle for Survival* (New York: Public Affairs, 1999). Ethnic Tibetans inhabit both Sikang and parts of Yunnan.

45. Wilfred Blythe, *Impact of Chinese Secret Societies in Malaya* (London: Oxford University Press, 1969), 190, 250.

46. Compare, for example, UN Commission on Narcotic Drugs, *Report of the Seventeenth Session*, E/CN.7/432, 15.

47. Blythe, *Impact*, 441, 449.

48. Blythe, *Impact*, 441–42.

49. Skinner, *Chinese Society in Thailand*, 120–21.

50. Skinner, *Chinese Society in Thailand*, 337.

51. UN Document E/CN.7/210, November 3, 1950, 3.

52. H. R. Isaacs, *The Tragedy of the Chinese Revolution* (Stanford: Stanford University Press, 1951), 81, 142–46; Y. C. Wang, *Journal of Asia Studies*, May 1967, 437; Blythe, *Impact*, 21, 28–29. See now McCoy, *Politics of Heroin*, 263–70. McCoy describes how Chiang mobilized Tu and the Green Gang into a secret police agency under General Tai Li, with whom OSS collaborated during World War II. As head of OSS wartime intelligence in China, Paul Helliwell dealt with Tai Li before going on to help organize Civil Air Transport as a CIA proprietary.

53. UN Commission on Narcotic Drugs, *Report of the Eighteenth Session*, E/CN.7/455, 10. Cf. McCoy, *Politics*, 269–82.

54. Will Oursler and L. D. Smith, *Narcotics: America's Peril* (Garden City, N.Y.: Doubleday, 1952), 87.

55. E/CN.7/394, April 29, 1960, 8. The United States knew very well that the operation was run by pro-KMT Chinese, but a CIA officer, George White, told the U.S. press that the heroin had come from *communist* China; see Scott, *Deep Politics*, 167.

56. Ross Y. Koen, *The China Lobby in American Politics* (New York: Macmillan, 1960), ix.

57. Joseph Keeley, *The China Lobby Man* (New Rochelle, N.Y.: Arlington House, 1969), 148, emphasis added.

58. Michael Straight, "Corruption and Chiang Kai-shek," *New Republic*, October 8, 1951, 12.

59. He was also Speaker of the Taiwan Provincial Assembly; for background, see George H. Kerr, *Formosa Betrayed* (Boston: Houghton Mifflin, 1965), 297–98.

60. *New York Times*, February 16, 1961, 9; *Singapore Straits Times*, February 20, 1961, 1.

61. Scott and Marshall, *Cocaine Politics*, 87. The Japan chapter of APACL was organized by Sasakawa Ryoichi, a *kurumaku* or fixer between Japanese intelligence, business, and organized crime.

62. *APACL: Its Growth and Outlook* (Taipeh: APACL, 1960). For CIA involvement in the creation of the APACL, see Jonathan Marshall et al., *The Iran-Contra Connection* (Boston: South End, 1967), 64–65.

63. *Christian Science Monitor*, June 16, 1970, 8; cf. May 29, 1970, 14: "Clearly the CIA is cognizant of, if not party to, the extensive movement of opium out of Laos. One charter pilot told me that 'friendly' opium shipments get special CIA clearance and monitoring on their flights southward out of the country. The same source alleged two or three flights without this 'protection' crashed under mysterious circumstances."

64. U.S. note of April 29, 1960, to UN Commission on Narcotic Drugs, E/CN.7/394, 2.

65. U.S. note of April 29, 1960, to UN Commission on Narcotic Drugs, E/CN.7/394, 1; *Free China and Asia*, January 1959, 10.

66. Bernard Fall, *Anatomy of a Crisis* (Garden City, N.Y.: Doubleday, 1969), 99.

67. The Thai police favoritism shown the KMT during 1952–1954 had been disavowed

in 1956; Prime Minister Phibun stated at a public press conference, "The Kuomintang causes too much trouble: they trade in opium and cause Thailand to be blamed in the United Nations" (Skinner, *Chinese Society in Thailand,* 343). The next year Phao was ousted from power by the present military rulers of Thailand, amid reports that Phao, "a sort of local Beria . . . ran the gold exchange and opium trade" (*New York Times,* November 6, 1957, 34). Cf. chapter 2 in this volume; McCoy, *Politics of Heroin,* 189–90.

68. UN Commission on Narcotic Drugs, *Report of the Seventeenth Session* (1962), E/CN.7/432, 11.

69. APACL, *Free China and Asia,* October 1959, 14.

70. *Free China and Asia,* October 1959, 31.

71. In fact Veha Akhat was little more than a front for the Nationalist Chinese airlines from which it chartered six planes and pilots. On February 19, 1961, four days after the CAT/FCRA plane was shot down by the Burmese, a Veha Akhat C-47 leased from a Taiwan company was shot down over Laos; four of the six personnel aboard were said to be Nationalist Chinese officers (*Bangkok Post,* February 22, 1961, 1; *Singapore Straits Times,* February 22, 1961, 3). The same year Taiwan's second airline, Foshing, reported a decrease in its air fleet from three C-47s to two. Foshing Airlines was headed by Moon Chin, a former assistant operating manager of Pan Am's China subsidiary, CNAC, under William Pawley.

72. *Bangkok Post,* April 18, 1964.

73. *San Francisco Chronicle,* August 16, 1971, 12. See McCoy, *Politics of Heroin,* xiv–xv, passim.

74. It is striking that in 1961, when the CIA inaugurated covert air operations from Saigon against North Vietnam, it spurned the available planes and facilities of CAT at Saigon's Tan Son Nhut Airport and set up a new, unrelated "proprietary," Aviation Investors, Inc., d/b/a Vietnam Air Transport. Vietnam Air Transport is said to have hired Nguyen Cao Ky and then fired him after learning that he used his "Operation Haylift" flights as a cover for opium smuggling from Laos to Saigon. Cf. McCoy, *Politics of Heroin,* 227–28, passim.

75. U.S. Congress, House, Committee on Foreign Affairs, *The World Heroin Problem,* Report of Special Study Mission, House Report no. 92–298, 92d Cong., 1st sess. (Washington, D.C.: GPO, 1971).

76. Stanley Karnow once named a "debonair, pencil-moustached Corsican by the name of Bonaventure Francisci" as one of the top opium runners in Laos ("The Opium Must Go Through," *Life,* August 30, 1963, 12). The Francisci family has been linked to the Spirito-Venturi arm of the Corsican Mafia in Marseilles, which in turn reaches to America through syndicate associate Vincent Cotroni of Montreal (U.S. Congress, Senate, Committee on Government Operations, *Organized Crime and Illicit Traffic in Narcotics, Hearings,* 88th Cong., 2d sess. (Washington, D.C.: GPO, 1964), 956, 961; cited hereafter as *Narcotics Hearings*). This Corsican traffic dates back at least to the 1950s, according to Martin Pera, a senior Narcotics Bureau official: "When French Indochina existed, there were quantities of opium that were shipped to the labs . . . around Marseilles, France, to the Corsican underworld there, and then transshipped to the United States" (U.S. Congress, Senate, Select Committee on Improper Activities in the Labor or Management Field, *Hearings,* 85th Cong., 2d sess. [Washington, D.C.: GPO, 1959], 12225; cited hereafter as *McClellan Hearings*). Cf. McCoy, *Politics of Heroin,* 296–99.

77. In 1965 Bird's air fleet was sold to Continental Air Services, a newly created subsidiary of Continental Air Lines headed by Robert Rousselot, a CAT and Air America veteran. The sale price was said to have been over $1 million (*Wall Street Journal*, August 23, 1965, 20; Continental Airlines, *Annual Report, 1965,* 13; *New York Times*, August 27, 1964, 6).

78. U.S. Congress, House, Committee on Government Operations, *U.S. Aid Operations in Laos*, House Report no. 546, 86th Cong., 1st sess. (Washington, D.C.: GPO, 1959), 2; *Hearings*, 327; *New York Times*, March 24, 1959, 19.

79. *New York Times*, February 2, 1962, 8.

80. Stanley Karnow, *Washington Post*, March 16, 1970, A10. Theodore Sorenson records that "Chiang was . . . vexed with Kennedy . . . over our quiet pressure for the removal of his foraging force from Burma" (Sorenson, *Kennedy* [New York: Harper & Row, 1965], 661). The KMT lobbied publicly for these troops to be given the job of stopping communism as a "volunteer force" in Laos (*Free China and Asia*, December 1960, 5–6). They were supported in the United States by elements in the Pentagon and American Security Council (including Admiral Felix Stump, Air America's board chairman). Western Laos was the area of the celebrated "opium battle" of July 1967 between 800 KMT troops and the forces of the opium-smuggling Laotian general Ouane Rathikone, who also figures prominently in the Laotian invasion fraud of September 1959; *San Francisco Chronicle*, August 16, 1971, 12; Feingold, "Opium and Politics," 323; Frank Browning and Banning Garrett, "The New Opium War," *Ramparts*, May 1971, 34. Cf. McCoy, *Politics of Heroin*, 355–61.

81. *New York Times*, March 19, 1964, 4; *Bangkok Post*, March 20, 1964; *New York Times*, August 27, 1964, 6; *South China Morning Post*, June 22, 1964, 1; *Saturday Review*, May 11, 1968, 44.

82. Starr's companies had a wartime connection to U.S. intelligence in China. Today they have evolved into the huge conglomerate AIG, which may still have intelligence connections. Recently AIG has been headed by Maurice Greenberg, who in 1995 was allegedly a candidate to head the CIA (*Washington Weekly*, March 17, 1997).

83. *McClellan Hearings*, 15262–72.

84. Hank Messick, *Lansky* (New York: Putnam's, 1971), 89. In 1968 Citibank refused to produce a $200,000 certificate of deposit that had been subpoenaed in an investigation of stock fraud (*New York Times*, December 1, 1969, 42).

85. *New York Times*, May 23, 1950, 34.

86. Pawley, on the advice of President Roosevelt and Tommy Corcoran, set up the Flying Tigers under a secret presidential executive order, exempting him from the neutrality provisions of the U.S. Code (Anna Chan Chennault, *Chennault and the Flying Tigers* [New York: Eriksson, 1963], 76–83). In 1949 Pawley petitioned the State Department to secure similar authorization for the Commerce International (China) mission but was turned down (U.S. Congress, Senate, Committee on Judiciary, *Communist Threat to the United States through the Caribbean, Hearings*, 86th Cong., 2d sess., testimony of William D. Pawley, September 2, 1960, 72, 9). Admiral Charles Cooke, later a member of the American Security Council, proceeded anyway.

87. *Washington Post*, September 9, 1951, A1, A8; reprinted in *Congressional Record,* Senate, September 10, 1951, 11066–67; *Reporter*, April 29, 1952, 10–11; Koen, *China Lobby*, 50. For more information, see Bruce Cumings, *The Origins of the Korean War* (Princeton: Princeton University Press, 1990), 2:509–12.

88. T. A. Wise, "The World of Alexander Guterma," *Fortune,* December 1959, 160. Also figuring in the Guterma scandals were Matthew Fox, a former registered lobbyist for Indonesia with possible CIA connections (Chester Cooper, *The Lost Crusade* [New York: Dodd Mead, 1970], 52), and Herman Brann, a U.S. intelligence agent in World War II. Guterma himself came from Shanghai and the Philippines and used Philippine capital to launch himself into Florida land development.

89. Through Chester's Seven Arts Productions; cf. Messick, *Lansky,* 228; Reid, *Grim Reapers,* 107.

90. Messick, *Lansky,* 211.

91. *McClellan Hearings,* 12246.

92. The company's president was an officer for the realty investment interests of Lindsey Hopkins Jr., himself an officer of CIA proprietaries in Miami (e.g., Zenith Enterprises and Melmar, Inc., in the 1960s). As a director of Sperry Corporation and its subsidiaries, Hopkins had been linked to William Pawley's establishment of the Flying Tigers in 1941 (through a Sperry subsidiary, Intercontinent Corp., of which Pawley was president). Through the Carl G. Fisher Corporation, Hopkins inherited a fortune in Miami Beach hotels and took part in the postwar land boom in the Bahamas.

93. *New York Times,* December 1, 1969, 42. Helliwell also served as counsel to the Miami National Bank. Miami National went through many changes of ownership, and in 1975 was forfeited to Citibank, the former National City Bank of New York, as collateral for an unpaid loan. The connection to Helliwell's law firm survived, even after Helliwell's death in 1976. Miami National's new counsel, and chairman of its loan committee, was Truman A. Skinner, a member of Helliwell's firm Helliwell, Melrose, and DeWolf. A Justice Department–organized crime strike force later accused Skinner of securities fraud and of making unauthorized loans from the bank to a condominium project with mob connections. See Penny Lernoux, *In Banks We Trust* (Garden City, N.Y.: Anchor Doubleday, 1984), 42–44, 84.

94. *New York Times,* August 14, 1959, 9; Messick, *Lansky,* 269. Allen Dorfman, whose friendship with Hoffa helped win the Teamsters insurance contract for U.S. Life in 1950, was indicted for accepting kickbacks on a Teamster loan to the Neisco Corporation (*San Francisco Chronicle,* July 15, 1971, 5). Neisco's chairman, G. A. Horvath, was board chairman and principal owner of the Miami National Bank in 1964.

95. The Thai king's general counsel in New York from 1945 to 1950, Carl O. Hoffmann of OSS, became board chairman of the First Florida Resource Corporation. This was at a time when "Kuomintang [KMT] money from Thailand and Burma came via Hong Kong to be washed through Lansky-related property firms" (R. T. Naylor, *Hot Money and the Politics of Debt* [New York: Simon & Schuster, 1987], 292).

96. Reid, *Grim Reapers,* 225–26.

97. Reid, *Grim Reapers,* 296.

98. Messick, *Lansky,* 241.

99. In March 1970, for example, Air America flew in several hundred Thai troops to defend the CIA's Hmong outpost at Long Cheng (*New York Times,* April 5, 1970, 22; *Flight International,* July 16, 1970).

100. Eliot Marshall, "Heroin: The Source of Supply," *New Republic,* July 24–31, 1971, 24: "Shutting down the Turkish opium route . . . is likely to do no more than drive the industry further east."

101. See chapter 3.

A Deep Politics Bibliography

Anderson, Scott, and Jon Lee Anderson. *Inside the League: The Shocking Expose of How Terrorists, Nazis, and Latin American Death Squads Have Infiltrated the World Anti-Communist League.* New York: Dodd, Mead, 1986.

Bamford, James. *Body of Secrets: Anatomy of the Ultra-Secret National Security Agency: From the Cold War through the Dawn of a New Century.* New York: Doubleday, 2001.

Beaty, Jonathan, and S. C. Gwynne. *BCCI: The Outlaw Bank: A Wild Ride into the Secret Heart of BCCI.* New York: Random House, 1993.

Block, Alan A. *Masters of Paradise: Organized Crime and the Internal Revenue Service in the Bahamas.* New Brunswick, N.J.: Transaction, 1991.

Brewton, Pete. *The Mafia, CIA, and George Bush.* New York: S.P.I. Books, 1992.

Chomsky, Noam, and Edward S. Herman. *The Political Economy of Human Rights.* Boston: South End, 1979.

Cockburn, Alexander, and Jeffrey St. Clair. *Whiteout: The CIA, Drugs, and the Press.* London: Verso, 1998.

Colby, Gerard, with Charlotte Dennett. *Thy Will Be Done: The Conquest of the Amazon: Nelson Rockefeller and Evangelism in the Age of Oil.* New York: HarperPerennial, 1995.

Cooley, John K. *Unholy Wars: Afghanistan, America, and International Terrorism.* London: Pluto, 1999.

Corson, William R. *Armies of Ignorance: The Rise of the American Intelligence Empire.* New York: Dial, 1977.

Cumings, Bruce. *The Origins of the Korean War.* Princeton: Princeton University Press, 1981, 1990.

Demaris, Ovid. *Dirty Business.* New York: Avon, 1975.

Denton, Sally, and Roger Morris. *The Money and the Power: The Making of Las Vegas and Its Hold on America, 1947–2000.* New York: Knopf, 2001.

Dorman, Michael. *Dirty Politics.* New York: Delacorte, 1979.

Ellsberg, Daniel. *Secrets: A Memoir of Vietnam and the Pentagon Papers.* New York: Viking, 2002.

Griffin, Michael. *Reaping the Whirlwind: The Taliban Movement in Afghanistan.* London: Pluto, 2001.

Haq, M. Emdad-ul. *Drugs in South Asia: From the Opium Trade to the Present Day.* New York: St. Martin's, 2000.

Hersh, Seymour. *The Price of Power: Kissinger in the White House.* New York: Summit, 1983.

Hougan, Jim. *Spooks: The Haunting of America: The Private Use of Secret Agents.* New York: Morrow, 1978.

Kaiser, David. *American Tragedy: Kennedy, Johnson, and the Origins of the Vietnam War.* Cambridge: Harvard University Press, Belknap Press, 2000.

Kwitny, Jonathan. *The Crimes of Patriots: A True Tale of Dope, Dirty Money, and the CIA.* New York: Norton, 1987.

Labévière, Richard. *Dollars for Terror: The United States and Islam.* New York: Algora, 2000.

Leary, William M. *Perilous Missions: Civil Air Transport and CIA Covert Operations in Asia.* Montgomery: University of Alabama Press, 1984.

Lee, Rensselar W., III. *The White Labyrinth: Cocaine and Political Power.* New Brunswick, N.J.: Transaction, 1989.

Lernoux, Penny. *In Banks We Trust.* Garden City, N.Y.: Anchor/Doubleday, 1984.

Loftus, John, and Mark Aarons. *The Secret War against the Jews.* New York: St. Martin's, 1994.

Logevall, Fredrik. *Choosing War: The Lost Chance for Peace and the Escalation of War in Vietnam.* Berkeley: University of California Press, 1999.

Marshall, Jonathan. *Drug Wars: Corruption, Counterinsurgency, and Covert Operations in the Third World.* Forestville, Calif.: Cohan & Cohen, 1991.

Marshall, Jonathan, Peter Dale Scott, and Jane Hunter. *The Iran-Contra Connection: Secret Teams and Covert Operations in the Reagan Era.* Boston: South End, 1987.

McClintock, Michael. *Instruments of Statecraft: U.S. Guerrilla Warfare, Counterinsurgency, and Counterterrorism.* New York: Pantheon, 1992.

McCoy, Alfred W. *The Politics of Heroin: CIA Complicity in the Global Drug Trade.* Brooklyn, N.Y.: Lawrence Hill, 1991.

McCoy, Alfred W., and Alan A. Block, eds. *War on Drugs: Studies in the Failure of U.S. Narcotics Policy.* Boulder: Westview, 1992.

Mills, James. *The Underground Empire: Where Crime and Governments Embrace.* New York: Dell, 1978.

Naylor, R. T. *Hot Money and the Politics of Debt.* New York: Linden Press/Simon & Schuster, 1987.

Newman, John M. *JFK and Vietnam: Deception, Intrigue, and the Struggle for Power.* New York: Warner, 1992.

Palast, Greg. *The Best Democracy Money Can Buy: An Investigative Reporter Exposes the Truth about Globalization, Corporate Cons, and High Finance Fraudsters.* London: Pluto, 2002.

Pizzo, Stephen, Mary Fricker, and Paul Muolo. *Inside Job: The Looting of America's Savings and Loans.* New York: McGraw-Hill, 1989.

Prados, John. *The Hidden History of the Vietnam War.* Chicago: Ivan R. Dee, 1995.

Ranelagh, John. *The Agency: The Rise and Decline of the CIA.* New York: Simon & Schuster, 1986.

Rashid, Ahmed. *Jihad: The Rise of Militant Islam in Central Asia.* New Haven: Yale University Press, 2002.

————. *Taliban: Militant Islam, Oil, and Fundamentalism in Central Asia.* New Haven: Yale University Press/Nota Bene, 2001.

Robbins, Christopher. *Air America.* New York: Avon, 1985.

Sampson, Anthony. *The Seven Sisters: The Great Oil Companies and the World They Shaped.* New York: Viking, 1975.

Scott, Peter Dale. *Deep Politics and the Death of JFK.* Berkeley: University of California Press, 1996.

————. *Drugs, Contras, and the CIA: Government Policies and the Cocaine Economy.* Sherman Oaks, Calif.: From the Wilderness Publications, 2000.

Scott, Peter Dale, and Jonathan Marshall. *Cocaine Politics: Drugs, Armies, and the CIA in Central America.* Berkeley: University of California Press, 1998.

Selden, Mark, ed. *Remaking Asia: Essays on the American Uses of Power.* New York: Pantheon, 1974.

Smith, R. Harris. *OSS: The Secret History of America's First Central Intelligence Agency.* Berkeley: University of California Press, 1972.

Spiro, David E. *The Hidden Hand of American Hegemony: Petrodollar Recycling and International Markets.* Ithaca: Cornell University Press, 1999.

Summers, Anthony, with Robbyn Swan. *The Arrogance of Power: The Secret World of Richard Nixon.* New York: Viking, 2000.

Tanzer, Michael. *The Political Economy of Oil and the Underdeveloped Countries.* Boston: Beacon, 1969.

Trento, Joseph J. *The Secret History of the CIA.* Roseville, Calif.: Forum/Prima, 2001.

Trocki, Carl A. *Opium, Empire, and the Global Political Economy: A Study of the Asian Opium Trade, 1750–1950.* London: Routledge, 1999.

Truell, Peter, and Larry Gurwin. *False Profits: The Inside Story of BCCI, the World's Most Corrupt Financial Empire.* Boston: Houghton Mifflin, 1992.

U.S. Central Intelligence Agency. Office of Inspector General. *Report of Investigation Concerning Allegations between CIA and the Contras in Trafficking Cocaine to the United States.* Washington: CIA Inspector General's Office, 1998. Also known as the Hitz Report.

U.S. Congress. Senate. Committee on Foreign Relations. *The BCCI Affair.* By Senator John Kerry and Senator Hank Brown. 102d Cong., 2d sess. Senate Print 102–140. Washington, D.C.: Government Printing Office, 1992. Also known as the Kerry-Brown Report.

U.S. Congress. Senate. Committee on Foreign Relations. Subcommittee on Terrorism, Narcotics, and International Operations. *Drugs, Law Enforcement, and Foreign Policy.* Washington, D.C.: Government Printing Office, 1989. Also known as the Kerry Report.

U.S. Congress. Senate. Select Committee to Study Governmental Operations with Respect to Intelligence Activities. *Final Report.* 94th Cong., 2d sess., Senate Report no. 94–755. Washington, D.C.: Government Printing Office, 1976. Also known as the Church Committee Report.

Weiner, Tim. *Blank Check: The Pentagon's Black Budget.* New York: Warner, 1990.

Yergin, Daniel. *The Prize: The Epic Quest for Oil, Money, and Power.* New York: Simon & Schuster, 1991.

Index

Abedi, Agha Hasan, 47, 48, 50
Abrams, Creighton, 172, 177
Abu Nidal, 47
Aceh, 82n30
Acheson, Dean, 109, 120, 188
Adham, Kamal, 47
Afghanistan, x, 27, 29, 30, 35n17, 36n33, 37n37; drugs and oil in, 27–33; Stingers in, 4–6, 18n23, 19n30; 2001 and 1979 compared, 43–50. *See also* mujahedin, Afghan
Agnew, Spiro, 148
AIPAC. *See* American Israel Public Affairs Committee
Air America, 1, 2, 3, 6, 9, 14, 16, 115, 150, 152, 153, 156, 160, 171, 174, 177, 178, 188, 190, 196, 197, 199; and drugs, 50, 51, 134, 138–39n13, 196; history of Laotian involvement, 119–38. *See also* Civil Air Transport (CAT); Kuomintang (KMT), and Air America/CAT
Air Asia, 123, 189
Airdale Corporation, 140n31, 189
airlift, 16, 101–2, 189–91
Air Vietnam, 181n27, 190
Alianza Anticomunista Americana, 85
al-Kassar, Monzer, 47
al-Qaeda, x, 32, 41. *See also* bin Laden, Osama
Alsop, Joseph, 52, 125, 130–31, 136, 189, 195

Alsop, Stewart, 126
American Bankers Insurance Company, 198
American Fliers for Laos, 131, 143n62
American Friends of Vietnam, 4, 40
American Israel Public Affairs Committee (AIPAC), 8–9, 20n47
American Security Council (ASC), xiv, 4, 6, 11, 14, 178
American Volunteer Group (AVG). *See* Flying Tigers
Amory, Robert, 114
Anderson, David, 119, 120
Anderson, Jack, 176, 177
Anslinger, Harry, 16, 194
antiwar movement, U.S., xv
APACL. *See* Asian People's Anti-Communist League
archival history, xiv, 6, 12–14, 22n63, 61, 62, 181n22, 199n3; from alternative archives, 13, 22n63; versus convergent overview, 14, 61–63; deep political analysis, xiv
Armenia, 7
Arnold, Thurman, 116
ASC. *See* American Security Council
Asian Development Bank, 168
Asian People's Anti-Communist League (APACL), 4, 52, 58n95, 163n3, 194, 195

About the Author

Peter Dale Scott was born in 1929 in Montreal, Canada. A former Canadian diplomat and professor of English at the University of California, Berkeley, he is both a poet and an author of political analysis. His chief prose books include *Deep Politics and the Death of JFK, The War Conspiracy, Cocaine Politics,* and *The Iran-Contra Connection* (the last two in collaboration). His most recent book of poetry is *Minding the Darkness,* completing his trilogy *Seculum.* In 2002 he received the Lannan Poetry Award. He is married to Ronna Kabatznick, and has three children by his former wife. His website is http://ist-socrates.berkeley .edu/~pdscott/.